OPEN AND RELATIONAL LEADERSHIP

Leading with Love

Roland Hearn, Sheri D. Kling, and Thomas Jay Oord, EDITORS

SacraSage Press
© 2020 Roland Hearn, Sheri D. Kling, Thomas Jay Oord, and Contributors
All rights reserved. No part of this book may be reproduced in any form without written consent of the author being quoted or SacraSage Press. SacraSage Press provides resources that promote wisdom aligned with sacred perspectives. All rights reserved.

Cover Design: Thomas Jay Oord (Three Finger Rock in Owyhee Mountains of Eastern Oregon)

ISBN 978-1-948609-22-7 *(Print)*
ISBN 978-1-948609-23-4 *(EBook)*

Printed in the United States of America

Library of Congress Cataloguing-in-Publication Data

Roland Hearn, Sheri D. Kling, and Thomas Jay Oord. Editors.
Open and Relational Leadership: Leading with Love / Hearn, Kling, Oord, Eds.

*Roland dedicates this book to his wife Emmy Hearn
for hours of support in the editing process.*

*Sheri dedicates this book to her mentor Philip Clayton
for beautifully modeling relational leadership.*

*Thomas dedicates this book to his friend Craig Drurey
for his leadership in promoting uncontrolling love.*

Table of Contents

Introduction i

Theory: Leadership in the Divine Model

1. Leading Without Authority - Bruce G. Allder 1
2. Leadership as Yielding - Vaughn W. Baker 5
3. Is Ambition Okay? - Roger Bretherton 9
4. Leaders as Energizers - Leading the Way God Leads -
   Roger Bretherton 13
5. Leading in the Light of God's Non-Anxious Presence -
   Joe Goodwin Burnett 17
6. Three-in-One Leadership: Creative, Sacrificial, and Transformative
   Emman T. Chapman 21
7. The Toughness of Grace - Hans Deventer 25
8. Does Godly Leadership Require Certainty About God? -
   Mike Edwards 29
9. Revelation in Relationship: Leadership as Affirmation and
   Spiritual Formation - Bruce Epperly 33
10. Godlike Dominion Not Human Opinion: Redefining
    Leadership in God's Economy - Rob A. Fringer 39
11. The Uncontrolling Leadership of God - Gabriel Gordon 43
12. Cutting Holes in Roofs: Making Paths for the Marginalized -
    Brittney Lowe Hartley 47
13. Allowing Good Things to Run Wild - Dana Robert Hicks ... 51
14. Lessons from the Break Room - Nancy R. Howell 57
15. God Leads Like a Midwife - Libby Tedder Hugus 61
16. Leadership in the Valley of The Madness - Dan Kent 67
17. The Humility of God - Bob Luhn 73
18. What Does Holy Leadership Look Like? - Glen O'Brien 77
19. Leading with Faith - Daniel J. Ott 81
20. Leading by Following - Dyton L. Owen 85

21. More Power II to You: Freedom and Trust in Organizational Leadership - Neil Pembroke 89
22. Relational Musings Concerning God and Politics - Tim Reddish 93
23. Going for the Gold - Omar Reyes 99
24. Leading Through the Contention: Guidance from Open and Relational Theology in Navigating Conflict - Kyle Roberts.......... 103
25. We Can't - Pete Shaw 109
26. Power-less Leadership - Jeffery D Skinner...................... 113
27. Are Some of the Best Leaders the Most Reluctant? - Ian Todd... 119
28. Waking up with Truman Burbank: Leadership alongside Spiritual Refugees - Jason Tripp....................................... 123

Application: Leadership in Church and Society

29. Loving and Relational - Donnamie K. Ali 131
30. Listening Together: Vision-Casting in Community - Chris S. Baker 135
31. Creating Open and Relational Communities - Peter Benedict and Miriam Chickering... 139
32. What We Know that Just Ain't So - Donna Bowman 145
33. Leading From the God-Shaped Pole - Tim Burnette..................... 149
34. Open Leadership as Creative, Loving, and Just - Joshua Canada . 153
35. To the Ends of the Earth and Beyond in the Spirit - Robert D. Cornwall 159
36. America: The Un-United States - Randall E. Davey...................... 163
37. The Home of the Brave - Beth Ann Estock................................... 169
38. Democracy and the Divine - Patricia Adams Farmer.................... 173
30. An Open Pulpit - JR. Forasteros... 177
40. God and Doctors - William Hasker and Jonathan Kopel 181
41. Pump, Pause, Release, Repeat - Beth Hayward 185
42. The Missing Finger: An Analogy of Love - Roland Hearn........... 189
43. Leadership after the Funeral of the Church - George Hermanson... 193

44. Passion, Authenticity, and Commitment: A Reflection on Theological Education - Sheryl A. Kujawa-Holbrook 199
45. Do Your Best to Present Yourself as One Trusted by God - Wm. Curtis Holtzen 203
46. Creativity, Community, and Transformation: Treasures Discovered through Dreams - Sheri D. Kling 207
47. The Living Earth as Teacher - Jay McDaniel 213
48. Leading by Listening - L Michaels 217
49. Open and Relational Leadership Is Like Coaching a Football Team - James Bradley Miller 221
50. Grace-fully Engaging Young Adults - Anita Monro 225
51. The Uncontrolling Track Coach - Craig Morton 231
52. True Leaders are Replaced - Seth Price 235
53. Toward Developing and Leading Open and Relational Organizations - Joshua D. Reichard 239
54. The Leadership of a Nurturant God - John Sanders 243
55. I'm Right, You're Wrong - Lemuel Sandoval 247
56. Seven Tips for Becoming a Better Leader - Wm. Andrew Schwartz 251
57. We are All Leaders - Michele Snyder 257
58. The God of Love Compels Me - Leann M. Van Cleef-Trimmer . 261
59. Organization as Family? - Wm. Paul Young 265

Introduction

Leadership studies have blossomed in recent decades. Many researchers and writers take recent developments in science, economics, medicine, or politics as their guide when advancing theories in leadership. Others seek insights from great leaders of yesteryear, presidents and prime ministers, coaches, or titans of industry today.

Leadership books from faith perspectives are also available. Many pick a sacred scripture or story from which to draw their primary leadership principles. Others look to great faith leaders for inspiration. Some explain and expand the virtues or gifts in light of leadership.

This book is unique on the leadership landscape. The essays in it explore leadership from a particular theological perspective: open and relational theology.

Open and relational theology has many dimensions and facets. But at its core are these ideas: 1. God is relational, which means God engages us in giving and receiving love. 2. Creatures and creation are relational, which means we all affect one another. 3. The future is not predetermined but open, which means our choices and decisions matter.

In light of these ideas, contributors to this book ask questions like, What would it mean to lead like a God who is open, relational, and loving? What does leadership look like in an open and relational world with open and relational people? What "style" of leadership fits this view? And so on.

Many readers will be surprised by the answers these chapters give to questions like these and others. Some answers upend long-held views of hierarchy, tit-for-tat exchange, separated, or controlling leadership. Those answers prompt us to wonder what good leaders might be like and do. They also might prompt us to wonder what it means to be a good follower, community member, or creature in the earth household.

The book divides roughly into essays exploring issues of theory and application. In reality, nearly every essay addresses both theory and application. After all, it's hard to keep issues in boxes when the overall themes are openness and relationality! But dividing the book this way makes some sense.

As editors, we want to thank the AMAZING group of contributors in this book. This collection was even better than we dreamed it would be! We are proud to be associated with this helpful contribution to contemporary leadership.

This is the kind of book readers should study, discuss, and share. We hope groups, organizations, leadership teams, and other communities explore these ideas together. The principles and insights are invaluable. We think this book could make a *real* difference!

Roland Hearn, Sheri D. Kling, and Thomas Jay Oord

Theory: Leadership in the Divine Model

1

Leading Without Authority

BRUCE G. ALLDER

Christian leadership involves authority grounded in relationship with Christ not a title or populist affirmation.

*A*uthority and power: these are often the first words that come to mind when the term "leadership" is mentioned. References to these are easy to find in relation to Jesus, and he is the one to emulate in Christian leadership, right? *All authority in heaven and on earth has been given to me. Therefore go...* (Matt 28:18); *Jesus entered the temple and drove out all those who were selling and buying in the temple...* (Matt 21:12). There are many more such examples in the Scriptures.

These words and actions by Jesus are usually read through the lens of institutional authority and hierarchy—authority and power. Jesus is God and has the absolute authority and privilege of interrupting people and events according to his will and purpose. However, to understand Jesus' actions in this way is to miss the foundation of Jesus' leadership. We can so easily drift into what Brueggemann calls *empire* (secular power), rather than *kingdom* (principles of the Kingdom of God). At the heart of this issue is that Jesus came to inaugurate the Kingdom of God (Mark 1:14; Matt 3:17). God reveals the nature of the Godhead and invites people into a life-giving relationship. The establishment of the covenant with the nation of Israel in Exodus 20 was an important step forward in that self-revelation. The Kingdom of God was established as a theocracy—God as king. God's people are to live and work under the rule of God to reach fully their created potential.

A theocracy sounds good in theory. But what does that look like? It is too easy to have leadership claim "theocratic leadership" when it is simply a guise for autocracy, or to run to democracy and have populism dictate what is right. Shaw says that both autocratic leadership and democratic leadership are built on fear. In autocracy, the leader fears a loss of control while in democracy there is a fear of autocracy. In the end, we are left with the choice between the tyranny of the one and the tyranny of the many.

A genuine theocracy is an alternative to these opposites. Jesus' leadership illustrates *Kingdom* leadership and the challenge is to look beyond the perceived demonstration of authority and power in his life to see the Kingdom principles at work. Under the leadership of Moses, God brought the Children of Israel out of slavery and through the desert to the threshold of the Promised Land. Moses, who did not enter the Promised Land himself, prepared this new nation for life there. His speeches are recorded for us in the book of Deuteronomy. Moses gave clear instructions about the kind of leadership (king) that the nation would need (Deut. 17) to be faithful to the covenant the people had made with God at Mt Sinai. The king of Israel was not to be like a king of other nations. Their king was to be a servant of Yahweh (God) and under authority himself. The king's authority was to be an inferred authority, based upon the quality of the relationship he held with Yahweh. In other words, the king's authority was only as good as his personal relationship with the God he was meant to serve. This is what the prophet Samuel warned the people about when they asked for their first king (I Sam. 8:10f). A title and endorsement by the people were insufficient bases for his authority as king of Israel. In an odd sort of way, leadership in this kingdom is not dependent on the response of the people served. Rather the quality of the relationship the leader had with God was the foundation from which the leader was to have influence.

By submitting to God, discernment of God's agenda and discernment of God's activity in the world becomes the focus of leadership. This is consistent with the New Testament teachings. The leader finds the authority to serve primarily in such a relationship (Matt. 5-7; Mark 10:43-45). Jesus shocked the religious people of his day because they anticipated that he would act like the kind of leader they were used to seeing—one that lorded it over those under them. Instead, Jesus sought out the marginalized, washed his disciples' feet before a meal, loved people unconditionally, and gave his life as a ransom to the undeserving.

We speak of Jesus as Lord, and he is that to those who follow him. But understand that Jesus is Lord, not because he has followers, but because that is who he is. Jesus' lordship is found in his relationship with his Father (God). This is the essence of Kingdom leadership. Perry W.H. Shaw says that when we find confidence in God through our relationships with Jesus Christ, we no longer need the praise or subordination of others. We are free to serve in authority and under authority.

Here is the genius of Christian leadership: in serving God as the essence of our leadership, we are not held hostage to the whims and opinions of those we serve, nor do we arrogantly usurp the authority that is God's. Once again the question is, what does loving God look like in our leadership? We love God by serving others. Our loving is expressed practically. It is not just saying "I love you" but actually engaging with people in the ordinary.

Samuel Wells identifies four different ways that leaders can relate to the people they serve. Namely, *working for* people, *working with* people, *being for* people, and *being with* people. He suggests that while all four have some place in Christian leadership, the most profound and deepest level of service is found in *being with* people. This is a profound shift in thinking about leadership. The default stance in being with people is not being a problem solver, nor one who comes from a place of authority and power, but being one who comes *alongside to empower* others.

Elements in such relational leadership include:

1. Presence: being in the same physical space with the people we serve.
2. Attention: not just 'showing up' but being present, focused, and vulnerable in the moment of interaction.
3. Mystery: acknowledging that in this unique encounter we find people and possibly ambiguous circumstances that cannot be fixed or broken down into various parts; however, we can enter into, explore, and appreciate the personhood of the other and their ability to find a way forward.
4. Delight: being glad to take time rather than being overtaken by urgency to "sort the issue."
5. Participation: having the patience not to leave people behind; replacing urgency with patient engagement with those who are seeking their own way into an optimistic future in relationship with their Creator.
6. Partnership: acting in community and seeing how respective gifts can be harnessed to enable a team to reach a common goal.
7. Enjoyment: enjoying time spent with those whom are often discarded as being of no use, yet who are actually of inestimable value because of God's love.

8. Glory: celebrating God's originating purpose of being in Christ

Here's the wonder: we can do all these things as leaders without the need for an authority that puts us at the center of the activity. Now that is counter-cultural! This kind of leadership moves us away from a transactional approach where we are "owed" certain benefits (authority, payment for services, etc.) to one of genuine transformation. The focus is on God's agenda of transforming people (including us!) and discerning well God's activity in the world. Institutional and traditional authority has more to do with the management of resources that we have before us, but management is not leadership. The danger in letting management set the leadership agenda is that it puts the focus on resources rather than relationships with people. The temptation is to manipulate resources to our own agenda because we can grab control. It feels good to be "needed" and to have a role to play, and is therefore so easy to drift into a leadership model that is self-focused rather than God-focused.

Being with people and relying upon our relationship with Christ to give us an inferred authority means that we are not the center of attention. It means that we are free to empower those around us to serve as we serve. It enables people to discover their own way forward in relationship with Christ. It opens the way for us to trust the Holy Spirit to lead and shape us as a community of Christ-followers. Maybe this is leading from the middle rather than the front. Sounds like leadership without authority to me!

Bruce G Allder is Asia Pacific Regional Education Coordinator for the Church of the Nazarene and Senior Lecturer in Pastoral Theology and Ministry at Nazarene Theological College in Brisbane, Australia. Research interests include the teaching of theological education, the influence of context in preaching, and leadership in the Body of Christ. He loves team sports, especially cricket, and enjoys hiking the Australian bush.

2

Leadership as Yielding

VAUGHN W. BAKER

The Trinitarian model of interdependence, self-giving, and honoring the Other gives us clear guidance for yielding leadership.

Blaise Pascal said God is not the God "of the philosophers and savants" but "the God of Abraham, God of Isaac, God of Jacob." God is also "the God of Jesus Christ."

Whatever else this might mean, it necessarily means that God is a person, and if a person, then essentially relational and if relational, then essentially related. Divine temporality, which is assumed here, can be found throughout the biblical witness. Describing open and relational leadership is another way of describing biblical leadership, for the witness in scripture to the God-world relationship is one of give-and-take. It describes interaction between God and humans, and humans among themselves, in which some things are settled, and other things remain open.

Leadership in the biblical sense is essentially relational and related! Women and men used of God to lead demonstrated the give-and-take of the divine-human relationship. This kind of relationship out of which leadership arises is not based on monergist visions of divine impassibility where, traditionally understood, God cannot be affected by creatures. Nor does this kind of relationship assume an unbridled omnipotence where God's power overrides all outcomes and human responses. God honors our responses, in fact, God encourages such. The divine human relationship is one based upon love in self-giving, much like is found in Philippians 2:6-8:

> *6 Who, being in very nature God, did not consider equality with God something to be used to his own advantage;*

7 rather, he made himself nothing by taking the very nature of a servant, being made in human likeness.
8 And being found in appearance as a man, he humbled himself by becoming obedient to death -- even death on a cross!

Such a description of Jesus' response to the Father is indicative of a leadership that exhibits the following characteristics:

1. For Jesus leadership meant "follow-ship!" God the Father sent Jesus. He himself said, "I can do nothing on my own. As I hear, I judge, and my judgment is just, because I seek not my own will but the will of him who sent me," (John 530, ESV). By taking upon himself the form of a servant, Jesus looked to God for direction and guidance. All leadership in this regard is Spirit-led and Spirit-directed.
2. For Jesus leadership meant being a servant. Jesus said, "The greatest among you will be your servant. For those who exalt themselves will be humbled, and those who humble themselves will be exalted," (Matthew 23:11, 12 NIV). Jesus' washing of the disciples' feet demonstrated visibly his approach to servant leadership.
3. Christ's atoning work on the cross gives us the ultimate sign of his leadership style. Jesus said, "Greater love has no one than this: to lay down one's life for one's friends," (John 15:13, NIV). The good shepherd lays down his life for the sheep, (John 10:11). As Jesus is the image of the invisible God (Colossians 1:15) then we can conclude that God is essentially self-giving, self-sacrificing, and therefore self-related to all creation in love. There never was a "time" that God was not self-giving, self-sacrificing, or self-related.

Given that leadership arises out of being related to God and others in love, how does that work out practically speaking?

1. Leadership begins by leading from God's presence. We cannot assume that God's will is already and always being done. We must seek God daily just as Jesus did. "Very early in the morning, while it was still dark, Jesus got up, left the house and went off to a solitary place, where he prayed," (Mark 1:35, NIV). Relational or open leadership is constantly open to the Spirit's leading from a God who does all things new, (Isaiah 43:19). Wesleyan disciplines would say that leading from God's presence and initiative involves a dedication to acts of piety: scripture meditation or *lectio divina*, prayer, Holy

Communion, fasting, worship, and accountable discipleship. The more we devote ourselves to these things the more we experience God's grace in our lives.

2. Leadership moves to affirm interdependence with others. We cannot affirm a God who is essentially related to others while seeking to be independent from others ourselves. God more often than not uses others—human, angelic, and even animals—to bring about God's purposes. The first Jerusalem Council makes a bold statement in saying "It seemed good to the Holy Spirit and to us not to burden you with anything beyond the following requirements," (Acts 15:28, NIV). Discernment is both an individual and a corporate experience. Otherwise, why have spiritual gifts? Why even have a body, i.e., the Church? God loves interdependence! Rarely, if ever, in scripture do biblical figures travel alone. We need each other to accomplish God's purposes!

3. Leadership is divinely chosen. Jesus said, "You did not choose me, I chose you and appointed you," (John 15:16, NIV). None of us is "freelancing" as leaders. We are related essentially to the One who called us and to one another. God takes the initiative in our calling as we respond either with a yes or a no or with delayed obedience. It behooves all who are called of God to respond in the affirmative in a timely manner. I have met individuals who felt called of God to the ministry while employed outside of the church and who said "no" to God's promptings for years, if not decades. But upon retirement decided that it was time to yield to God's grace and enter the ministry. God is very patient, but in each of those who delayed their response to answer the call to ministry I heard only regret for not obeying sooner.

In conclusion, we can find clear guidance about relational and open leadership by looking at the relationship between the Persons of the Holy Trinity as found in the New Testament. Interdependence and not isolation, love shown in self-giving, and showing honor to the Other is modeled between Father, Son and Holy Spirit. Such a demonstration and such a divine Presence exists in all who yield to God.

Serving as Pastor of United Methodist churches for over forty years, Vaughn Baker shares a belief with others that the God of the philosophers is not the God of the Bible.

Vaughn has engaged in writing and research leading to a doctoral degree in theology and missiology. In addition to serving as pastor in local congregations, he also has taught in the summer course of study school at a local seminary. The Trinitarian model of interdependence, self-giving, and honoring the Other gives us clear guidance for yielding leadership.

3

Is Ambition Okay?

ROGER BRETHERTON

Why we do what we do, is more important than what we do.

An Unconvincing Substitute

I regularly receive a philosophy lecture from my ten-year-old. Usually when we are driving home from school, he regales me with whatever insights into life's mysteries have struck him over the course of the day. Some of these are quite profound. Like how Marvel movies would be much shorter if the baddies just learned to forgive. Or how the indisputable purpose of dogs is fun. The other night he offered me a short synopsis of his developing philosophy of euphemism. He wondered if I'd noticed that swear words (as we quaintly call profanity in England) are just naughty words for normal things. He had a few examples to share. But ultimately I felt the need to stop him, while causally wondering aloud whether he'd recently been hanging out with Jonny, the hands down sweariest kid in his class. But his main thesis was solid. Some words are dirty and we find other words to replace them.

The church often resorts to euphemism when it comes to leadership. On the one hand, we are more obsessed with leadership than any other group of people I can think of. We want good leaders. We want people to lead well in church, at work, and wherever they find themselves. We talk up leadership and train more leaders than any other organization on the planet. But at the same time, we are mindful of all the biblical injunctions to humility: the first is last, the servant is the leader, the least is the greatest. It's a fundamental tenet of Thomas Jay Oord's relational and open theology: we love, live, and lead like Christ in giving up status and giving away ourselves. We are rightly wary of the need for dominance that often drives those who seek to lead.

While our instincts are right, our solution is often wrong. We resort to a euphemism that wouldn't fool a ten-year-old. Given that the pursuit of power is obviously wrong, we swap a dirty word for a slightly less dirty word. We don't want power, I hear people say, we want *influence*. It's not a very convincing substitute, but it is symptomatic of our confusion around leadership. We don't always know how to make sense of ambition.

Two Worlds of Ambition

Our translations of the New Testament don't help us very much in this respect. The word ambition is used in most English translations to render Greek words that could not be more different. One of them (the root word *eritheia*) is usually translated *selfish ambition*. Paul says it is unanimously bad. So bad in fact, that he tells the Philippians (2:3) not to do *anything* out of selfish ambition. It's a work of the flesh (2 Cor, 12:20; Gal 5:20). It leads to disaster (Rom 2:8). It connotes strife and electioneering—the kind of self-interest that creates factions for its own advantage. Not one for the character wish list.

The other New Testament word often translated as ambition strikes a markedly more wholesome tone. Paul uses it to describe his ambitions to preach (Rm 15:20), and his desire to please God (2 Cor 5:9). At root, it's the word *philotimeomai*, and it forms the basis for what is arguably one of the most beautiful instructions in the entire New Testament: make it your ambition to lead a quiet life: You should mind your own business and work with your hands," (1 Thes 4:11). It speaks of the love and honor connected to the privilege of rising to a task.

These two Greek words that have both been translated as "ambition" belong to different worlds. One is disastrous and should never motivate us. The other gives life and is a core motive of who we are. Both have been translated as "ambition," so it's no wonder we're confused.

Do it for its Own Sake

Psychologists have also picked up this duality in ambition. Some would draw a distinction between extrinsic and intrinsic motivation. Put simply, extrinsic motivation is when we do what we do not because we inherently care about it, but because we want to obtain the external rewards of doing it. The student volunteers to help the homeless because it looks good on their resume. The employee seeks promotion for the money, status and power. Intrinsic motivation on the other hand is when we do something because we value it in itself. The teacher who really cares about the kids, the artist who delights in subtle explorations of color, the basketball player who leaps through the air with the joy of skill and elegance, and the leader who leads from a deep sense of inner conviction. Intrinsic motivation means we value the thing we do, not just the glittering prizes that accompany it.

Our lives are a complex web of extrinsic and intrinsic motivations. Sometimes we go to work just to put food on the table. Sometimes we do things just for the fun of it. Occasionally work and play are the same thing. But the big challenge of the motivational literature is this: extrinsic motivation eats up intrinsic motivation. We start to do something because we love it. We then are rewarded for being good at it. And if we're not careful, our motives are undermined by the external rewards. We switch tracks. Eventually we will only do it if we are rewarded. The footballer who once played with the verve and appetite solely reserved for those who love the game, fades in energy as the money, the celebrity, the supercar and the glamourous wife take his attention. The worship leader enamored with sharing the love of God struggles to retain this focus as the pressures of management, touring and album sales mount.

When extrinsic rewards distract us from the joy that first inspired us to do what we do, we start to feel trapped. It's a common dilemma for those who rise to leadership. It's tempting to believe that guy from Galilee was right when he told us to beware of performing our righteous acts for the approval of others, because in the pursuit of an immediately bankable reward we can lose sight of the ultimate lasting reward—the God who dwells secretly in every given moment.

How we Live our Passions

Psychologist Robert Vallerand brings another distinction to the table in his work on passion. Our passions, he says, are the things we consider important. We devote time and energy to them. And we attach a large part of our identity to them as well. We all need our passions; we really care about them. For those of us who call ourselves Christians, we may say that our passion is to know Jesus and to be like Jesus. Or, as Thomas Jay Oord puts it, to live a life of love. Our passion is what we live for.

But what Vallerand notes is that no matter how worthy the cause may be, *how* we live our passions has a profound effect on who we become. He draws a dividing line between obsessive passion and harmonious passion. In obsessive passion, we risk workaholism. We sacrifice health, family, friendship and whatever needs to go in order to pursue our ambition. We cannot help ourselves.

Our worth hangs on the success and status that come with the passion. We are what we do.

On the other hand, in harmonious passion, what we do has a deep resonance with who we are—that's why we give ourselves to it so vibrantly and with such dedication. We feel that we have freely chosen our passion, like answering a call. Consequently, we can step back from it for a time if we need to, and our passion then finds a balance among all the other spheres of life: friends, family, and health. The formula of obsessive passion is reversed in harmonious passion: we do what we are. It won't be any great surprise to know that obsessive passion has been linked to burnout, derailment and dissatisfaction in high performers. Harmonious passion, on the other hand, leads to satisfaction with life, sustainable accomplishment and a long list of benefits to psychological and physical health.

Our Motives Matter

Our motives for leading matter. That's why one of my favorite questions to ask leaders, in church, in education, in health, in business, or wherever, is: *what first drew you to do what you do?* It's an invitation to recall their intrinsic motivation, before the red tape, the pressures and the demands of the role dulled their passion and obscured their vision. It reminds them to examine the harmony between who they are and what they do.

At no point in over two decades of posing that question to leaders in various settings has any leader worth their salt ever said that they were aiming at influence. They aimed at something else, something that mattered to them. At times, this made them influential: as the voice that speaks up, or the person people trust, or the one who takes responsibility for the team. Overall, they were ambitious to make the world a better place, and influence was a by-product.

Roger Bretherton, Ph.D. is Associate Professor in Psychology at the University of Lincoln (UK). He is a Clinical Psychologist specializing in the definition and development of Character Strengths. He frequently consults, coaches, and trains leaders in large organizations.

4

Leaders as Energizers: Leading the Way God Leads

ROGER BRETHERTON

If we want to lead the way God leads, we need to create culture in the same way God created the world.

God the Collaborator

The passage in Thomas Jay Oord's writing that mystifies me most when I first read it is his account of God creating the universe. Surely if there's any case for a God who can do what God likes, initiating actions entirely autonomously, it's creation. No one else was there. No one was praying. Nothing stood in God's way. All God had to do was apply the metaphorical jump leads, and boom—it would all roll from there.

But no, in *The Nature of Love*, Tom claims that God "'does not coerce when creating. God's creative love does not entirely control or fully force the coming to be of new creation.'" It confused me, because it made pre-human creation sound almost sentient. It made God a collaborator with the world rather than its absolute master. Here was a God who was responsive to creation right down to the subatomic level. This was not the command-and-control God I'd come to know and love—and loathe. This God was unfamiliar, but also a pretty good model of how really good leaders change the world.

Just as the notion of the command-and-control God doesn't appear to be going away any time soon, neither does the notion of the command-and-control leader. Our world is filled with people who think that being the boss means being bossy; that the principal role of the leader is just to tell people what to do. To hear some CEOs talk, you'd think not only that they built their company single-handedly, but that they created the world too. As a consequence, our world is filled with bemused leaders, terminally frustrated that their staff won't do as they've been told. Sooner or later every good leader becomes an amateur psychologist, if only because they are trying to work out why it is that so many people don't seem to get it, don't do as they are told, and, more often than not, don't even seem to understand the instructions.

Leader as Energizer

In recent years, psychologists have proposed multiple models of leadership that move away from the command-and-control leader who just issues instructions. Many Christians have been deeply taken with Robert Greenleaf's idea of the servant leader. It certainly aligns with New Testament notions presented by Jesus of the one who serves all being the greatest. Others place the essence of leadership not in the individual or in their actions, but in the relationships they form with others. The stand-out definition here comes from leadership expert, Jim McNeish: *the leader is the person who forms a relationship with the leader in each of us.* It involves a calling out of something good within other people. It's so close to Oord's picture of God hovering over the world, drawing out the energetic potential of creation rather than hectoring it into action. The role of the leader in this definition, as Peter Drucker liked to phrase it, is *to make strengths effective.* It requires a belief that people have wonderful things to contribute to our organizations if only we can find the way to create the opportunity for them to do so. That's leadership.

Kim Cameron is one of the founders of Positive Organizational Scholarship—the academic study of organizations working at their best. If teams perform super-productively, or leaders lead towards the wellbeing of their workforce and the world, then they may find themselves the subject matter of positive organizational scholarship. Cameron uses a different motif for leadership. He says that leaders are energizers. Cameron and his team have done some fascinating work mapping how energy moves through large organizations. They do this by getting employees to list all the colleagues they spend time with and then giving a rating from -7 to +7 for how energizing or de-energizing they found those contacts to be. An energizing contact lifts our mood and sends us out the door with the sense that our work is worthwhile, valued and meaningful. A de-energizing contact does, well, the opposite. Our mood lowers, we wonder if anyone cares, if our work is really worth doing, and whether we may even be better off working elsewhere. It's no wonder that the number one reason people often give for seeking alternative employment is not salary or work-life balance, but simply that they feel underappreciated.

When all those ratings are entered into social networking software, what emerges is a picture of the organization as an energetic system. And what really stands out, even in an organization of thousands, are the bright nodes of vitality; those individuals or groups where lines of positive energy converge. The energy network shows us who the real leaders are. They're the people who pump energy and vitality into the system and everyone they meet. Sometimes they occupy the corner office and earn the big bucks, but often they don't.

Good for the Whole System

What do these energizers do? To cut a long academic reference list short: they recognize, celebrate and make effective the strengths of others. They invite others to bring their best to the table. And something really interesting occurs when we get to express our best selves in the workplace. Yes, our energy goes up. But also the levels of positive emotion in an organization increase. In an organization where people can bring their best to work, we are also more likely to find hope, love, interest, humor, joy, serenity, inspiration, and trust. And these so-called positive emotions don't just leave us feeling good, they actually do us good. A meta-analysis of numerous studies on positive emotions suggested that a workplace high in positivity not only sees more motivation, higher job satisfaction, greater innovation and collaboration on projects, but also lower staff turnover, fewer absences, and less burnout. Leaders as energizers are not only good for their immediate colleagues, they are good for the whole system.

Here's the advantage of the leader as energizer motif: As opposed to the notion of leader as influencer, which implies leadership as a controlling activity—pulling the levers that move the engine of the organization—the idea of leader as energizer opens up a much wider understanding of what it means to lead. It means we can lead with whatever we have at hand. Whatever strength we naturally bring to the table can at times be a source of leadership. Even if we are not the boss, our honesty, our creativity, our wisdom, our prudence, our passion, our bravery or whatever it is that we naturally contribute, can energize and elevate others. And at times, our contribution will be the weight that swings the balance. Sometimes we will have the casting vote. In such times, it may look like we were in control—but only by accident.

The Way We Talk

One of the ways energizing leaders breathe life into a system is through the way they talk. Not just *to* people, but *about* them. Perhaps the most powerful thing we can do to change the culture of an organization is to gossip positively about people behind their backs. Sooner or later this spills out in the casual feedback we offer in passing comments to others. These offhand appraisals have been likened to the suits in a deck of playing cards. We can tell people what we think of them in four different ways. *Clubs* feedback involves telling people that they did things wrong without any further detail. It can be a sharp rebuke. It guarantees they won't do it again but goes no further. *Spades* feedback on the other hand indicates where they got it wrong and digs deep into the detail of precisely what they got wrong and how. Conversely, *hearts* feedback is positive; it tells someone they are fantastic, but not much more. It may leave them wondering why we think that about them and whether we are really sincere. It can be difficult to tell the difference between a vague compliment and an insincere platitude.

All three of these styles of feedback to other people—clubs, spades and hearts—have their place, but the research suggests that if we really wish to bring the best out in other people we will learn to give *diamonds* feedback. This means that we attend to the good in them in great detail. We apply Paul's advice in Philippians 4:8 to our relationships: we look for the good, the true, the noble, the pure, and we make the most of it wherever we find it. We become every bit as skilful in commending the good as we are in complaining about the bad.

And here's the thing. When we lead in this way, drawing the potential out of all around us, we rarely need to coerce or command or control. We create culture in the way God created the world. We lead the way God leads.

Roger Bretherton is Associate Professor in Psychology at the University of Lincoln (UK). He is a Clinical Psychologist specializing in the definition and development of Character Strengths. He frequently consults, coaches and trains leaders in large organizations.

5

Leading in the Light of God's Non-Anxious Presence

JOE GOODWIN BURNETT

Non-anxious leadership is a way of being that reflects and is grounded in God's own eternal and non-anxious presence.

*I*n a parish I served as rector many years ago, a controversy erupted between my Christian education director and the director of our parish's playschool, a popular child development center for two to four year-olds. The education director reported to me that the playschool was seeking additional space that would compromise our parish Sunday school programs.

Taking her word for it, I became concerned enough to carry an urgent request to our vestry for their counsel in seeking a resolution. Sensing my anxiety around this matter, they quickly moved to support me in any decision I made, including shutting down the playschool altogether.

Soon thereafter at a meeting with the playschool director I learned that her request for more space had been misrepresented by our education director. I also learned that for some time there had been some festering conflict between the two of them. It was true that the play school did want more space, but they were also quite willing to cooperate in any way to reach a solution.

I realized that I had overreacted to the whole situation and had "bought into" the anxiety of the education director regarding this issue. In so doing, I came close to setting in motion a series of events that could have had negative results for the health of the parish, the playschool, and the wider community.

I immediately directed the two parties to sit down and come to a resolution that could be presented to the vestry. They did so, and by the time of the next vestry meeting the plan had been agreed to and implemented. The vestry, after being "stirred up" by my initial anxiety, went on with other business. No one even asked a follow up question. All was well.

Not long after this episode, I became familiar with the groundbreaking work of Rabbi Edwin Friedman in his 1985 book, *Generation to Generation: Family Process in Church and Synagogue*. In the decades since, his application of family systems theory to the nature, behavior, and functioning of churches and church leaders has become widely known and used.

Utilizing the insights of family process to understand the dynamics of a congregational system is not just another pastoral "tool," or method of problem solving. Rather it goes to the very heart and soul of what it means to be a pastoral leader.

When clergy (and lay) pastoral leaders can self-differentiate, remain non-anxious, and yet stay deeply connected to others, the inner integrity that emerges from that identity can empower mature relationships that fuel congregational health, ministry and mission.

What is crucial here is not knowledge or technique, but the leader's own deep awareness of his/her place and role in the system. When leaders focus not on a system's pathology, but on their own emotional presence and participation in it, they are much more likely to foster healing, promote vision, and instill in others the courage and capacity to treat crisis as an opportunity for growth.

As I began to reflect on my experience with the parish playschool, I saw how my anxiety played right into the issues presented to me, and how close we came to open conflict. Over time, I became more adept at not being drawn into another's anxiety, and better able to grasp what was most needed in a pastoral situation. As Friedman might say, I came to realize that my main responsibility was not the organization, but leadership.

For example, years later a neighbor who lived down the street asked if she could come to my office for a visit. When she arrived, she shared the problem she and her husband were having with their twenty-year-old son, John, who was living with them at the time. He was attending a local college part-time, not working, and leading a very active social life.

She and her husband felt that they had lost control of their own home. She reported that John's room was a wreck, and that he would come and go at all hours of the day and night. He was unresponsive to their attempts to bring some order into the chaos. Her husband had become so frustrated that he tended to lose his temper with the son very easily.

She then asked if I would be willing to meet with her son. After a moment's reflection, I decided not to insert myself in this situation, but to guide them instead to assume their rightful leadership. I suggested that she and her husband draw up a list of basic areas where John's cooperation would be necessary to restore peace, and then call him in for a conversation. The bottom line would be this: John could continue living at home, but only if he could abide by a few basic house rules—all of which are generous to him, but also necessary for her and her husband's emotional health.

Some days later, she told me that she and her husband had the conversation with their son, and that things at home were much better. In fact, she said John had made some remarkable changes, had gotten a part-time job, and was now looking at moving into the dorm for the coming semester.

Countless persons have benefited from this simple and direct approach to leadership. Friedman often referred to it as "headship." In this understanding, leadership is much more than a collection of honed skills. It is a way of being, a "discipleship," a *spirituality*. Indeed, the very notion of a "non-anxious presence" is laden with biblical and theological roots and implications.

For example, Matthew's gospel is dotted throughout with language about worry, fear, and anxiety. At the announcement of Jesus's birth. Joseph is told by the angel of the Lord not to be "afraid" to take Mary as his wife. When "wise men" from the East come seeking the newborn king, Herod, "and all Jerusalem with him," are "troubled," or "anxious."

In the Sermon on the Mount, Jesus affirms God's providential care in the midst of the disciples' fretting about the so-called "necessities" of life. He tells them, "Do not worry," "take no thought," "do not be anxious." Later on, when the disciples are caught in a small boat in the middle of a storm, he asks, "Why are you afraid?"

The chief priests and the Pharisees are stung by his parables and want to arrest him. But they do not, because they "fear" the crowds. In Matthew's story, anxiety is all around. And in the midst of it stands Jesus. He remains, from start to finish, the quintessential, non-anxious one.

Rabbi Friedman once observed, "There is a chronic anxiety that comes with the territory of living." In that observation are echoes of a theme common in the work of a twentieth century theologian named Paul Tillich, who spoke of human anxiety as estrangement "from the origin and aim of our life." The only remedy for this, in Tillich's thinking, was the pure gift of God's grace.

OPEN AND RELATIONAL LEADERSHIP

In one of his most famous sermons, he affirmed that grace strikes us as though a voice were saying: "You are accepted. You are accepted...by that which is greater than you, and the name of which you do not know...do not try to do anything now...do not seek for anything; do not perform anything; do not intend anything. Simply accept the fact that you are accepted!" When that happens, "everything is transformed."

At a workshop he led, I once asked Edwin Friedman if he had ever thought about the relationship between his concepts of a non-anxious, differentiated, and yet connected self, and that of Paul's teaching about justification by faith. He replied that he had not, then paused, and added, "That's interesting. I'll give it some thought." (A few years later, he developed a fascinating program on the relationship between family process and process theology.)

I think it is well worth our giving that some thought as well. What might it mean that we can stand, justified in Christ, as a non-anxious presence before God? One of the Eucharistic prayers in *The 1979 Book of Common Prayer* puts it this way: "For in these last days you sent him to be the Savior and Redeemer of the world. In him, you have delivered us from evil, and made us worthy to stand before you."

Those who exercise leadership—however imperfectly—from a non-anxious presence must be immersed in a way of being that enables their graces and gifts to flow from that deep divine well of acceptance. Tillich referred to this God as "the ground of being."

For Christians I believe this means being rooted in the way of love to which Jesus calls us. The origin, source, and end of that love is the God of Jesus—who is holy, inexhaustible, and eternal non-anxious presence in and through all creation.

Joe Goodwin Burnett was Episcopal bishop of Nebraska from 2003-2011. Prior to that, he served twenty-five years as a priest in Mississippi, and later taught pastoral theology at the School of Theology in Sewanee, Tennessee. More recently, he was assistant bishop in Maryland, and interim rector at St. Columba's in Washington, DC. He currently resides in Rapid City, South Dakota.

6

Three-in-One Leadership: Creative, Sacrificial, and Transformative

EMMAN T. CHAPMAN

Leading with love is modelled in the active presence and work of our creative, sacrificial, and transformative Three-in-One God.

Shalom!! That has been my heart's cry for as long as I can remember, although I did not always have that Hebrew word for "peace" to describe it. At the age of three my parents divorced. My sister and I stayed with our mom. My biological father all but disappeared. Like any child, I loved my dad and missed him deeply. My mom told me of times in the first couple of years, when I looked longingly out the front window of our house, desperate for him to come see me. But he never did. I saw him only a handful of times after the divorce.

The most recent time was almost 20 years ago. I rode an emotional roller coaster of loving and wanting to see him to hating him and never wanting to see him again. My father's rejection of me created a deep-seated shame within me. I blamed myself. I thought there was something wrong with me. I was not good enough for my own father. I was broken and unlovable. At the same time, I longed to be loved. I felt a huge void in my life and desperately needed to fill it. My mother poured as much as she could into me. But she could not replace my dad or heal the hurt that I felt in my heart because he abandoned me. His absence continued to mold and shape me throughout my childhood, adolescence and into early adulthood.

OPEN AND RELATIONAL LEADERSHIP

My life's goal has been to find *shalom*, a peace that only exists in a deep sense of well-being and right relationship with self, others and God. I need to know and experience a love that offers a genuine self-worth that cannot be shaken or taken. Along life's journey I have looked for *shalom* in a lot of places and people. All of those places and people resulted in more hurt for me as well as for others. Eventually, I found the love I was looking for in Jesus. And for the past 30 years I have been on a journey led by the love of God into my own worth and lovableness in Christ. Daily, the Holy Spirit leads me, in love, farther into peace.

As a husband, father, pastor, mentor, counsellor, and friend I have influence in a lot of people's lives. I am seen as a leader and guide toward a vision of well-being and peace. I am responsible, and accountable, for the impact my leadership has on the people around me. I can honestly say that my deepest longing for all people is *shalom*. I want us all to experience, express, and expand God's Kingdom of well-being and right relationships by being transformed through the love of God. I want only to lead people into that space of grace and peace. But how do I do that? How do I lead others as God leads?

In looking back over my life, I can see God's presence throughout my journey. God was with me through my Mom. God was with me through my friends, teachers, family, and even pets. God was with me wherever I felt love, courage, comfort, encouragement, acceptance, strength and hope. Ultimately, I believe God's presence is the key. God-With-Us reminds us that we are not alone, that we are deeply loved by the Creator of all things, and that we are worth God's time, efforts, and sacrifice. To genuinely find rest in God-With-Us is to truly experience well-being and right relationship that fills us with a worth and love from which we cannot be separated.

As leaders, we are called to be with others in the particular way God is with us. God is not just sitting there and watching. But God is not controlling us either. We find God's way of actively present love in the unique works of the Trinity, our Three-in-One God. God is actively present with a Three-in-One Love that is creative, sacrificial and transforming.

As we see in the Genesis creation stories, God the Father creates spaces of right relationships between all people, animals, plants and God. God creates space in which God enters to spend time with creation. And in these spaces, we are free to love and be loved. We are free to make choices. Even choices to reject God's space and break our relationship with God. Throughout the Old Testament, we see that God continues to create space after space and opportunity after opportunity for all people to come back into right relationship with themselves, each other, and God. God never stops creating space for people. God never abandons us.

In the gospels, God the Son humbly pours out his status as God in order to be born and live among us in the space God the Father creates. God the Son is Jesus the Christ, Emmanuel, God-With-Us. Jesus embodies love because God is Love (1 John 4:7-21). Hebrews 1 and Colossians 1 tell us that Jesus is the exact revelation of God's fullness and character. In his birth, life and death, we see God, who is love. A love that is present, sacrificial, honouring, compassionate, embracing, encouraging, and empowering. Jesus ultimately expresses the love of God in his willingness to be vulnerable to rejection and crucifixion at the very hands of those he came to love.

In the book of Acts and throughout the epistles of the New Testament, we see the active presence of God's love in the work of the Holy Spirit. When people enter into the space created by God the Father and experience the sacrificial love of God the Son, they begin to open up their hearts, minds and bodies to the transforming work of God the Holy Spirit. The Holy Spirit renews willing minds and sanctifies willing hearts, transforming people into new creations compelled by Love, who is God. People begin the journey toward perfection in love as God the Father is perfect in love (Matthew 5:43-48).

I affectionately call my Uncle Dan, Superman. I was four years old, around a year after my father abandoned me, when my Uncle Dan took me to see the original Superman movie at the theatre. A couple of my earliest memories are of holding his hand as we walked into the theatre and the scene of baby superman in the capsule being hurled toward earth, where he would be embraced and loved by someone other than his biological father. Throughout my life, Uncle Dan continued to create space for me in his life. And in that space, he actively loved me and helped me to feel like I was worthy.

As a young adult, I met with him and talked about the challenges of life. Even when I made bad choices (and I made many), he made time for me, listened to me, loved me and encouraged me. He has been, and still is, a consistent presence of worth and love in my life. His influence is a large part of who I am today. And throughout our sharing of life together, Uncle Dan has allowed himself to be influenced and impacted by my presence in his life. He allows me to inspire and encourage him in his life and ministry. I know and experience *shalom* when I am with Superman.

In my Uncle Dan I see and experience the love of God. He has led me by creating spaces of grace for me, sacrificially loving me in those spaces, and allowing the Holy Spirit to work freely in those spaces to influence and transform us both in the process. This is what it looks like to lead with God's love. We create space for others without oppressive expectations or rules. Spaces that are open to all people, regardless of who they are, who they were, or who they are becoming. We embody the sacrificial love of Christ in those spaces. We do not judge or shame others. We are patient, compassionate, gentle, honoring, and sacrificial. We seek to help others see their beauty and potential that God has created within them. Our active presence has the single aim of revealing to all people that they are beloved and worthy children of God. We trust the Holy Spirit to transform us and everyone else in those spaces. We let the Holy Spirit do the saving and renewing of people through right relationships that meet each person at their own brokenness and love each person toward freedom and healing in their own time.

If we lead with Three-in-One Love, then we will see the fruit of transformed people leading in the same way; by creating spaces, embodying sacrificial love, and participating in the transformation of others and themselves along the way. And thus, the Kingdom of God's *Shalom* is continuously experienced, expressed and expanded.

Emman T. Chapman is an Ordained Elder in the Church of The Nazarene. He is currently pastoring in Brisbane, Australia at Place of Peace Church of The Nazarene, a member of the ANWD Missional/District Superintendency Team and of the Board of Trustees for Nazarene Theological College – Brisbane. He earned a M.Div. from NTC-Brisbane and a master's degree in Counselling from Trevecca Nazarene University.

7

The Toughness of Grace

HANS DEVENTER

Open and relational leadership is accepting grace for yourself and looking out for what grace can do in the life of others.

One of the greatest challenges of the Christian life is to accept grace. This seems like a weird statement because, what can be better than to know you are forgiven? You'd think that the whole world would run to this experience like bees to honey. And yet, it is not so. German theologian Dietrich Bonhoeffer, in his book *The Cost of Discipleship*, famously talks about costly and cheap grace, explaining that the latter is a system. Though he does not mention it, to me it looks like an apt description of relational grace and non-relational grace. For non-relational grace is like a dogma, a belief that does not actually change you. Like the knowledge that the earth is not the center of our solar system, but our sun is. For your daily life, either of these options don't change a thing. In fact, when faith functions like a system, it becomes unhelpful, if not, in fact, damaging.

To me, one of the best examples of a damaging non-relational belief is the infamous penal substitution theory of the atonement. As with all the other theories, it is a metaphor that inevitably breaks down at some point, but this one breaks down really quickly. The Scriptures do speak of justice and of punishment, even of God being a judge. But a judge is one who sets things right. He or she defeats the enemy, liberates the people of God and restores the relationship between God and the people.

We, however, have a judicial system in which people are declared "not guilty," and released, or "guilty," and sentenced to a punishment, a fine, time served in jail, or even face capital punishment. In this system, if it were possible for someone to fulfil the conditions of the sentence on behalf of the accused, the judgement would effectively be removed. Subsequently the judge too is removed from any necessary or essential relationship with the defendant. This is not at all the central idea of the Christian faith. It in no way represents the heart of all that is being presented by the prophets and ultimately by Jesus.

A relational view of atonement should definitely include us, and it should restore the relationship between God and us. It should not merely deal with guilt and punishment, but rather with restoration and reconciliation.

This short example tells us something about a relational view of leadership, and obviously God is our prime example of that. God is the ultimate parent and leader, which has huge implications for our own leadership.

From the very start in the creation story, God gives humanity room. YHWH brings animals to Adam in order to see which names he would give them. As early as Genesis 2, we are able to identify a very open and relational approach to leadership. God is working with humanity in a way that honors humanity's choices. In fact, throughout the Scriptures, humanity is taken very seriously. Love does that. In Matt 23:37, Jesus laments that he desired to gather Jerusalem under his wings, but they did not want to do that, implying that he could not, in fact, make them come.

Of course, this applies totally to our own leadership. We must give room, because we cannot force people. We cannot lead those who do not want to be led. We cannot convince those who do not want to be convinced. And we cannot heal those who do not want to be healed (even apart from our skills and knowledge). Open and relational leadership might therefore be considered "weak leadership," but I would contend it is the only *real* leadership. Trying to enforce anything might produce short term results but will eventually always break down. Obedience is not God's goal. Again, also from the very beginning (Genesis 3:9), God is in search of humanity. God is seeking response and seeking a relationship.

We also find God changing God's plans based on the realization that it "is not good for the man to be alone" (Gen 2:18). It is interesting to see God declaring all God created to be "good," yet within that process, seems willing, and not at all shocked, to adapt. The concept of "good" is not static, and neither is God's open and relational approach to creation and humankind.

This has significant implications for leadership. We may want to "stay the course," considering the goal of restoration and reconciliation, but the road to that goal is not fixed, not even for God. The Messiah was born from David's line, through Batseba, despite David's personal sin. Even Israel's consistent disobedience becomes the context in which the whole world is brought the gospel. Good can indeed come out of bad situations. This is not to deny the evil or sinfulness of these circumstances but highlights our understanding that God is able to somehow work good out of bad situations. The crucial thing here is that God can do that. Therefore, part of being "open" in our leadership is to remain open to God and what God can do.

Finally, God forgives. If there is one key concept that runs throughout the Scriptures, it is forgiveness. Actions have consequences. God takes us seriously and so God takes our actions seriously. But forgiveness is primarily about the restoration of the relationship that we have broken by these choices. It is not that our guilt and punishment are removed, as if that were the exclusive goal. They are removed, but the goal of forgiveness is restoration and reconciliation to God and others. Prime examples of those are Psalm 103 and Jesus' famous parable on the prodigal son in Luke 15.

This, of course, is crucial for leadership, primarily because we must first accept that grace ourselves in order to be able to lead. Unless we thoroughly and deeply know ourselves to be forgiven, we will transmit our lack of grace rather than God's love. We cannot share what we have not received. But real grace is tough. It is a death. A death to all our foolish pretence that we are not so bad ourselves. Jesus exposes that notion for what it is in Luke 18 in his parable of the Pharisee and the tax collector. Grace starts with stark honesty.

Also, grace is fundamentally unfair. Therefore, this starting point is so important. Unless you see who you are yourself, it is so easy to look down on others in a judgemental way. And declare they do not deserve grace. Which, in fact, is true. They don't. And you don't. But that is exactly what grace is: unmerited favor.

Open and relational leadership is looking out for what God can do in any situation. It is being open to the work of the Holy Spirit and understanding that the world is not a predetermined play that God is watching, but rather an adventure in which new things are possible.

With this relational concept of leadership, God's laws and commandments can be understood in terms of guidance for liberated people that gives them direction in their lives. They point towards God. They are not the goals, let alone boundaries, to keep others out. They are Torah, or teaching, they primarily show Israel how to live in relation with God. As the Word incarnate, Jesus has shown us the most effective example of that very principal. And he wants to dwell in us! How much more relational can it get?

Hans Deventer is an ordained elder in the Church of the Nazarene, serving the Dordrecht Church in the Netherlands. Through the years, he has served the church in numerous ways, as a layman and more recently, as an elder. He loves mountains and hiking.

8

Does Godly Leadership Require Certainty About God?

MIKE EDWARDS

Leaders proclaiming certainty have not allowed God's open and relational ways to guide individuals in their own time.

I am grateful for pastors of churches I attended in the past who encouraged getting to know God. In retrospect, it seems pastors felt compelled to proclaim certainty of what God thought, according to their understanding of Scriptures. Perhaps they felt an internal pressure due to leadership expectations from parishioners. Didn't pastors, though, read books where biblical scholars, who respect the authority of Scriptures, do not always agree? Total certainty is an illusion because even if God is Truth, we still have to discern what is Truth. For example, can preachers or priests be women or gay? Many are leaving the institutional church because of the lack of honest, open dialogue. God's example seems more open and relational because of the freedom given to understand God in our own time.

It's hard to be relational when you are so damn certain.

One would think Christians would be the least judgmental people in the world. After all, they believe in loving others like they want to be loved. Catholics and Protestants, or whatever other representation of the church may apply, seem compelled to establish creeds, as if uncertainties about God are a sign of weakness. It isn't always voiced that you are required to accept their doctrines to participate, but try challenging them and see where that gets you! If God was so concerned about beliefs such as the Trinity, angels, the Bible, the Virgin

Mary, or hell, it seems there would be more agreement. Maybe Christians would be more united and less judgmental if religions only encouraged the Creed of Love as the Spirit guided individuals.

No, uncertainty doesn't have to lead to lawlessness!

I am not suggesting anything goes in the declaration that we can't be certain. No one questions laws against murder. Criminals don't deny their actions are wrong; they deny they committed such a crime. Unless you are a terrorist, it is almost universally accepted that it is morally wrong to kill or behead someone because of his or her beliefs. We don't have to fear uncertainty. Different opinions, expressed without physical or verbal aggression, can stand side by side, as we continually evaluate the most loving approach or understanding of God.

The idea of an infallible or inspired Bible may be a reason Christians claim certainty.

The Bible certainly is a resource to discover what God is like, though the majority of people born into this world didn't have a Bible or knowledge of Jesus. There must be other ways to know God! Infallibility is a non-starter because we don't have the original manuscripts. The many translations or versions of the Bible we have today suggest copying is not an exact process. Even if we had the original autographs, interpretation is still required. Scholars who believe in the authority of Scriptures disagree regarding what the Bible says about critical issues such as homosexuality, gender roles, divorce, and hell, among many other things.

Interpretations are fallible, but most people do not begin a discussion with "I may be wrong..." Keep in mind that we can't prove that God inspired every word of the Bible, unless you argue a biblical writer making such a claim is definitive evidence. The possibility of a fallible book encourages questioning rather than demonizing views to the contrary. We have every right to question interpretations that suggest a Creator does not love in the way we were created to love. God-followers seem unaware of how often they appear to be unopen and morally superior based on their assumptions about the Bible.

How can we know God?

Some declare God is mysterious when their interpretation of the Bible makes God appear immoral, but how can we have a relationship with a God we can't understand with the brain God gave us? Is evil sometimes mysteriously good?

The Bible assumes we can understand God by challenging us to be perfect like God (Mt. 5:48). We can only understand God's perfect love by the way we humans were created to love perfectly. It is intuitive to think that the perfect love of God and human are the same. That is why the mystery card is used when God seems unloving from a human perspective. A Creator surely loves others and us in the same way that we were seemingly created to love others.

Where has certainty in God's name gotten us?

It is logical to suggest we can't be certain of what an invisible, inaudible God thinks. But supposed certainty has led to justifying slavery. It has led to revered theologians such as St. Augustine and John Calvin not firmly opposing the execution of those who didn't agree with their theology. The Bible can't be the definitive guide to what God would do because scholars who respect Scriptures disagree on so many issues. And it clearly is wrong to behead people because they don't share your personal beliefs about God.

Jesus didn't judge uncertainty.

Jesus performed many miracles, but his disciples/followers still didn't believe. Jesus didn't cast away Peter when warning him he would deny Jesus three times; I believe Peter now is called the "Rock." Jesus hung out with all kinds of people that didn't share his certainty. Jesus didn't unload on others when their beliefs weren't his, unless you were a religious authority who was misrepresenting God. My hunch is that God, like parents, would rather be doubted than ignored.

Is God unloving by not being more visible, thus more certain?

We may wonder why God isn't more obvious in our lives. God's awe-filled or overpowering presence may only lead to fearful obligations to obey. When parents push their agendas, even if in their children's best interests, a child may resent or rebel against coercion and never turn back from that rebellion. If God communicates in less demonstrative ways, this may allow for heartfelt choices. God may know what a controlling parent never learns: the road of learning, reflecting, and non-coerced choices may best lead to lasting convictions.

God's love is not controlling. Controlling love is an oxymoron. Authenticity, the highest good in relationships, is impossible without freedom. Not even an almighty God can force true love. It isn't that God has the power to do something and doesn't. God can't control or violate freedom and love perfectly. God, like parents, had a choice—not to create or to create knowing suffering was a possibility in the pursuit of intimacy. Divine love limits divine power. God is open to changing the world at relational speed.

Uncertainty can lead to acting more lovingly.

Being unable to declare the certainty or morality of our opinions forces us to listen and express ideas openly. God understands, as much as humans do, that forcing beliefs does not lead to long-lasting changes. Starting a conversation with "I may be wrong…" will more likely lead to new understandings and creative solutions. Conversations change when humility is part of the tone. Certainty, when it comes to political matters such as taxes or health plans, has led to justifying verbal or physical violence in the name of God or morality. Differences don't have to lead to chaos but can be resolved by remaining open-minded to the most loving ways.

The Bible tells us the Word of God is not the Bible; it is flesh in the body of Jesus (Jn. 1:1-14). Jesus, when leaving this earth, didn't promise to leave us with a Bible, but with God's Spirit to aid in discerning good from evil (Jn. 14:16). Doesn't the Spirit speak to us somehow when we have thoughts to be the perfect partner, parent, or friend we desire to be deep down, despite our constant failures? It may be good that that the Spirit doesn't communicate audibly. The Bible may be more direct communication, but it has been used to force beliefs on others despite being subject to interpretation. Leaders who admit uncertainty, rather than certainty, about God, keep from imposing beliefs on others, which is just not in God's open or relational nature.

Mike Edwards earned his M.Ed. in Counseling at Georgia State University. Mike blogs at what-god-may-really-be-like.com and donewithreligion.com He asks questions in hopes that individuals may reconsider any beliefs they hold about God that discourage pursuing God and spirituality. Mike loves to play tennis, read, and spend time with his family.

9

Revelation in Relationship: Leadership as Affirmation and Spiritual Formation

BRUCE EPPERLY

Open and relational theologies prize the interplay of relationship, reciprocity, and revelation, and this encourages healthy and affirmative relational styles.

Theology matters. Our theological viewpoints can be a matter of life and death, health and illness, and positive and negative approaches to leadership. Our images of God, God's relationship to the world, and our relationships with one another can be factors in promoting authoritarian or collaborative leadership styles. Open and relational theologies prize the interplay of relationship, reciprocity, and revelation, and this encourages healthy and affirmative relational styles.

Open and relational theologies affirm the statement: "God in all things and all things in God." The affirmation "God in all things," the divine ubiquity, has profound implications for interpersonal and institutional relationships. From this perspective, regardless of our awareness, God's Spirit speaks within each of us "in sighs too deep for words," providing possibilities for immediate and direct insight as well as more nuanced unconscious inspiration and synchronicity. (Romans 8:26) There are no God-free or Godless zones nor is any creature bereft of divine guidance. Unlike traditional Calvinist theologies which separate the world in terms of saved and damned, elect and reprobate, and by implication, god-inspired and godforsaken, the ubiquity of divine revelation makes each encounter and every individual a potential revealer of divine wisdom. This insight can significantly shape our professional and personal relationships. Wise leaders recognize that those with whom they work are influenced by God and, thus, may become sources of institutional, congregational, and workplace insight. Moreover, revelation inspires reception and reciprocity, the willingness to be transformed by others' experiences, whether at the divine or human levels of experience.

In over nearly forty years of institutional, classroom, and congregational leadership, I have tried to approach leadership in terms of God's ubiquitous revelation and the importance of being shaped by others' insights. While my leadership role gives me primary responsibility for maintaining the right blend of order and novelty, and structure and freedom, in any given institutional setting, my perception of this "democracy of revelation," grounded in divine ubiquity, has encouraged me to look for truth and guidance from others in every relational setting. I have discovered that healthy leadership provides a "playing field" that promotes mutuality and creativity. As an academic, congregational, or classroom leader, I seek to look beneath the surface of those whom I teach and supervise to experience and support their deeper holiness and divinity as well as spiritual and scholarly initiative. From this perspective, every person and every encounter can be a medium of revelation for those whose senses are trained toward divinity.

This democracy of revelation invites leaders to be on the lookout for wisdom and insight wherever it is found, often in the most unlikely places. The universality of revelation grounded in the vision of a relational God transforms our understanding of power dynamics. Bernard Loomer, with whom I studied at Claremont Graduate School, described two kinds of power, unilateral and relational. These two power dynamics relate to God-world as well as interpersonal relationships.

These two approaches to power reflect radically different understandings of revelation. Unilateral power, grounded in authoritarian understandings of the relationship of God and the world and, accordingly, promoting authoritarian understandings of the relationship of leaders and followers, sees revelation as limited and binary in nature. Those in authority "know" what's right and divide the world into the informed and uninformed, competent and incompetent, and saved and lost. They don't need, and can't be bothered with, alternative viewpoints, which, by definition, have nothing of value to offer. From the perspective of unilateral power, knowledge and insight is understood as finite and zero-sum in nature. Accordingly, the knowledge and viewpoints of "inferiors" are always a threat to those in authority. "My way or the highway" is an appropriate leadership style if leadership is seen as unilateral in character.

If others have insights—and in a binary world this is unlikely—then it is possible that I (the leader) may be wrong or, more charitably, need to learn from those whose credentials I perceive as inferior to my own. If they are permitted to be knowledge bearers or have a role in shaping the classroom, organization, or congregation I lead, then my monopoly on knowledge and power is put at risk. Their self-affirmation and self-expression threaten my understanding of leadership.

In contrast, relational power and knowledge is based on a perception of inspirational abundance which welcomes diverse viewpoints and multiple intelligences and ways of knowing as contributing to a growing body of knowledge, power, and effectiveness. In an open and evolving universe, we are always in process and growing. This is even the case for Jesus of Nazareth, who "grew in wisdom and stature and favor with God and humankind." (Luke 2:52) Relational knowledge and leadership is always incomplete, subject to change, and communal in spirit. In an affirmative community, the gifts and gains of one member positively impact the totality and promote greater creativity and achievement. (I Corinthians 12:7-30, especially 12:26)

Revelation leads to reciprocity as leaders are transformed by their relationships. Bernard Loomer, who coined the term process-relational theology, asserts that "size" or "stature" is fundamental to spiritual growth and healthy relatedness. According to Loomer:

By size I mean the stature of a person's soul, the range and depth of his love, his capacity for relationships. I mean the volume of life you can take into your being and still maintain your integrity and individuality, the intensity and variety of outlook you can entertain in the unity of your being without feeling defensive or insecure. I mean the strength of your spirit to encourage others to become freer in the development of their diversity and uniqueness.[1]

Leaders of stature, such as Abraham Lincoln who gathered a "team of rivals" to be his cabinet in the darkest days of the United States Civil War, welcome diverse and creative viewpoints, including those that critique and challenge. They see differing viewpoints, shared civilly and for the well-being of the community, as aesthetic contrasts rather than win-lose oppositions. Large-spirited leaders are cosmopolitan in outlook, seeking to go beyond their own parochial viewpoint to embrace wider and wider circles of concern. As Mahatmas on the job, these leaders encourage wholeness and collaboration in the contexts where they lead. They recognize that professional, classroom, and workplace well-being and growth are contingent on appreciation and affirmation, of supporting as much creativity and freedom as possible given the overall needs of the specific context.

In my own approach to leadership, whether in congregation, classroom, or seminary, I am guided by the following theological and spiritual affirmations. I make these evident to colleagues and students by my words and actions:

There are many ways and many possible "right" answers to life's most important questions. (Sometimes the "right" answer depends on our perspective or the dynamics of institutional, congregational, or classroom life, as well as the realities of change.)

Each person has inner wisdom that can be shared for the well-being of the classroom, congregation, or community.

Our workplace, congregation, or classroom is a laboratory for recognizing your gifts and cultivating your voice for leadership.

Our workplace, congregation, or classroom is a laboratory for recognizing your limitations and fallibility and cultivating your need to hear other voices.

Expressing gratitude and appreciation encourages partnership and creativity.

Leadership involves looking for insight and guidance in unexpected places. (For example, listen to the children of the congregation; pay attention to the quiet members of the group; heed the helpful comments of "naysayers" as well as "positive thinkers.")

Speak your truth, but share it with humility and love, recognizing others' different perspectives and need for self-esteem.

Accept the insights of others and let them widen your perspective and practice as a community and in your leadership role.

In an open and relational world, there is no final answer. We are constantly in process and are at our best when we initiate novel responses to the novelties of our environment.

Theology makes a difference. Prizing relatedness and possibility makes leadership the art of spiritual midwifery for leaders, colleagues, students, and institutions. With the poet Rumi, I believe that there are (at least) a hundred ways to kneel and kiss the ground. Accordingly, entertaining a variety of perspectives, coming from various members of a team or class, brings forth new perspectives, expands ownership and commitment, and opens the door to new possibilities. This is the way God works in the world, nurturing creativity in our world, receiving our creative contributions, and inviting us to be partners in healing an unfinished world.

[1]Bernard Loomer, "S-I-Z-E is the Measure," Harry James Cargas and Bernard Lee, *Religious Experience and Process Theology*, 70.

Bruce Epperly is Senior Pastor and Teacher, South Congregational Church, United Church of Christ, Centerville, MA, and professor in the areas of theology, spirituality, and ministry in the D.Min. Program at Wesley Theological Seminary. He is the author of over fifty books, including The Mystic in You: Discovering a God-filled World; Become Fire: Guideposts for Interspiritual Pilgrims; and Process Theology: Embracing Adventure with God.

10

Godlike Dominion Not Human Opinion: Redefining Leadership in God's Economy

ROB A. FRINGER

Leadership is redefined in terms of God's mandate to live Godlike dominion in our world.

Corruption of power is an everyday occurrence in our world. Sadly, it has not escaped the institutional church. People are increasingly skeptical of Christianity and its leaders. As a result, God's name is blemished in the court of public opinion, and the opinion is that God no longer matters. Maybe the problem isn't power, but how we, the church, wield it. Maybe the dilemma arises out of our misunderstanding of power and its purpose. Instead of looking to God for our example, we have too often emulated the world around us. This must change!

In the opening chapter of Genesis, we learn of humanity's creation and of God's first mandate to us.

> *26 Then God said, "Let us make humankind in our image, according to our likeness; and let them have dominion over the fish of the sea, and over the birds of the air, and over the cattle, and over all the wild animals of the earth, and over every creeping thing that creeps upon the earth." 27 So God created humankind in his image, in the image of God he created them; male and female he created them. 28 God blessed them, and God said to them, "Be fruitful and multiply, and fill the earth and subdue it; and have dominion over the fish of*

the sea and over the birds of the air and over every living thing that moves upon the earth." (Gen 1:26-28, NRSV)

There is a clear parallel between the image of God in which humanity was created and humanity's charge to have dominion over God's creation; it is repeated twice. We were given the opportunity and the responsibility to be the leaders. We were called to rule over the land and the animals of sea, air, and land, but not over other humans. Unfortunately, we quickly got it wrong. We mistakenly assumed that dominion and rule meant controlling and exploiting those persons and things that should have been under our protection. We used power for our own personal gain. In the Fall, there was another significant shift that took place; the harmony and union of humanity was disrupted, and a hierarchical system emerged as the inevitable consequence of sin—man began to rule over woman (Gen 3:16).

Is this what dominion was supposed to look like? In order to answer this question, we must address one of the most significant questions set before the church in each and every generation— *"Who is this God?"* Is this God a malevolent overlord hell-bent on judgement and completely self-absorbed, or is this God a benevolent and loving parent desiring intimate relationship with humanity? Obviously, there are other options in the middle. Nevertheless, the point is that our understanding of God significantly influences our self-understanding. We have been created in God's image and charged with having dominion over creation in the same way God exercises dominion. If God is relational, then our leadership must also be relational. If God exercises dominion through loving influence, then we must abandon coercion and manipulation and find ways to lead in love.

It is sometimes claimed that we get two contradicting pictures of God between the Old and New Testaments. In other of my writings, I have argued strongly against such an assertion. Throughout the Old Testament, we see examples of God's relational nature. God's unrelenting forgiveness toward individuals and whole communities (e.g., Israel in the book of Hosea, and Nineveh in the book of Jonah) attests to God's unbounding love. God desires relationship and continues to provide avenues to make this possible. God's calling of Abraham (Gen 12), Moses (Exod 3-4), and the whole people of Israel is proof that God's overarching plan of salvation, redemption, and restoration includes human involvement. Rather than ruling with an iron first, God invites participation in mission.

In case we are still in doubt concerning the Old Testament representation of God, we must remember that Christ is the ultimate revelation of the Father. This is clearly articulated in John's Gospel—"Whoever has seen me has seen the Father" (John 14:9, NRSV). Furthermore, Christ is sent by the Father (John 12:44), abides in the Father's love (John 15:10) and only does what he sees the Father doing (John 5:19). In other words, the Triune God (Father, Son, and Holy Spirit) is united in a single-minded mission to restore all of creation one relationship at a time. Christ reveals the fullness of God's love and shows us what Godlike dominion looks like. God's dominion is defined by God's love! Therefore, just as God's love is epitomized in self-emptying surrender, so is God's power (Phil 2:5-8). And God extends this kind of Godlike dominion to us, the Church.

The New Testament uses a family of Greek words (*oikonomia* and cognates) to refer to the position and act of managing or stewarding the people and possessions under one's care (Luke 12:42; Titus 1:7). This language is used to reference those entrusted by God (Eph 3:2; 1 Cor 4:1-2) and to speak about God's divine plan or economy of salvation (1 Tim 1:4-5). In a very real way, Scripture teaches us that all Christians have been entrusted by God and given stewardship over God's creation and over God's mission of reconciliation and restoration of all creation back to God. In other words, all Christians are leaders; and as such, we are called to lead in a very specific way, through personal relationship that flows out of our relationship with God. This kind of divine economy is only possible as we walk in relationship with God and as we live by the power of the Holy Spirit. We glorify God by reflecting God's image to a watching world. In the words of 1 Peter 4:10-11,

[10] Like good stewards of the manifold grace of God, serve one another with whatever gift each of you has received. [11] Whoever speaks must do so as one speaking the very words of God; whoever serves must do so with the strength that God supplies, so that God may be glorified in all things through Jesus Christ. To him belong the glory and the power forever and ever. Amen. (NRSV)

Through the incarnation, cross, and resurrection, the image of God can be fully restored in humanity as we place ourselves in Christ and are filled with the Holy Spirit. And with this renewed image, the creation mandate is reiterated and reestablished. We are once again entrusted to steward God's creation through God's love.

The wonder of God's dominion is that God yields power rather than wields it. This is because God is love (1 John 4:8, 16). God is, therefore, the definition of love. Love is always expanding, encompassing, encouraging, and empowering. If we are going to lead like God, then we must lead with love. It is not about controlling others. It is about releasing them while still walking alongside of them and seeking to help them be the best steward of the resources and gifts with which God has entrusted them. This kind of leadership will not be easy, and it will not be quick. Relationships are never easy or quick. But in God's economy, every person has value and every relationship is worth it.

By way of benediction, allow me to paraphrase John 3:16 as a mandate to us, God's church:

"For the Church so loved the world that she gave herself away in sacrificial leadership, so that everyone might come into relationship with Christ, might escape the destroying grip of sin, and might experience God's everlasting love both now and forevermore."

Go! And be this kind of Church and this kind of leader.

Rob A. Fringer, PhD (Manchester) is Principal and Lecturer in Biblical Studies and Biblical Language at Nazarene Theological College, Australian & New Zealand. Fringer is the author of Paul's Corporate Christophany (Pickwick, 2019) and Engaging the Story of God (Global Nazarene Publications, 2018), and co-author of Theology of Luck (Beacon Hill, 2015) and The Samaritan Project (The House, 2012).

11

The Uncontrolling Leadership of God

GABRIEL GORDON

> *God's nature of Uncontrolling Love is non-hierarchal, and we should model our own leadership after God's leadership.*

*I*s leadership the same as hierarchy? Within my personal experience, as a member of the Anglican Communion our leadership structure is three-tiered with Bishops, Priests, and Deacons, which seems hierarchical. We have what might be called a top-down or pyramid model. We share this same basic structure with Roman Catholics, and the Eastern Orthodox. Lest anyone think hierarchy is just found in these traditions, let me assure you they are in the majority of the Christian world. In fact, this system of leadership is in most of the world, Christian or not!

However, is hierarchy the model of leadership that aligns with who God is? My opinion (as an edgy Anglican) is that it is not. God's nature, as Uncontrolling Love, exhibits itself not in hierarchy. Since hierarchy seems to be at some level controlling, there can be no hierarchy found in God. As the author of the epistle of Diogentes says, "There is no compulsion found with God," thus if hierarchy is controlling it is not compatible with God's nature of Uncontrolling Love. Instead, God's nature is enacted in egalitarian ways—what we may call a flat model of leadership. As an example, the Incarnation itself is an egalitarian, non-hierarchical action of God. Through the Incarnation, we get a glimpse into the nature of God. God relates to free creatures not as an *overlord*, that is by being over them; instead, as shown in the Incarnation, God relates to free creatures by being *among them*. "And the Word became flesh and lived *among us*." This was not a one-time event where God was not Incarnational prior to that point. Rather, *the Incarnation reveals what God has always been like*. There has never been a time in which God has not interacted through and in creation in a similar way to the *Incarnation* of Jesus Christ. Creation itself has always served as a vehicle for God enacting God's presence among God's creatures. In this way, God has always been *among* creation rather than *over it*.

When discussing leadership, one also thinks about authority. Leadership and authority go hand in hand. But what is authority? How do we define it in light of God's nature of Uncontrolling Love? Society has been built on a distorted and misunderstood definition of authority and power. The church is no less built on these same assumptions as the rest of society. According to the popular definition, authority is over and above, top down. It assumes that coercion is in reality the essence of power and authority. Servant leadership has been a concept used to dull the edge by the church. Or perhaps used to deviously cover-up our shared desire to rule over our fellow human beings. Too often, those who espouse servant leadership also assume the same faulty definition of power and authority; whereas true servant leadership is non-hierarchical.

For Christians, this worldly definition of authority is rooted in their view of God as one who controls. They see God as over and above creation. As ruling from the top down. They see God's Trinitarian nature as hierarchal. The Father is at the top giving command to the Son, who further delegates command to the Holy Spirit. But as we have already seen in the Incarnation this is not how God relates to creation, as an over-and-above type of leader. Otherwise, why did God come as a marginal Jew rather than as the king of the Roman Empire? Why would God have come *among* us humans at all? Yet, God comes *among us*, instructing us to reflect God's nature in how we do leadership. Indeed, it is because we are created in the image of an uncontrolling and non-hierarchical God that all humans are called to model that image. We do this by being uncontrolling and non-hierarchical. Just as the members of the Trinity are all equal before one another, so are all human beings equal before one another and the rest of creation, of which we are one part.

This also seems to be what Jesus teaches in regard to leadership. Jesus' teaching to his disciples is always a call to imitate God. "*Do this, because God is like this.*" As image bearers, we are to reflect God's nature by being like God. In Matthew, Jesus contrasts Rome's "over them" leadership by using the phrase "among you" to indicate how his disciples were to practice leadership. "But Jesus called them to him and said, 'You know that the rulers of the Gentiles *lord it over them*, and their great ones are tyrants *over them*. It will not be so *among you*; but whoever wishes to be great *among you* must be your servant, and whoever wishes to be first *among you* must be your slave; just as the Son of Man came not to be served but to serve, and to give his life a ransom for many.'" Jesus calls his disciples to practice a flat, among-them type of leadership rather than the common over-and-above leadership.

While hierarchy may still be assumed among church leadership, practicing hierarchy in other aspects of life are frowned upon. One of which is hierarchy in marriage. Some still believe the man is the head of the household, where he alone is the leader, over and above his wife. However, this view is starting to fall out of favor in Western culture, especially among mainline Protestant churches. Another example where a hierarchical practice was initially upheld but then stopped was slavery—humans owning other humans. In the 19th century, this was such a heated topic it created schisms in various denominations. Many denominations believed hierarchy between a slave and master was not only acceptable but part of God's design. This view has largely, if not completely, been abandoned in the Western church.

There seems to be a slow but steady abandonment of hierarchy in the church. First with hierarchy between slaves and masters, now steadily between husbands and wives. However, hierarchal leadership is still largely accepted and assumed. Even mainline or evangelical churches that have rejected hierarchy in slavery or marriage still hold over-and-above forms of leadership. This seems inconsistent to me. Why would hierarchy be bad in marriage but not in church leadership? Or between a slave and a master? Or a Jew and a Greek but not in church leadership? Is it consistent to reject hierarchy in one situation but not another? It seems as though we are in need of a fundamental redefinition of power and authority. Especially in the light of God's nature as Uncontrolling Love. When concepts like leadership, authority, and power are defined in terms of a person holding position over another, it can too easily become a justification for the act of devaluing our fellow human beings, plants, animals and the whole of creation. The language we use forms us into a certain kind of people. When we use this kind of hierarchical language, we become the kind of people who abuse others and use creation for our own selfish gain.

The theology of the Uncontrolling Love of God says God's very nature is love. Love, as the apostle Paul says, is never controlling. God acts in ways that are always consistent with God's nature. A truly orthodox view of the Trinity accepts that no one member of the Godhead is above or over the other. All stand on equal ground with one another. If they did not, could we say that God was truly one God and not three? If this is the case for God, then it also should be the case for humans in how we interact with one another. Particularly in our models of leadership.

Good theology should be practical. The study of theology is never an end in and of itself, but rather it is a means to an end. The goal is that through our study of theology we become more like God. If God is truly Uncontrolling Love, and by extension non-hierarchal, then to become more like God we must conform our whole lives to this image of God. This includes our notions of leadership. The church has begun this process by rejecting slavery and in some circles by rejecting one spouse as the head of the household. Yet, if we are to be consistent in our transformation into the likeness of Christ, we must also reject hierarchal leadership in all its forms.

Gabriel Gordon graduated with a double major in anthropology and cross-cultural ministry from Oklahoma Baptist University. He is currently working on his master of theological studies at Portland Seminary. He is the director of student ministries with Christ Church Episcopal and a co-founder of The Misfits Theology Club, a blog dedicated to working towards unity amongst diverse Christians.

12

Cutting Holes in Roofs: Making Paths for the Marginalized

BRITTNEY LOWE HARTLEY

Leaders are those who create paths for the marginalized to find the love of God.

It is not controversial to say that coercive leadership is unhealthy. Any obedience obtained through shame, guilt, or authority is shallow at best. It can even be said that humans have a natural proclivity for turning love into power when given the opportunity. But it is not as easy to agree on how to prevent love from becoming power. How do we better protect ourselves from ourselves?

As a Mormon, I especially witness the tension between communal love and hierarchical power. While Mormon doctrine claims Priesthood to be maintained "only by persuasion, by long suffering, by gentleness, and meekness, by love unfeigned, and by kindness," the reality is the Priesthood often feels like authority, required submission, coldness, judgment, misogyny, or dismissal. This is especially true for the marginalized including women, people of color, the LGBTQ community, intellectuals, single people, doubters, and those with mental or physical illness.

Joseph Smith himself sensed this tendency in human nature when he said, "We have learned by sad experience that it is the nature and disposition of almost all men, as soon as they get a little authority, as they suppose, they will immediately begin to exercise unrighteous dominion" (D&C 121:39). Unrighteous dominion to some degree happens so frequently as soon as any human comes into authority; it almost becomes the norm rather than the rare.

When coercion happens, the actor is no longer using Priesthood power at all. Like with the powers of God, Priesthood power cannot be "controlled nor handled only upon the principles of righteousness" (D&C 121:36). Joseph Smith even went so far as to say when we use Priesthood to "cover our sins, or to gratify our pride, our vain ambition, or to exercise control or dominion or compulsion upon the souls of the children of men, in any degree of unrighteousness, behold the heavens withdraw themselves" (37). Not only do the heavens withdraw themselves, but "Amen to the priesthood or the authority of that man" and "he is left unto himself" (37-38).

Herein lies the current predicament of the Mormon Church. There is tension between the doctrine of what Priesthood leadership is, which is described as non-coercive service that brings a people together in relationship, and the practice of how Priesthood leadership is done. There is currently no system in place by which a member may claim unrighteous dominion. While there may be doctrinal precedent, it is difficult practically speaking to say "Amen" to the Priesthood of the leader over him or her. What we are left with is Priesthood power acting as a vehicle for abuse.

One parable that highlights a solution lies in Mark 2. In it, a sick man cannot enter the house through the front door to reach Jesus. But there were four who did not take no for an answer. When there was no way in, they cut a hole in the roof to lower the man into the room to be healed. The parable reminds us that true leadership is not a seat of honor in the house, but on the roof, making paths for those who are unable to enter. Without those leaders, those who are the most sick will never be reached. All that will remain inside the house are the Pharisees jockeying for position. The most important question for a leader is not "how will I be seen?" but instead "where can I cut a hole in this roof for another?" Leaders are path makers.

Today, the prophets in Mormonism are not those who preside over the business affairs of the Church. They are those who break open our theology, Church culture, or power structures in order to make room for the marginalized. One modern example is Sam Young, a former Bishop who began gathering accounts of abuse by Mormon leadership. He brought forth hundreds of accounts of children being abused by Priesthood leaders. Mormonism is the only organization in America that currently allows a man in power to talk to a minor about sex behind closed doors, due to the Priesthood claim that they are judges in Israel. When a child was being abused, or reported abuse, the Bishop's hotline did not go to counselors, police officers, or experts in pastoral care. The abuse helpline goes to Church lawyers, who do what lawyers do: minimize the damage, protect the good name of the Church, and close the case with as little attention as possible. The idea of tithed money from members going to support non-disclosure agreements of abused, silenced children while the perpetrators are not reported to the police or even removed from positions of power seems just about as un-Christlike as one can get.

Sam Young, as with many of the prophetic voices in scripture, was eventually rejected by the power structure through excommunication. Rather than notice that this man was cutting a hole in our procedural roof in order to give voice to the abused children, the top leaders saw him as a rabble-rouser, and chose to protect Priesthood power and their claim that change only comes from the top down. Mormon men still have the power and authority to ask girls even under the age of 12 about sex, masturbation, and their bodies with no background check, no parent in the room, and no window on the door.

What we need from leadership today is the ability to inspire the angel within us while also providing measures to protect us from the devils that are so easily tempted by power. In each congregation there is a fair chance that there is a woman being beaten by her husband, a child being sexually abused, a family at risk of homelessness, a gay teenager who is being bullied, an immigrant who is not accessing available resources, a mentally ill adult, an addict on the brink of relapse, a widow forgotten by the world, and other modern lepers who live on the fringes. True leadership is the ability to create pathways to reach these most suffering of God's children. It is on the fringe of Jesus' clothing, where a woman was healed of her illness. A leader provides paths to allow her passage to Jesus while also preventing the worst of human nature from being able to stop her easily.

In the case of Sam Young, he presented ways in which our most vulnerable children among us could find the love of God and community. This included measures that requested an end to one-on-one interaction between adults and children, no one-on-one communication via technology between adult leadership and children, no private discussions relating to sex, criminal background checks for leaders, professional training on youth protection for leaders, establishing a complaint process for reporting leaders acting in ways not consistent with child protection, required reporting of child abuse, and an independent verifier to evaluate how well we are doing. What this did is create a path for children, when dismissed by men of power, to be able to reach a loving person who can help him or her in the way that Jesus would. Jesus called the children to him and chastised his followers from diminishing them. Sam Young made a path to prevent our community from being able to push away the child.

All acts of leadership require the question, "can I make a hole in the roof here in order for someone to experience God more fully?" It is the character of men to create clubhouses out of religion. The Church keeps out the marginalized in many ways. Leaders are the ones who break open the roofs and make room for more expansive love. The leaders in Mormonism today are the ones cutting open our theology in order to fit LGBTQ individuals into our heaven. They make paths by giving talks in our widely public General Conferences normalizing depression and mental illness. Such an act is as simple as telling a young woman she is welcome in class rather than condemning her for her immodest clothing. Or it can be as big as challenging the Church at large when it invades the separation of Church and State.

The true leaders in my community are the hell raisers, both in and out of the official ranks. Some may complain that they are damaging the roof of unorthodoxy. The community may exile some. But so were the leaders in the scriptures who came before them. Jesus warned that the path of leadership may well lead to persecution from the very Church that you serve. To lead, raise some hell so that more people can experience heaven.

Brittney Hartley is a history teacher in Boise, Idaho. She is the author of the book Mormon Philosophy Simplified: An Easy, LDS Approach to Classic Philosophical Questions. *She is a feminist voice in the Mormon community and writes often in various journals in Mormon thought highlighting the complex history, philosophical strengths, and blaring weaknesses of the Mormon tradition. When not writing she enjoys eating ice cream with her husband and four children.*

13

Allowing Good Things to Run Wild

DANA ROBERT HICKS

Worshipping a God that is open, changing, relational, influential, and empowering inspires us to create space to allow good things to run wild.

"And the more I considered Christianity, the more I found that while it had established a rule and order, the chief aim of that order was to give room for good things to run wild."
-- G.K. Chesterton

I don't remember much from my Introduction to Sociology class with Dr. Stellway 30 years ago, but he made a comment that stuck with me—"Sociologically speaking, a conservative is someone who has something to conserve." People who benefit from the status quo do not usually want the status quo to change.

While true in a political sense, this observation is also accurate when it comes to theology. Those who hold God as unchanging, immutable, and all-powerful tend toward a theology that is static and fixed. Some people are even willing to use coercive power to ensure the status quo. Rousseau, Mark Twain, and Voltaire have observed that God created people in God's own image and people returned the favor. When people don't want things to change, their god also tends to be unchanging.

But God's love is uncontrolling, influencing, empowering, and never coercive. Consequently, the most basic definition of healthy leadership is "influence." Great leaders lead through influence, not by control or coercion. Usually the people who make the deepest and most positive impact do not hold the titles of power; rather, it is those who operate from a moral authority and create change through influence. Martin Luther King, Jr., Mother Theresa, Albert Schweitzer, Desmond Tutu, and Malala Yousafzai are all examples of people who had no formal position of power, yet wielded incredible influence.

Leaders who lead with moral authority and influence change the course of human history. Leaders who lead with power, fear, and control are at worst despots and at best control behaviors through fear of punishment. Henri Nouwen observed, "It seems easier to be God than to love God, easier to control people than to love people, easier to own life than to love life."

Jesus is the ultimate example of a leader with no formal position who changed the course of human history. He never wrote a book, never commanded an army, never held a political office, never wielded power of any kind, was never on TV, and did not even have his own website. Yet no person has had a greater influence on the trajectory of Western Civilization than Jesus has.

Jesus did not come to start an institution or a religion; he came to start a movement. Movements are going somewhere and have end goals. For Jesus, that *somewhere* was what he called The Kingdom of God—a topic he talked about more than any other subject. The Kingdom of God is a place where everything is exactly the way God wants it to be: a place where nobody is marginalized or left out. It is a way of life in which love and not power is the currency. It is a place where good things have the room to run wild.

The early followers of Jesus were not initially known as "Christians," nor did they claim to be starting a new institution or a new religion. They were simply called "Followers of the Way" (Acts 22:4). They were part of a movement that had no power, no money, no military, and no clout in the Roman Empire in which they lived. Yet within 300 years, they had re-ordered the entire culture of the Roman Empire by following this "Way" of Jesus. As a matter of historical record: The Jesus movement transformed the way the Roman Empire viewed women, children, minorities, the sick, and the marginalized.

Every movement follows a predictable pattern. Movements begin as decentralized, small, and not very organized. They are usually just a handful of passionate people who believe in a great vision for the future. As the movement grows, gains ground, and things begin to change for the better, someone in the movement observes, "We have put a lot of effort into this movement. We need to find a way to preserve the gains of the past for future generations." It is at that moment that a movement starts to become an institution. Somebody must be a steward of the assets and resources—to make sure the staff has health insurance and that all the correct forms are filed with the IRS.

This isn't all bad. Movements and institutions should have a symbiotic relationship: movements progress; institutions preserve the gains of the past. Movements create culture; institutions preserve culture. Almost every great institution in our world finds its roots as a radical movement. This is why the old joke rings so true: "A conservative is someone who worships a dead progressive."

Institutions are not bad, but when we confuse the institution for the movement, we can trick ourselves into thinking we are serving the movement when we are actually only propping up nostalgia from the past in the form of an institution, or thinking that managing the organization is the same thing as being the church. Brian McLaren once observed:

One of our most common temptations is to turn the way into a place, to turn the adventure into a status, to trade the runway for the hangar, to turn the holy path into a sitting room—even if we call it a sanctuary. When the movement becomes an institution, those whose hearts call them to pilgrimage get restless.

Christianity represents its founder best when it is a movement. When the Jesus movement was "The Way," it changed the world. When it became "Christianity," it relinquished most of its power to the Roman government. The Jesus movement went from a force to be reckoned with to the ushering in of the Dark Ages. I saw a tweet recently that summed up the history of the Jesus movement this way: Christianity started out as a movement, moved to Greece and became a philosophy, went to Rome and became an institution, spread to Europe and became a government, and came to America and became an enterprise.

Many people admire the life and teachings of Jesus but tell me, "I am not really in to organized [institutional] religion." Most people do not want to join an institution, but a movement can be inspiring. What might it mean to re-capture the ethos of the Jesus movement in our day? What would it look like to create avenues to allow good things to run wild?

The Book of Acts describes the very beginning of the Jesus movement in which tongues of fire rested on the disciples' heads. Peter then preached to the bewildered crowd and quoted the prophet Joel:

In the last days, God says, I will pour out my Holy Spirit on all people. Your sons and daughters will prophesy. Your young men will see visions. Your old men will have dreams. In those days, I will pour out my Spirit on my servants. I will pour out my Spirit on both men and women. When I do, they will prophesy. (Acts 2:17-18; NIRV)

My Pentecostal friends like to focus on the tongues in this chapter: when the Spirit comes, people will speak in tongues. My Evangelical friends like to focus on the 3,000 who joined their ranks: when the Spirit comes, people who are far from God will find their way back to God. But the crux of Peter's message is found in this short statement: When the Spirit comes, people prophesy. They will dream dreams and see visions.

When people are in captivity or are oppressed, one of the first things they lose is their ability to dream, to hope for a better future, to dream that our lives will be better tomorrow than they are today, that our children will have a better life than we had. We lose the ability to dream that everyone will have food, clean water, and shelter, that people's bodies will not be violated by slavery or violence, that racial inequality will be something only read about in history books. So, Peter says when the Spirit comes, people will dream dreams and have visions of a better world.

In the movement of Jesus, there have been moments in which his followers were the dreamers and visionaries of the world. They lived on the cutting edge of innovation, change, and social issues: ending or healing human trafficking, sickness, the marginalization of women, and child exploitation. Sometimes Jesus' followers were on the cutting edge of art and technology. They dreamed dreams and saw visions of the Kingdom of God here on Earth as it is in Heaven. They created space for good things to run wild.

Sometimes when I am speaking to groups, I ask them to participate in a thought experiment with me. I ask, "What was the greatest innovation or social change in the 20th Century that was spearheaded by the church?" Without exception, whenever I ask this question, I get blank stares. There in fact may be some great innovation or social change that the church has spearheaded in the 20th Century, but the fact that they really must dig deep to think of it is telling. The movement of Jesus used to be on the edge of social issues, but now the church reacts to technology, change, and justice issues by trying to preserve the past rather than leading into the future. The church today is not a movement of dreamers and visionaries for what the future can be. In the United States, at best, it is an organization for people who like to study and are nostalgic for the past. At worst, it is an institution for administrators and managers who are attempting to control others' behavior through power and domination.

On the day of Pentecost, Peter speaks to the huge crowd and tells them that when the Holy Spirit comes, not only will they dream dreams and see visions, but they will prophecy. By prophecy, I don't think Peter was talking about some spooky foretelling like a tarot card reader. I think Peter is referring to the rich tradition of the prophets from the Hebrew Scripture who spoke truth to the powerful. Prophets in the Hebrew tradition were quirky people who were not very popular in their day, but looking back, everyone realized they were way ahead of their time. They did not defend the values of their day. They shaped the values of the future. Instead of blind allegiance, they questioned, examined, and took a knee to the moral defects of their time. They dreamed dreams and saw visions of a better world, they prophesied by speaking truth to the powerful, and they brought the Kingdom of God to Earth a little bit more.

The kind of people who dream dreams, see visions, and speak truth to the powerful have a very particular kind of God that they worship. If we worship an unchanging, all-powerful, dominating god, we will create institutions in "His"[1] image that are unchanging, static, controlling, and coercive. If we worship a God that is open, changing, relational, influential, and empowering, we will create life-giving movements as we dream dreams and see visions of the possibilities that God has for our world. We will create space to allow good things to run wild.

Dana Robert Hicks is the founding pastor at Crosspoint United Methodist Church in Boise, Idaho. He also serves as the Director for Leadership and New Campus Development at the Cathedral of the Rockies and as adjunct professor of Missional Leadership at Northwest Nazarene University. He earned his D. Min. from Asbury Theological Seminary. You can find his personal website at www.danahicks.org.

---

[1] The gender-exclusive language in reference to God in this context is intentional and meant to be ironic.

14

Lessons from the Break Room

NANCY R. HOWELL

Creativity is the key to transformative, relational leadership built on empowerment, encouragement, and passion of co-laborers and coworkers.

We all meet in the break room at some time because that's where the truth is told. The break room is the space where workers share their misery and discontent. "No one appreciates my work, and I spent hours on that project." "Are you kidding? I nearly killed myself on a job and the boss cancelled the project all together." "The worst thing about being here is that the work is boring, and I have no idea why we're doing it." I've never even seen the boss except when we're being criticized. I'm not even sure the boss knows what I do." Even when the work seems good and our coworkers are great, the break room is the space where we learn the best lessons about how a business or school should be run and what kinds of leaders are the best—at least, that's where I learned my lessons about leadership.

Being in a variety of jobs, we all know that we want our work to be meaningful, valued, and interesting (and fairly paid!). We want supervisors to know who we are and to respect us. We want leaders to understand the challenges and processes that come with our work assignments—and to trust our skills and knowledge. We want to know how our work contributes to a common goal and product. We want to value and respect those who lead us because we trust them both personally and professionally.

The good news is that new forms of leadership are emerging (in innovative tech companies, for example). The bad news is that poor leadership continues to frustrate workers and undermine their well-being. But, if we're creative and build good relationships, maybe new kinds of leaders will emerge, and the workplace will be a welcome space we're eager to see each day. The lessons I've learned from both good and poor leaders give me a vision for the possibilities we might realize in our working collaborations.

We've become accustomed to top-down leadership and associate leaders with power. No matter how confused or counterproductive a decision may be, we simply follow orders. Yet on the other hand, we know brilliant leaders whose skill invites us into a common project or idea, and we enthusiastically join their vision.

Whether we drag our feet or rush eagerly to our job sites depends on the kind of power wielded by those who supervise us. Speaking for myself, I know I'm a bit resistant when power is used to force me into an assignment that I don't understand, or suspect is based on a poorly developed plan. Am I just supposed to complete the assignment, preoccupied with the thought that I'm just wasting my time?

My attitude shifts, however, when I'm working with a confident and knowledgeable leader who shares and inspires power. Imagine a supervisor who does more than "boss." A wise leader empowers others by recognizing and appreciating the diverse talents, expertise, and skills each worker contributes. To share the stage with gifted employees, a leader must have both confidence and humility—equally engaging workers in her thoughtful planning while learning from workers the practical and insightful perspectives they bring from their desks or benches. Sometimes roles may be reversed when a leader must learn or even tackle a supportive (or even servant) role under the skillful tutoring of an employee. A great leader embraces her power and ability, but also respects the power of others as key to the success of a common project.

A leader who empowers others leads by encouragement. One image I've encountered depicts a leader as an orchestra conductor. Picture being faced with a stage full of extremely talented musicians who have been competitively auditioned for their seats in the orchestra. Each plays at least one instrument among the many that make up the brass, woodwind, string, and percussion sections. The leader-conductor is charged with knowing musical scores and then discerning what music best fits the talents and training of the musicians. With the concert performance in mind, the conductor must call the musicians to their best work: by rehearsing music that challenges and inspires the players, features their unique abilities, and doesn't underestimate their skills or deaden their enthusiasm. At the same time, the leader inspires musicianship with music that motivates the players, she must also be aware of what fits and enhances their talents.

In the ordinary workplace, a leader also motivates and inspires, and good relationships are essential to understanding what fits and enhances the talents of workers. A good leader knows the skills and knowledge she lacks and must hire well those employees whose expertise compensates for her vulnerabilities. Respecting employees for the experience and skill they contribute is vital, but leadership must neither overburden nor bore workers (of course, while doing what is appropriate for a thriving business, school, or church). Attentive leaders know people—not just workers. Genuine relationships with people enable leaders to craft assignments that lure individuals and teams toward their best work and senses of self.

Knowing persons with whom we work requires something deeper than a resume with previous jobs, skills, and accomplishments in a list. A good leader recognizes where the passion of coworkers lies—in other words, the leader has compassion. In an essay called "From Hospitality to Shalom," Elizabeth Conde-Frazier writes that compassion facilitates transformation or movement. Her essay teaches that compassion is a way to know others deeply, especially those who differ from us by gender, race or ethnicity, class, religion, nationality, ability, and other self-identifying traits. In a diverse workplace, leaders who are open and knowledgeable of co-laborers—collaborators—enter into solidarity and empathy in working relationships.

Where passion and compassion are nurtured, collaborators and coworkers create a common vision. Their work is not simply the maintenance of an institution or system because their solidarity (internally as a team and/or externally in service to the community) is moved by passion. The orchestra leader-conductor sees musicians through messy rehearsals, but on concert night, they express a common vision of a moving musical performance. As a teacher, I've read about the importance of connecting with the students' passion as a way to motivate learning that persists long after the semester ends. For students, musicians, and other coworkers/co-learners, the power of passion reminds us that people are more than their knowledge; they are people with feelings that move them to work and service that bring change.

Because Christianity is my spiritual tradition, I think of God as the One who leads us into transforming possibilities and who blesses us with divine compassion. Christians often speak of the leadership of the Holy Spirit, who moves us toward unimaginable adventures. God's leading has the potential to generate a common vision or goal. Christian leaders open to divine inspiration and to the deepest passions of coworkers may create a community with meaningful work dedicated to a common purpose.

A common goal, vision, or purpose is generated in community, in relationships of trust, respect, and passion. A leader (even the founder or owner of a company) can be the sole source of an institution's purpose, but even someone as innovative as Steve Jobs needed Steve Wozniak to create a company like Apple.

Creativity is the key to generating vision and empowering collaborative relationships. Creativity is the emergence of something fresh and novel that could not arise from a single leader. Perhaps there are two sources of creativity relevant to leadership. One source is God's novel purposes or possibilities acting as inspiration for both leaders and teams. Another source is the diversity of participatory "leadership" in a setting where all voices are valued and heard.

Mutuality in the classroom, workroom, or community enables diverse persons to contribute creatively to the common vision. When I visited various schools to discern where to study, I saw two contrasting settings: one was competitive and belittling among students, but another was collaborative. In the latter classroom, I watched students creatively layer ideas into an ever more insightful and complex discussion (under the leadership of a very skilled teacher). Transformative leaders can engage their coworkers and co-learners in creative layering of ideas and actions. The more diverse the participants, the greater the creative potential. Creativity emerges for the sake of the common good when greater awareness of diverse perspectives enhances a common vision.

Creativity is the key to transformative, relational leadership built on empowerment, encouragement, and passion of co-laborers and coworkers. For those who claim the Christian tradition, the compassionate God is the Creator who empowers and encourages both leaders and their collaborators.

Nancy R. Howell is Professor of Theology and Philosophy of Religion and Oubri A. Poppele Professor of Health and Welfare Ministries at Saint Paul School of Theology (Leawood, Kansas, and Oklahoma City, Oklahoma). She completed her doctoral work on Alfred North Whitehead and process theology at Claremont Graduate University. Howell has practiced leadership in both the academic dean and president's offices at Saint Paul.

15

God Leads Like a Midwife

LIBBY TEDDER HUGUS

Understanding how God leads like a midwife inspires us to lead by invitation.

When I was preparing to give birth to our first child, we chose the midwifery model of care for prenatal through postpartum provision. We did so for many reasons including a belief that birth was not something "done to the mother" but rather a cooperation of the mother with the miraculous power of her own body to birth in a way she was designed to. We researched, interviewed and hired a midwife who jived with our values when it came to birthing. She had a practice of having an assistant midwife attend every birth: one tends to mother; one to baby; both team together toward a successful labor and delivery.

We also hired a doula to assist during and after our pregnancy as well. I remember the first time I met her, shook her hand and we smiled into each other eyes; it was clear this woman would be a powerful witness and servant in my birthing experience. A doula's role is to nurture, support and offer expert guidance to a mother, her partner, and other family members in the birthing transition. Where a midwife's care is medically and physically centered, a doula's is emotionally and practically centered in evidence-based information.

On a bright and early summer's morning, our little one was born at home under the watchful care and witness of our birthing team. We bonded with her as sunlight poured through our windows. Our birth was a mutually empowering shared experience. I was free to cooperate with my body giving birth, unrestricted and well supported by a team of expert witnesses. They were able to provide direct assistance at every step of the way, while not forcing my body to do the work of birthing our child from my womb. In the blissfully high oxytocin-soaked first moments postpartum as a newly emerged mother, I was able to celebrate what I had accomplished by the power of my own body while acknowledging how necessary the presence, knowledge and physical support of each women in the room had been.

I sense that this is exactly how God leads: like the trifecta of a midwife, midwife's assistant and doula. What if we reimagined the relationship God shares within Godself this way? God the midwife, God the assistant and God the doula. What a team they make! What beautiful, powerful presence they offer to those they are in relationship with.

Open and relational theologies affirm that God interacts in an uncontrolling, mutually empowering, cooperative way with all God creates. A midwife enters the particular story of a mother and growing baby to work with that person in her current circumstances. She does not assume or force practices that are outside the scope of a mother's needs or desires. She listens, suggests, monitors, provides, and cooperates with the mother's specific experience. A doula comes alongside a mother and family to listen, ponder, question, suggest and participate with the family's needs during pregnancy, labor, delivery and postpartum. She does not coerce, dominate, or lord her power over them. Devoting herself to the particularities of this mother and partner and baby in this birth leads to a participative, shared experience for all involved.

This kind of leadership is invitational and cooperative. This kind of leadership loves. This kind of leadership necessitates a posture of *alongside* and *with* not *over* or *against*. God leads like a midwife and invites us to do the same.

Community Organizers follow a model of leadership that defines a leader as anyone who invites another to the table. The table may represent a shared goal or need, or a shared community or identity. Anyone is invited to meet said goal or fill the gap between need and provision. Leadership is not understood as the hierarchical model of someone in charge who hoards all the authority. It is not a buck-stops-with-one-dictator kind of leadership. Leadership is engaged as a shared kind of power that engages the capacity, ability and willingness of others to act cooperatively. Power is shared and built together in order to accomplish a common goal. Leaders may have different abilities and capacities to share, but each one matters in the movement toward the shared result. Along the way, participation by each leader in knowing and exercising their own power is more important than who is in charge. Shared power is greater than the sum parts of any one authoritative leader. The common goal is collectively discerned and decision making found among all the leaders at the table. In this way, authority is shared and mutually agreed upon. A question often asked by such leaders is, "who is missing? Who haven't we considered as a possible leader toward this goal?"

Through the lenses of open and relational theology, God comes alongside each individual and community to share power with all willing participants. The ability to act toward a whole and peaceful creation belongs to all of us. This is ultimately God's desire for creation: holistic well-being for all, in all spheres, in all ways, across all spectrums. Genesis chapter one affirms that all of humanity, every single human being, is created to reflect God's image. We are imbued with the very essence of God's own heart and given agency to steward and lead on earth.

We can all lead in God's kin-dom. "Kin-dom" offers an alternative to the more widely used kingdom. Kingdoms are dominions where power is hoarded at the top of a sliding scale of power. Kingdoms determine who carries the power based upon birthright, sexual identity or gender. In kingdoms, the power only trickles down from those who hold status, wealth and ideal social pedigrees. Kin-doms are realms were all perceive themselves as siblings in God's family, sharing the power to act and influence and change and cooperate amongst each other. Every sibling in the kin-dom knows their inherent worth and dignity, because they are created in God's image. Inside kin-doms, power is identified according to creative capacity, imaginative ability, and enthusiastic willingness to respond. In the peaceable kin-dom, like a trifecta birthing team, God as midwife, assistant, and doula enters the particularities of a given individual's or community's experience to listen, influence, and support the shared goals of the whole gathering.

Perhaps this model of leadership doesn't settle easily with you. Perhaps you prefer the idea of a determined future where God is in control. Perhaps it is easier to respond to an authoritarian leader who wields the power from a throne on high. Perhaps recognizing the responsibility required of those of us who love and desire to imitate God in a model like this is intimidating.

But how does it replenish your love for, and desire to cooperate with, God when you consider God like a midwives and doula team? To consider God coming alongside of you, joining you in your particular quirks, desires, joys, and hopes to assist you in an end goal—like birthing a new dream into the world? What if God's leadership is invitational and cooperative, not domineering and controlling? What if this is how God woos each of us to lead as well?

God leads like a midwife. God's leadership is not authoritative, coercive, or determined. God leans with us into an open future, with possibilities as endless as we have the capacity, ability and willingness to help co-create. God joins with us by relating to us inside the experience of our humanity. God invites us to lead alongside others in the kin-dom who desire to realize God's dream for shalom on earth.

Who is missing from your life right now? Who haven't you invited to help give birth to God's creative, imaginative dream for shalom on planet earth? Maybe it's you. Maybe you have been hiding behind a non-relational view of God and waiting for God to act unilaterally. The leadership of God is opposite of this kind of view. God is extending the invitation to you. God is establishing a reign of peace on earth, and wants your responsive, cooperative participation.

St. Teresa of Avila lived in Spain in the 16th century. She was a participant in the Carmelite order of sisters and wrote prolifically on prayer, despite physical ill health and struggling against earthly attachments. One of her best-known prayers is below. You may want to consider praying this prayer and to ponder Christ as "The Midwife's Assistant."

> Christ Has No Body
> *Christ has no body now but yours*
> *No hands, no feet on earth but yours*
> *Yours are the eyes through which He looks*
> *Compassion on this world*
> *Yours are the feet with which He walks to do good*
> *Yours are the hands with which He blesses all the world*
> *Yours are the hands*
> *Yours are the feet*
> *Yours are the eyes*
> *You are His body*
> *Christ has no body now on earth but yours*

God the midwife, God the assistant, God the doula is extending their hand to you right now. "Lead with me," God says, "Let us bless the world together."

Libby Tedder Hugus is founding Pastor of The Table in Casper, WY. She is co-author of "Marks of the Missional Church" and contributing author to multiple anthologies. She is a pastor, wife, mama, coach and obsessive podcast and audiobook consumer. She believes there is always room for one more around the table and generous hospitality will heal the world.

16

Leadership in the Valley of The Madness

DAN KENT

Good leadership empowers and nurtures autonomy; bad leadership seeks automation and control.

𝒜 type of madness threatens each of us. It stalks us, surrounds us, and whispers sweet promises in our ears.

I first confronted The Madness shopping at Target twenty years ago. My truck blew a headlight, so I found a new headlight and brought it to the checkout counter. The cashier put my headlight in a plastic Target bag.

"No bag, please," I said. It was, after all, only a headlight.

She said, "It's our policy to put merchandise in bags."

"But I don't want one," I said, a little annoyed. Then I remembered I needed toothpaste, too. "Oh, can you hold this here for a minute? I'll be right back."

She took the headlight while I hurried to the hygiene aisle. I grabbed a tube of Colgate, and then returned to the cashier. I saw my headlight on the floor by the cashier's feet. She had put it in a bag!

I paid for the toothpaste and she tossed that in the bag with the headlight.

"I didn't want a bag for the headlight," I said, "I thought I made that clear?"

She hardened her eyes, "it's our policy to give everyone a bag. It's for your protection."

"Protection? From what?"

"So we know you purchased your goods."

Of course, anyone could sneak a Target bag in and fill it with stolen goods, but I decided against mentioning that. Instead, I grabbed my bag and walked away.

As I approached the automatic doors, her voice cried out again." Sir, sir, you forgot your receipt."

I turned and, lifting the plastic bag above my head like a trophy fish, proclaimed, "I don't need a receipt. I have a *bag*."

She didn't seem to appreciate my sarcasm. I could almost hear her thoughts: *it's just a bag, jerk*. And it was *just a bag*. No big deal. But that's exactly why it exposed The Madness. If the bag really didn't matter that much, if it wasn't a big deal, then refusing the bag shouldn't have caused a problem. Yet giving a bag to each customer seemed critical to this poor woman. Why?

Because she had succumbed to The Madness.

The Madness can creep into you unexpectedly. It might gain a foothold in you with something as simple as a nametag, then a uniform, a job description, a customer service script, an employee handbook outlining corporate policy on hair length, tattoos, and vacation requests. Each of these innocent little tokens can chip away at your autonomy, democratize your individuality, and automate your personality. You begin to think and act less and less for yourself.

A hilarious representation of this insanity can be found in the movie *Idiocracy*. The movie tells the story of an average guy transported fifty years into the future—a future so dumbed down by The Madness that he now exists as the smartest person on earth. At one point, he visits a Costco where a store greeter, with sleepy eyes and a dull slouch, mumbles, "welcome to Costco… I love you." The dolt-greeter utters this numbing chorus to each customer entering the store. "Welcome to Costco, I love you. Welcome to Costco, I love you."

Each time we utter, "It's just my job," "it's company policy," or "I'm just following orders," we've surrendered a little more of ourselves to The Madness. Have you tried to use telephone customer service lately? They're almost all computer programs now, programmed to sound human. Humanity literally automated. Welcome to the dystopian now.

I see scripture hollering out against this automation of self, this loss of autonomy, and this over-conformity. I see David telling King Saul: "I'm not wearing that!" when Saul tried to get David to wear a kingdom-branded uniform (Saul's armor) before David fought Goliath. I see Mary shirking her duties (violating her job description, if you will), so she could sit at Jesus's feet—to the dismay of Martha, who was *just doing her job* (Luke 10:38-42). And don't forget Jacob physically wrestling with God for a blessing.

Boldness pleases God more than meaningless conformity. Jesus only praises three people throughout the gospels. I already mentioned Mary. The other two boldly confronted Jesus with supposedly inappropriate requests—with which Jesus complied! One, who worked in the violence profession as a centurion, asked the non-violent, peace-promoting messiah to heal his servant (Matthew 8:5-13). The other was a Canaanite woman who, because of hostility between Jews and Canaanites, had no business approaching Jesus, either. In fact, Jesus calls her a dog. But she boldly persists (Matthew 15:21-28). Jesus answers both of their bold requests, and then celebrates their great faith.

God wants us to be in agape-love relationship with each other and with God. In order to pull this off, God had to create us with something special: autonomy. When God breathed that special breath into the dust and brought us to life, God created a source of say-so, a source of initiative and proactivity that can transcend, in some degree, cause and effect. Made in the image of God, we have the power to originate events, to bring forth realities that wouldn't otherwise occur without us. This power fills us with vitality.

We put this precious autonomy in danger when we thoughtlessly submit to things like corporate culture, branding, or marketplace expectations. Protecting individual autonomy stands at the center of the battlefield in our spiritual war against the principalities and powers. I'm not saying we should necessarily disobey orders, shrug off job requirements, burn our uniforms, or blow off customer expectations. I'm simply trying to expose how the principalities and powers can smother autonomy and can draw us into a tug-of-war for our soul.

For my part, I offer three strategies for Open-and-Relational Leaders to help their people fight against The Madness, and to maybe even help them foster that beautiful boldness God enjoys so much.

(1) Mandate the *what*, not the *how*. When you give someone work, tell them clearly the result you want. Avoid getting hung up on the method for achieving that result. Nothing chokes vitality like some grabby micromanager looking over your shoulder saying, "no do this, no not like that, like this." For example, imagine you are the manager of a mega-store. You could be a manager who mandates method: *For each customer who enters, tell them: 'Welcome to Costco, I love you.'* Now consider managing from an open-and-relational perspective. Instead of dictating method, you state your desired result: *I want customers to feel like they are personally welcome in our store, and I want them to feel appreciated.* Watch how this approach allows employees to make their own decisions and to figure out how to give you what you want in a way that feels natural to them. You get what you want, and they maintain their autonomy.

(2) Fight to remove as many policies, requirements, and rules as possible. Yes, we need some of these bureaucratic ornaments. But bureaucracy inherently wants to take over the world. You can always come up with a good reason for a new rule, a new policy, or a new required form. And, creating these precious little burdens creates the warm feeling of *managing*. For every ten people who propose new rules, policies, or documents, I've found only one who fights to remove them.

New controls come easy, but never for free. They accumulate fast, and eventually create a spiritual claustrophobia that can crush employee vitality. The more you press an employee to conform and comply, the less likely your job role will appeal to high quality candidates. You'll see employee quality diminish, requiring more bureaucracy, which will reduce future employee quality. This downward spiral of bureaucratic sadness continues until the job begins to feel like jumping rope: something is always happening, but…nothing meaningful. Who wants to work under such heavy loads? Policies, requirements, procedures, dress codes…they always cost us something. Get rid of them!

(3) Give away as much power as possible. God does. God hands over such abundant power that we can even reject God and sabotage God's will. The more say-so and input employees have, the more empowered and proactive they become. When I go into convenience stores or coffee shops, I often ask employees, "Do you get to choose the music? Or does management decide what plays here?" Usually, management decides, which makes me sad because, well, usually the music is terrible. It's usually Classic Rock. Ugh! I'd much rather hear whatever music employees enjoy. And you know what? They'd be a whole lot happier, too, if they had even that small amount of say-so.

An Open-and-Relational Leader promotes autonomy, not automation. They seek to empower, not control. God formed humans out of dust, and then enlivened that dust with a special breath. Subversive forces seek to turn that breath back to dust. The Open-and-Relational Leader works to guard and foster God's holy breath in each of us and works to give that breath space to expand and to accomplish whatever wonderful things it hopes to accomplish.

Dan Kent authored the best-selling book Confident Humility: Becoming Your Full Self Without Becoming Full of Yourself (2019). He serves as Teaching Pastor at Woodland Hills Church in Maplewood, Minnesota and hosts the wildly popular podcast "Greg Boyd: Apologies & Explanations."

17

The Humility of God

BOB LUHN

Humble service is an essential characteristic of God and Jesus repeatedly manifested it in the life, teaching, and sacrificial death. Humble service should inform our own leadership.

As I grew up attending church with my family every time the church doors were open, I developed a concept of God that focused primarily upon God's majesty, power, justice, sovereign control, and righteous anger. God was big. A Being to be feared and served, not a God to be loved and with whom to relate. There are many commands in Scripture to bow down before God; to worship God in fear and trembling; to acknowledge God as King of kings and Lord of Lords; to exalt God's name on high; to understand God as All-Mighty and All-Powerful and All-Sufficient. It almost led me to think God was egotistical, to believe God would never share glory with any other creature. God was "God Most High."

When I was 18 years old, I encountered in a very real way the God who is love (1 John 4:8). My understanding of God began shifting at that time, a shift that continues to this very day. One of the theologians who has been very helpful in this ongoing shift of understanding has been Thomas Jay Oord. His writings on the uncontrolling, non-coercive love of God have been instrumental in helping me embrace the God who is loving, compassionate, caring, serving, self-effacing, and yes, humble.

Recently I was reading Genesis 2:18 where it is written, "The Lord God said," It is not good for the man to be alone. I will make a helper suitable for him." At that point in the story, Adam had not been alone. He had been placed in the garden, a place of perfection, by God. He was given a task to "work it and take care of it." (Gen.2:15) He was in communication with God and in partnership with God. There were no barriers of sin or selfishness to disrupt fellowship. Surely, this would be ideal, the man and his God in perfect harmony. And the Almighty, All-Sufficient One would be everything the man needed. But for the first time in the salvation story, God says something is not good. It wasn't good enough for the man to enjoy unblemished fellowship with God. The All-Sufficient One was not enough. The man needed someone other than God.

To me this speaks of an inherent humility within God's self. God does not keep Adam all to God's self. Rather, there is the humble love admitting that a person needs something more, that people need other people. Men and women need loving partners and friends, and parents need children and children need loving parents, grandparents, aunts and uncles and cousins and playmates. An essential humility says, "I am not enough."

This humility is seen most clearly when God became one of us. The birth of Jesus was a remarkably humble affair. Oh yes, there was an angelic choir announcing the birth, but only a handful of humble shepherds saw and heard the choir. And when they got to Bethlehem, what they found was a baby wrapped in swaddling clothes like every other baby born before and since. For a bassinet, there was a simple manger quite possibly carved out of stone that would need hay or straw to soften the hardness. A stable is certainly a humble place for God to make an appearance on Earth.

From Bethlehem came the flight to Egypt, during which the Son of God was a refugee fleeing violence in his home country. Eventually returning but this time to Nazareth ("Can anything good come out of Nazareth?" John 1:46), Jesus grew up in obscurity and became a "blue-collar" worker, a carpenter. We might think this humble beginning was just an accident of history except that humility was a trademark of Jesus. He said things like, "Take my yoke upon you and learn from me, for I am gentle and humble in heart...." (Matthew 11:29). When dealing with disciples jockeying for position, Jesus shared revolutionary teachings on servant leadership that have found fresh emphasis in my own lifetime. Jesus turned leadership completely upside down in Mark 10:42-45. While the leadership style of the world is primarily authoritarian, controlling, dominating, and one of "power over" others, leadership in the Kingdom follows the loving leadership style of God; it is not "lording it over" anyone or exercising "authority over" others.

The followers of Jesus, too, were called to servant leadership, to putting others first, to meeting others' needs. And who was the example of this servant leadership? None other than the Son of Man, who "did not come to be served but to serve and give his life as a ransom for many." Once again, we see a humility that was essential to Jesus's being and way of living.

In the last week of Jesus's earthly life, we see this very servant leadership modeled. "He got up from the meal, took off his outer clothing, and wrapped a towel around his waist. After that he poured water into a basin and began to wash his disciples' feet, drying them with the towel...." (John 13:4-5). Although Jesus was worthy of being served, he acted in accordance with God's true nature and took the servant's role and performed the servant's function. And of course, from there Jesus went to the cross where he became the "ransom for many" (Mark 10:45).

Humble service was not just an act with God. It is an essential characteristic of God's self and was manifested repeatedly in the life, teaching, and sacrificial death of Jesus.

In 1998, my wife was diagnosed with Parkinson's disease. This progressive neurological disorder has very gradually robbed my wife of coordination, balance, speech and other cognitive functions. She is today dealing with terrible hallucinations and paranoia. She was very creative: painting, doing fine needlework and made some gorgeous banners exalting God that are still in use today. She developed a Women's' Christmas Tea that blessed hundreds in our community. She worked as a school secretary, a job she absolutely loved. She raised our three beautiful daughters who have become loving wives, mothers, and much-valued employees. Parkinson's has robbed her of all of that. She cannot do anything that she did before.

Her disease caused us to have to live a completely different life. I had to pick up the load she had carried so capably for all our earlier years of marriage. I cannot do it as well as she did; my learning curve is steep! But, in this lifestyle change, I have entered a graduate school of servanthood. And it just may be that God has revealed more of God's essential humility to me than through any other means. It is humbling to get on my hands and knees to put on my wife's shoes and socks. It is humbling to burn a meal or singe the clothing because the iron is too hot. I am learning what it means to be a servant to someone who doesn't always appreciate it because she is confused or frightened at that moment.

I have also noticed a new tenderness in my heart towards her and others who are struggling with less ability. Patience is growing. And maybe, just maybe, a little more Christlikeness is being worked into my life. It isn't easy. I don't always have a good attitude. Some days I want to run away. But I have been placed into this school of servant leadership. And here is where I encounter our humble God who is with me on the floor as I gently put on shoes and socks.

Bob Luhn retired in 2014 after 34 years of pastoring his beloved Othello, WA, Church of the Nazarene. Since then he has served as interim pastor in a variety Nazarene churches in eastern Washington, northern Idaho and northeastern Oregon. Bob and his wife Kathy have three daughters, three great sons-in-law, and seven grandchildren.

18

What Does Holy Leadership Look Like?

GLEN O'BRIEN

Relational leaders need to admit their fallibility and proneness to sin. They should walk with Jesus in solidarity with others.

"*H*oliness" is an increasingly "insider" concept, rarely used outside of a religious context. In fact, it's very difficult to think of its occurrence in the present culture of the West except as something very negative. Someone might say, "He's a bit of a holy Joe" or "she's a bit of a holy roller." Of course, this kind of statement is not meant as a compliment! What does it mean, then, to offer genuinely holy leadership?

In a relational theology, holiness is characterised by love and by openness toward others. It isn't about being separated from the "impure" or the "unclean," but about the power of presence. Think of how Jesus, surely the holiest of all spiritual leaders, touched and healed the unloved, the impure, and the rejected. Yet his holiness was not tainted by this contact in any way. Rather, those he touched were healed and themselves made holy. His was a contagious holiness.

In the nineteenth century, Protestant churches were very much engaged in a project to transform culture through the application of Christian principles to social problems. This was as true for Liberal advocates of the "social gospel" as it was for the Evangelical revivalists. In some circles, this ethic of *transformation* began to be replaced by an ethic of *separation* so that withdrawal replaced engagement. This created a leadership gap in the public square as the focus shifted from contributing to the common good to purifying the holy community from within.

Of course, the church no longer has the privileged place it once had in society and there are good reasons why it should not assume the sole place of moral leadership in a plural society. Yet Christian leadership still has an important role to play alongside other people of good will in seeking human flourishing across cultural and religious boundaries. Any concept of holiness as separation will not be up to the task of such engagement. Only a relational concept of holiness as transformative presence will do.

While there is a public role for relational leadership, there are also internal dimensions to church leadership to be considered. In Holiness churches, uncritically received teachings about sanctification, and in particular "entire sanctification," have sometimes resulted in rather toxic patterns of leadership. I have known leaders who could not admit responsibility for the harm caused to others through their words and actions. "My motives are pure because my heart is fully sanctified. If you are harmed by something I said or did, I'm sorry, but it was not intended by me." This is not an apology at all but merely an evasion of responsibility. Even the most fully sanctified are aware of their proneness to error, to fault and yes, to sin. No one ever outgrows the prayer Our Lord taught us to pray—"Forgive us our trespasses as we forgive those who trespass against us." Relational leadership is the kind of leadership that is honest about failure, open to correction, and willing to admit fault.

Too often we think of leadership as exercising authority over people in order to get things done. It is something quite different to that. The relational holiness to which Christian leaders are called does not treat people in an instrumental way—simply as tools to achieve some purpose. Rather it wants to learn from others and is open to the contributions and insights of all, including (indeed especially) the humblest and simplest of fellow travellers. When reflecting on the people you think of us as the holiest "saints" you know, they are likely to be people who are too humble to speak of themselves in such terms. They don't need their holiness announced, it announces itself. These people are true leaders, even if they have no official leadership role in the church, because they are models for us to follow.

In the 1980s I was involved in attempting to plant a church in a little seaside village on Australia's east coast. Around 60 people attended a public service, interested in what the introduction of a "Holiness" church might look like in their region and whether they might like to be involved. The invited speaker gave his testimony with great boldness and confidence. "Forty-five years ago, God sanctified my heart at an altar of prayer and since that day my heart has been as pure as the driven snow." My heart sank and I knew we had lost that crowd. Sure enough, no one showed any interest except to say, "If that's what a Holiness church looks like, we don't want to be a part of it." That kind of testimony might have gone well in a camp meeting in rural Tennessee within a revivalist subculture, but in beachside New South Wales it failed to communicate. It was heard only as prideful boasting. It didn't point to Jesus (as the speaker probably intended), but only to the person speaking. As such it failed the test of genuinely relational holiness—it spoke of the "purity" of the preacher but did not evoke the "presence" of Christ.

One of the key insights of the theology of Openness is that God is a relational Being who does not simply act in an arbitrary way over against people from a position of ultimate power. Instead, God makes covenants, keeps promises, grows frustrated, dances with joyful celebration and occasionally even has a change of mind. God's people, made in the divine image, are also called to be relational beings expressing a range of responses in a dance of mutual connection to others.

Christianity certainly affirms the oneness, the unity, and the power of God, but it does so in a very particular way. God is not simply a Divine Being, but a being who exists in communion. The Father loves the Son. The Son asks the Father to send the Spirit as our Helper, and the Spirit speaks not of herself but of the Son.[2] Terms like "Father" and "Son" can seem very gendered (and very male!) but if we think more deeply about them it is not their gender that matters so much as their *relational* nature. The relationships that exist within the very being of God are mutually reinforcing relationships of others-focused love. There is nothing jarring, competitive, selfish or abusive within God. Relational leaders will exhibit a similar kind of holiness, even if of a less perfect kind. They will not demand a predetermined set of responses from others, but be open to their uninvited, unexpected (even sometimes unwanted), insights. Relational leadership will ask how best to provoke love even in the most surprising and disarming of circumstances.

There is a very short answer to the question of what holy leadership looks like. It looks like Jesus. Not the Jesus who is morally perfect (though he was that) but the Jesus who loved perfectly. Most people do not become (or stay) Christians because they become convinced that Jesus is God the Son, the Second Person of the Holy Trinity or any similar theological description. Somehow or

---

[2] The use of the feminine pronoun in reference to the Spirit seems allowable given that the Greek word *pneuma* is neuter. The author is aware that male pronouns are used of the Spirit in the New Testament.

other they encounter him, maybe through reading the Gospels, maybe through seeing a movie, maybe through a conversation. They are drawn to him, not as an idea, or as a concept but *as a person* and they find they want to follow him. It's for this reason that Christianity is not first a system of beliefs or religious practices (even though it involves such things) but a way of living with and for Christ in solidarity with others. A person may be a religious leader but can only be a genuinely holy leader when their response to others is in line with the love most fully exhibited in Jesus of Nazareth.

Glen O'Brien is Research Coordinator at Eva Burrows College within the University of Divinity and Chair of the University's Research Committee. He is a Uniting Church minister with an ecumenical placement to The Salvation Army. He is the author and editor of several books including (with Hilary Carey), Methodism in Australia: A History (Ashgate 2015) and Wesleyan-Holiness Churches in Australia (Routledge, 2018).

19

Leading with Faith

DANIEL J. OTT

Leading with faith is to be aware of and appreciate the goodness of people, the beauty in work, and the creativity that emerges when we are open and present.

"I think it pisses God off if you walk by the color purple in a field somewhere and don't notice it." These words punctuate Shug and Celie's theological discussion in Alice Walker's novel, *The Color Purple*. Celie seems convinced that Shug is probably right that God is not some old, white man and more of an "it" than a "who." God is best seen in the bird and the air and in other people. And these notions are quite consistent with the kind of faith I have in mind when I think about leading with faith.

Theologian Bernard Meland called this kind of faith an "appreciative awareness." Faith is not so much assent to a set of beliefs and it is even less the assurance of any future outcome. Faith is a kind of trust. Meland says that there are two dimensions of faith. The first dimension is essentially just the trust one needs to live, it "is simply a will to live." Here, faith is a trust that life is worth living and that we can keep our fears at bay and feel secure enough to keep going. The second dimension is a more conscious and more appreciative awareness of that which is creative and good in life. It's noticing the color purple. It's valuing all of those moments when something good or beautiful emerges. It's appreciating the goodness in the people that surround us.

So what would it mean to lead with this kind of faith? It seems to imply a different kind of leadership. Too often, we think of leaders as strong, decisive, and even impassive. Many people who write about leadership advocate creating urgency and give advice about how to persuade people to see things as you do.

Leaders rush to think about how they can make change and transform organizations. I would like to suggest that leading with faith implies being mindful, present, and available.

It's not surprising that just about every recent book on leadership that you might pick up deals with the complexity and rapid change that mark our lives today. Military leaders, who seem to have a great proclivity for acronyms, call this VUCA – volatility, uncertainty, complexity, and ambiguity. What may surprise you is that many of these books on leadership advocate some sort of mindfulness in the face of VUCA.

Mindfulness is a concept taken from Buddhism. In its simplest form, mindfulness is attending to the present moment; not allowing the mind to race to the future or mull in the past. There's an old story about a farmer who was jealous of the attention and reverence paid to the monks who lived on the mountain. One day, while the farmer was working in his field, one of the monks walked by on his way to town. The farmer called out to the monk, "Pardon me, but may I ask what it is that you monks do up on the mountain that is so special?"

"Nothing special," replied the monk, "this morning I woke and prayed, I worked in the garden, and I ate my breakfast."

"Yes, that isn't special," the farmer agreed, "I prayed, and worked, and ate this morning as well."

"Oh," said the monk, "perhaps the difference is that when we pray, we know we are praying, and when we work, we know we are working, and when we eat, we know we are eating."

This is the kind of attentiveness that mindfulness involves, and it is the basis for an appreciative awareness. When we attend to the present moment, we can notice the color purple and be aware of the goodness that surrounds us.

Another aspect of mindfulness is what Buddhists would call "right intention." Being mindful includes understanding the impact of our words, acting compassionately toward others, and conducting our business with ethical standards. Jerome Murphy in his book, *Dancing in the Rain*, calls this "minding your values" and sees it as the first step toward mindful leadership. He advocates that we take a careful inventory of our values and effort to always act and lead from a place of minding our values. This involves a deep faith and trust in goodness and truth. Transformation and change are always possibilities, but the transformations and changes that we seek should be consistent with what we take to be good and true. Transformation and change are not ends in and of themselves.

Leading with faith may also require us to understand being present as more than just attending to the present moment, however vital that may be. Otto Scharmer has coined the term "presencing" to indicate something like what I have in mind. Scharmer invites us to imagine the basic image of a "U." We move down the left side of the "U" in the present and up the right side toward the future. The movement down the "U" toward the middle is the practice of mindfulness that I've been describing: being present in the moment, observing well what is going on around us, connecting with our deepest selves and our dearest values. What the movement up the right side of the "U" adds is an imaginative engagement with the future. This is a place of being present to the moment, present to our best selves, and being present to the emerging future, being present to creativity, being open to acting anew.

Here, leading with faith is not only attending to the already present goodness and beauty, but also opening to and trusting new instantiations of goodness and beauty as they emerge. We then engage those possibilities and release our creativity. So often the future can feel like a threat because of VUCA, but leading with faith is trusting the future can be better than the present. Notice, I did not say that leading with faith is believing that the future *will* be better, but trusting that the future *can* be better.

Leading with faith will also require that we are available to the persons that we lead. Leaders need to be available to those we lead in order to receive their best contributions and in order to help them feel valuable and valued. We need to be appreciatively aware of the people we work with. Schein and Schein, in their book *Humble Leadership*, call this kind of appreciative awareness of the persons around us, "personization." They use the simple example of a surgeon who found that recognizing the people on his ever-changing surgical teams as persons was invaluable to successful results. He took extra time in the pre-surgery meeting to look each member in the eye, to listen well to their overview of their part of the task, to smile at them, and to thank them for their coming contributions.

As I have reached higher levels of leadership within my college, I've noticed that the higher the level of meeting the more likely there is to be chitchat and personal checking in as the meeting starts. At first, I thought this was a kind of largesse of leadership. I prided myself on running tight meetings, starting on time, moving efficiently through the agenda. Now, I'm realizing that this is the practice of skilled and effective leadership. They are taking time to make sure they recognize the personhood of those with whom they work and make themselves personally available. They are indicating that the members of their team are valuable, both for their work, and in their personhood. This sort of appreciative awareness of the people with whom we work, not only makes people feel more comfortable and valued at work, but it also takes seriously the relational and human qualities of the systems that make up organizations.

One of my favorite lines from the Bhagavad Gita says, "You have a right to your actions, but never to your actions' fruits. Act for the action's sake. And do not be attached to inaction." Leading with faith is a way to take joy in the work of leadership and detach a bit from the fruits that our leadership may yield. In an age of VUCA, we can get lost in a world of results and bottom lines. We can get drunk on transformation and change. We can get frustrated by rough waters and thwarted efforts. Leading with faith is a way to calm the waters, to notice the color purple, to be aware and appreciative of the goodness of the people around you, the beauty in the work itself, and the creativity that emerges.

Daniel J. Ott is Associate Dean for Academic Initiatives and Chair of the Department of Philosophy and Religious Studies at Monmouth College, Monmouth, Illinois. His articles and review articles have appeared in Theology Today, Political Theology, and the American Journal for Theology and Philosophy. He is co-author with Hannah Schell of Christian Thought in America: A Brief History (Fortress Press).

20

Leading by Following

DYTON L. OWEN

Leadership is grounded in relationship between us and God, but a leader must first follow.

While in college, I received my first appointment to serve a church as pastor. My father, who had been a pastor for over thirty years by that time, gave me a piece of advice that has stuck with me for the past 35 years of my ministry: "Relationship will always be the most important factor in your leadership as a pastor. Keep your relationship with God strong first, and your ministry will flourish."

To be honest, I have sometimes failed to follow that advice, but the truth of it has never failed to make itself known. Leadership is grounded in relationship.

Over the past 40 years, the topic of leadership has mushroomed in the publishing industry. According to the Bowker Report, the number of self-published leadership books alone was 458,564 in 2013, an increase of 437 percent over 2008. And, according to Cairnway (ServeLeadNow.com), over 1240 books with the word "leadership" in the title were published just through the third quarter of 2015. Seminars and workshops on leadership are plentiful and growing. It seems that everyone has an idea on what leadership is all about, preaching and proffering all sorts of advice on the subject. Even in the life of the Church, leadership is most often portrayed as something a person does based on his or her personality, skills, or authority.

What is sorely lacking in leadership—even (or especially) leadership in the Church—is the idea that leadership is rooted in relationship, and that the primary relationship required is with God. It is from this relationship with God that leadership flows naturally, effectively, and sincerely.

Yet, how someone understands God will have an undeniable effect on his or her leadership. If God is understood as aloof and distant—as One who is not affected by human creatures—then leadership may be viewed as power over others, as authoritarian, or manipulative. On the other hand, if God is understood as open, relational, and loving, leadership is experienced as partnership with One who guides and influences the leader and his or her leadership.

The scriptures show us that God is a relational God who actively seeks a loving relationship with us. James Weldon Johnson speaks to this understanding of God in his poem "The Creation." In the poem, after God had created everything except humanity, Weldon says God sat down, looked at all that had been created, and then said to himself, "I'm lonely still." Then, writes Johnson, "God thought and thought, till he thought: I'll make me a man!"

God desires and pursues a relationship with us. Leadership as relationship understands that this relationship between God and human creatures makes an essential difference in how our leadership is played out.

There are many examples of an open and relational God in scriptures. In the book of Genesis, for example, God's desire to interact with Adam and Eve is evidence of God's open, loving, and relational nature. God goes in search of Adam and Eve after they disobeyed God's command not to eat of the fruit of the tree of the knowledge of good and evil. Yet, in spite of their disobedience, God desired to remain in relationship. Furthermore, Adam and Eve's actions affected God, as seen in God's act of seeking after them. While God was disappointed, God continued to remain in relationship with humanity in spite of their acts of disobedience and its consequences.

Another example of God's open and relational essence can be seen in the story of Moses and the people of Israel. In the giving of the Ten Commandments, we clearly see God's desire and intention to be in relationship with creation and creatures. The Commandments were given as a way to reestablish a relationship that had been severely broken—a relationship between God and humanity as well as between human beings themselves.

In fact, the entire Bible, from cover to cover, is one story of how God desires to be in relationship with God's creation; indeed, God pursues such relationship. Beginning with Adam and Eve and moving through the Ten Commandments, the prophets, priests, and kings, we see God actively seeking a relationship with humanity. In the course of time, God chose to make God's self known in the human being, Jesus.

Jesus is God's ultimate act of relationship with humanity and all creation. In Jesus, God becomes that with which God desires relationship. In Jesus, God no longer relates to creation—to humanity—through laws, rules, regulations, or propositions; God relates to humanity through one of us, through a human being. It is through this self-revelation of Jesus that God relates to creation in a new way. Through Jesus, we undoubtedly see God relates to and is affected by humanity, because God became one of us. We also see that humanity relates to and is affected by God in how Jesus relates to others. The act of God becoming human is a reciprocating event that affects both the Creator and creation.

In God-in-Jesus, we realize that no further attempts by God to relate to creation are necessary: Jesus is the unsurpassable relationship between God and humanity. In Jesus, God responds to creation's need for relationship. As French philosopher and mathematician Blaise Pascal wrote, "There is a God-shaped vacuum in the heart of each man [sic] which cannot be satisfied by any created thing but only by God the Creator, made know through Jesus Christ."

Having said all this, it is important to understand that relationship in regard to leadership begins with being first a follower. That is to say, I am a leader only insofar as I am first a follower of Someone greater. That "someone" is God in the person of Jesus. We cannot be good leaders until we are first good followers. Being followers enables and empowers us to be leaders. Leonard Sweet reminds us that the Church is not led by leaders, but by Christ. Everyone else is a follower (*I Am A Leader*, p. 24). Our followership enables, empowers, and influences our leadership, not the other way around. We lead others only as we are first led ourselves. We cannot out-lead our Leader; we can only lead others as followers first.

This relationship deeply influences our leadership. An open and relational understanding of God helps us appreciate that human creatures have an influence on God, and that our relationship with God consequently influences how our leadership is carried out. This relationship-leadership interplay can be seen in Jesus' words to his disciples in the Gospel of John:

I am the vine, you are the branches. Those who abide in me and I in them bear much fruit, because apart from me you can do nothing. Whoever does not abide in me is thrown away like a branch and withers; such branches are gathered, thrown into the fire, and burned. If you abide in me, and my words abide in you, ask for whatever you wish, and it will be done for you. My Father is glorified by this, that you bear much fruit and become my disciples (15:5-8).

Here, we see how an open and relational understanding of God shapes us and our leadership, as well as how this understanding affects God. Jesus states that without an interdependent relationship with God, we can do nothing. But with such a relationship, we can "bear much fruit." This implies that God relates to humanity and that relationship makes an essential difference in how we lead and "bear fruit." It further implies that we affect God in the relationship: our "bearing fruit" glorifies God. However, despite the fact that human beings have an influence on God, God's open and loving nature is unchanging. That is to say, regardless of how our leadership plays out—for good or for not so good—God always loves us. God's essential nature is to love despite our own failures and broken nature.

As my father told me, leadership is first a relationship. That relationship is firmly grounded in the understanding that God is a living and loving Creator who desires and pursues a relationship with us. But a genuine leader must first be a follower: someone who follows Jesus first, and from that relationship leads others.

Dyton L. Owen is a United Methodist pastor serving in Kansas. He is the author of Jesus: God Revealed and Remembering Who We Are. Owen has also written several articles and essays for various publications on the topics of theology, worship, and church leadership.

21

More Power II to You: Freedom and Trust in Organizational Leadership

NEIL PEMBROKE

Rather than deterrence-based leadership, a model in which leaders risk trusting imitates God's covenant, and it produces work, creativity, and fidelity to mission.

J teach Christian Studies in a public university. I well remember the first retreat led by our new Head of School. He adopted a fairly grumpy tone. At one point I thought I was back in high school and my Headmaster was laying down the law: "I want you to know that I'll be checking your phone bill. If you go over $30 for the month, expect me to come knocking on your door!"

This is an example of deterrence-based trust. Managers trust their subordinates because there is close monitoring and sanctions against opportunistic behaviour. It fits within the command-and-control approach to management. A little bit of this may be okay, but there is a better way.

I offer a more intelligent and productive way for leaders to handle trust and risk. Let me introduce you to Power II. Power II is a concept developed by the political philosopher, Sverre Raffnsøe. It's trust-as-power. When leaders trust their subordinates they hand over part of themselves. They run the risk that those they place trust in will disappoint them. In this sense, they are placing themselves in the hands of their subordinates, to an extent. So Power II is really about a gift exchange—like we see in preliterate societies. In that cultural context, if I give you a gift you are under a moral obligation to reciprocate. A moral contract is set up. Similarly, when leaders take a risk and trust their subordinates (by delegating, for example), they lodge a moral claim: "I've stepped out on a limb and placed trust in you. Don't disappoint me." It is the moral duty of the subordinate to work diligently and creatively, and in line with the leader's vison and aims. In trusting subordinates, leaders are em-powered. By taking a risk and offering a gift to their subordinates, they create a condition in which it is quite likely that the outcomes they are looking for (hard work, creativity, and fidelity to the corporate mission) will actually eventuate.

You may be thinking, "That's a nice theory, but how does it work out in practice? We can all tell stories of people engaging in opportunistic behavior. It could be anything from pilfering items from the work supplies cupboard, to pushing work on others down the line and claiming credit, to serious misappropriation of funds. I found this in my ABC News feed a couple of days ago: "Former senior public executive Paul Whyte and another man, Jacob Anthonisz, have been charged with using fake invoices to fraudulently take $2.5 million in taxpayers' money. Police later revealed in court the final amount allegedly stolen could be up to $25 million."

So does the Power II theory really work? I'm not absolutely sure, but there is a body of empirical research that suggests that it does. Feeling trusted by one's leader is associated with increased performance, greater job satisfaction, and increased commitment to organizational citizenship. "Organizational citizenship" refers to behavior that is discretionary; it's not part of the job description and is not recognized by the formal reward system. The end result is promoting efficient and effective functioning of an organization. An example would be helping someone out in a different section who is snowed under when you have a little space in your workday. We need more research to confirm this, but it does seem that the thinking behind a Power II approach has a basis in reality.

A number of scholars interested in leadership in organizations have worked with the concept of God-as-leader. Neil Remington Abramson sets up a comparison between God's leadership in the Abraham story and modern vision-casting and ethical leadership. His conclusion is that God's leadership approach is very modern, but God accords a high value to something that is not nearly so prominent in contemporary leadership theory—namely, quality of relationship. Matthew Viau analyses Psalm 91 to show that God's leadership behavior suggests an addition to the existing model of transformational leadership. The divine leadership displayed in the psalm manifests the four factors in traditional transformational leadership theory, and indicates inclusion of a fifth element: personalized protection. Reflecting the accent in open theology on the freedom God grants to human beings, Carolyn Bohler offers the provocative metaphor of God as jazz band leader. God evokes certain themes in the "music" that humans play (beauty, peace, love, and justice), but God grants freedom to us so that we can play the song according to our own particular style.

I like the God-as-leader approach to theological reflection on organizational leadership very much. It strikes me that what we see in the God-David relationship as it is narrated in 2 Samuel 9-20 and 1 Kings 1-2 is God adopting a Power II approach. In discussing this covenantal relationship, I aim to draw out the crucial role that freedom plays. (Here I want to thank Walter Brueggemann for his very helpful lead.) In a bold and risky move, God chooses to grant David a largely free run.

God (Yahweh) is present and involved in the narrative, but human choices and human actions are accorded a significant role in determining historical events. What really stands out in this narrative history is the freedom granted to David and to the other actors. Naturally enough, Yahweh takes a lead role and establishes boundaries. David is not free to act just as he pleases; he must align his decisions and actions with the divine requirements of righteousness, justice, and compassion. But the scope for free thought and action that God grants is astonishing.

We see in the succession narrative a new casting of the divine presence. Yahweh's role is essentially to create a context. The context that God constructs has two sides. On the side of Yahweh, there is absolute fidelity, wise counsel, and superabundant blessing. On David's side, there is faith and fidelity. David is free, but he is not emancipated from faith. Faith and freedom here are two sides of the one coin. David trusts in Yahweh; Yahweh trusts David with freedom and grants him a large swath in which to exercise this freedom.

The oracle in Second Samuel 7 is also very significant in terms of our story of Yahweh's loving gift of freedom and remarkable display of trust in David. What we see here is an astonishing transformation by Yahweh of David's situation in life. The change is patently the result of Yahweh's action, not David's: "Thus says the Lord of hosts, I took you from the pasture, from following the sheep, that you should be prince over my people Israel" (2 Sam 7:8b). Then comes an amazingly generous and risky promise: "I will make for you a great name, like the name of the great ones of the earth. And I will appoint a place for my people Israel, and will plant them, that they may dwell in their own place, and be disturbed no more…Moreover the Lord declares to you that the Lord will make you a house. When your days are fulfilled and you lie down with your fathers, I will raise up your offspring after you, who shall come forth from your body, and I will establish his kingdom. He shall build a house for my name, and I will establish the throne of his kingdom forever (2 Sam 7: 9b-13).

What is particularly noteworthy here is the unconditional nature of Yahweh's promise to David and to his house. David will surely fall. He may have a strong faith and (for the most part at least) display good moral character, but he is also frail, weak, and a sinner. That is to say, he shares in the human condition. His descendants will just as surely fall. But God will not fall back on his promise; the covenant is an eternal one. Amazingly, Yahweh has signed a blank check. That is not his usual way of doing business.

The four sin stories in the succession narrative speak to Yahweh's expansive love and buoyant commitment to freedom for David. Yahweh continues to trust even when David shows himself to be untrustworthy. There is a risk in trusting a subordinate. God refuses to step back from that; God absorbs all the risk of opening up a free space for his king to think, plan, and act. When David falls, as is inevitable, Yahweh naturally enough requires repentance and amendment, but Yahweh does not cease to trust; the gift of freedom is given unconditionally. David needs the security of knowing that Yahweh is constant and his promises eternal in order to develop as an innovative and ultimately truly great ruler of God's people.

I say to leaders of organizations: "More Power II to you." Trust-as-power is the smart and generous approach to leadership of the modern organization. From a biblical perspective, there is clear evidence that God's leadership style is of the Power II variety.

Neil Pembroke is an ordained minister in the Uniting Church in Australia and Associate Professor of Christian Studies at the University of Queensland, Brisbane, Australia. Neil is the author of 7 books and more than 60 articles in the field of practical theology.

Relational Musings Concerning God and Politics

TIM REDDISH

God's relationship with political leadership requires citizens to exercise free will wisely and responsively, mindful of God's priorities.

As I write, my home country of Canada has just returned Trudeau's Liberal Party to power (but as a minority government), Britain is undergoing a general election and wrestling with the complex matter of Brexit, and the United States is gearing up for 2020 elections while embroiled in an impeachment inquiry. Democratic politics can be very messy! Where does God come into all this? Does God *already* know who our future elected leaders will be? More to the point, does God manipulate circumstances—so to speak—so that *God's* pick wins? In other words, is it true that, as Paul says in Romans 13:1, "The authorities that exist have been established by God"?

In responding to these questions, I think it's helpful to begin by reviewing God's relationship with his people throughout history, beginning with Moses. God called Moses to lead the people from bondage in Egypt and later established a covenant with them, as summarized in the Ten Commandments. Joshua took them over the River Jordan into the Promised Land and, in time, God called special individuals— "judges" —to lead the people. A judge was a combination of a military deliverer, a magistrate, and an administrator. Being a judge was not an inherited right; God continued to appoint God's leaders. The last judge was Samuel and, in his old age, the people came to him desirous of a *king* as his successor so they could be like the other nations around them. Samuel was unhappy; so—we are told—was God. The LORD told Samuel,

"Listen to all that the people are saying to you; it is not you they have rejected, but *they have rejected me as their king*" (1 Sam 8:6-7). Samuel warned the people of the consequences in having a monarchy, namely taxation and conscription, but the people still wanted a king and the LORD relented (1 Sam 8:19-22). Guided by God, Samuel sought out a suitable king and anointed tall and handsome Saul. Initially popular, he soon disobeyed God's instructions and we are told God "regretted appointing Saul as King" (1 Sam 15:11).

Let's pause for a moment: *God regrets*?! Did God not *know* beforehand that Saul would turn out to be a disappointment? Apparently not, according to this biblical writer. (See also Gen 6:6.)

Now kingship normally begins a hereditary line but, curiously, rather than simply continue with Saul's noble son, Jonathan, God decided to start again with David. Kings were meant to be shepherds of the people, caring benevolently for their subjects as a surrogate for God. But this didn't happen; Israel's history is of a few good kings and many corrupt ones. To counteract this tendency, God raised up *prophets* to speak truth to power, to encourage kings to exercise social justice and remind them to worship the one true God. In the end, Israel was repeatedly taken captive by various empires and lost their right to self-determination—the Roman Empire in New Testament times being just one such example. The Jewish *religion* and the Jewish *nation*, then, were strongly interlinked. As Israel self-analyzed their plight, they understood their predicament to be a consequence of their repeated failure to keep the covenant made at the time of Moses (see Deuteronomy 28). They therefore longed for a *political* deliverer in the Messiah, and many religious leaders sought to hasten his arrival by encouraging everyone to recommit themselves to following the Mosaic Law. Christianity was born in this environment as an emerging, minority religion within the Roman Empire.

It was not until Emperor Constantine's edict of Milan in 313 CE that Christianity become acceptable—even respectable—within the Roman Empire. Before long (in 325 CE), Constantine wanted one religion for one empire and he established the first Church Council of Nicaea (in modern-day Turkey) to begin thrashing out church doctrine, create a formal Creed, and formalize the New Testament. Prior to that, the churches around the Mediterranean were semi-independent. The effect of all this was a merging of Church and state and the formation of "Christendom." This infused power, money, and influence into the Western Church and lasted for 1600 years! Even the Protestant Reformation required new national marriages of Church and state to sustain its rebellion from Rome.

In the last few centuries, two important political developments have occurred: the rise of nationalism together with modern forms of democracy. Moreover, in the last 60 years there has been the collapse of Christendom, which many churches are only just recognizing. All three affect this question of God's relationship with political leaders today. First, nationalism strives for territorial self-governance, free from outside interference. Coupled with this, however, is an expected sense of prime loyalty to the nation state and its flag. Such loyalty can usurp God and become idolatrous. Second, in modern democracies, a monarch's influence is minimal (or non-existent) and public elections take place to choose a country's leaders. Such a notion was unheard of in biblical times! Consequently, simply translating biblical ideas, which we can see *evolved* from the times of the judges to that of the early Church, into our contemporary political scenes is fraught with difficulty. Third, the collapse of Christendom has created not only a crisis for the place of the Church within society, but a re-evaluation of the Church's relationship of power and privilege that it previously had with the Establishment, (i.e., its influence in politics, ethics, education, healthcare, taxation, etc.).

Some see this demise as a tragic loss of what was previously deemed a "Christian nation." But that "loss" —if that's the right word—really began centuries earlier in Western culture, during the Age of Reason and the Enlightenment and with the emergence of an individualistic, secular society. Frankly, that is where we find ourselves today and I think it is foolish to waste effort trying to put the genie back in the bottle. It would be better if the (Western) Church recognized we are now in a situation not unlike the first century Christians: as a minority religion in a pluralistic society and one where the prevalent culture is not neutral to Christianity.

Given this background, we could ask, "What would Jesus do?" This not as simple a question as it might seem, because Jesus was more political than many people recognize. For example, in choosing *twelve* disciples, he was making a political statement as this signified establishing a new Israel, echoing its original twelve tribes. Jesus also confronted the religious and political leaders of his day; his overturning of the moneychangers' tables in the Temple court was a public act of rebellion against corruption. Moreover, as we see throughout the gospels, Jesus keeps talking about the "*kingdom* of God." He, therefore, sounds and acts political. Yet John reports that at Jesus' trial before Pontius Pilate, he stated,

"My kingdom is not *of* this world" (John 18:36). And Pilate was so convinced Jesus was not a *political* threat that he wanted to release him![3] In light of this, trying to establish or maintain an idealized "Christian nation" is precisely what the gospel is *not* about—despite many Christians today thinking the contrary! The ministry of Jesus was *not* an attempt to re-establish a pre-monarchical, territorial form of governance. Nevertheless, it is still theologically appropriate to say, "Jesus is now King." Through Jesus, God has given his people new hearts, ones renewed by the Holy Spirit, and Jesus is the king of *hearts*.

We can therefore see that God's relationship with political leaders has *adapted* with the times. In that process, it is not unreasonable to say that throughout history God respects human free will and does *not* override it. Instead, the divine Spirit tries to influence hardened hearts through those whose hearts are sensitive and responsive to God's desires. This being the case, in a democracy, where the public choose their leaders, dare I suggest that God has relatively little to do with the outcome. Once everyone has cast their vote, however, God will certainly be the first to know who has won the election! But if God is not coercive, and if free will is genuine, then it is *not* a foregone conclusion that the result of an election will also be God's preference. Consequently, I am not convinced that Paul's bold claim, "There is no authority except that which God has established" (Rom 13:1) is literally true.

Instead, I think a better way to understand God's relationship with leaders is to begin with the proclamation, "God is the ultimate ruler" and acknowledge that a leader's authority is always *in relation* to God. Our political rulers, then, don't have absolute authority—even though some act and behave as if they do! Ideally, our leaders are benevolent and just. Their role is to create and maintain social cohesion, for God desires order not chaos. But if our leaders claim for themselves the absolute authority that belongs to God, or become agents of evil rather than of good, then I don't think the appropriate Christian response is to cite Romans 13:1 and passively see their acts as divinely mandated. After all, we believe the biblical prophets were *inspired* to speak out courageously *against* the established authorities, don't we? If such a government no longer functions as a responsible servant of God, it is not to be blindly obeyed as such.

---

[3] John 18:38b; Luke 23:4, 14-15, 22. Jesus' claim was, therefore, *not* one of *political* kingship. But his radical upside-down "kingdom" was most definitely *for* this world. That's why it's better to think of the kingdom of God not as a *place* but as a *time*—not a location but an era. And this also explains why the kingdom of God doesn't recognize national boundaries.

The civil rights movement in America can be recognized as legitimate in this light. But in resisting the state, we are to follow Christ's example and seek to do it non-violently, and always wisely counting the cost. Paul gave no advice on knowing when a government or a leader has crossed a "red line" and become a force for evil and injustice. That we have to figure out for ourselves, preferably collectively, and always with the help of the Holy Spirit, who—amongst other things—may still be speaking through prophetic voices today.

Tim Reddish (PhD, M.Div.) is the Minister at St. Andrew's Presbyterian Church, Amherstburg, Ontario, and the author of three books, including Does God Always Get What God Wants? (Eugene: Cascade, 2018). Prior to being ordained, Tim was a professor and researching in atomic and molecular physics. See asamatteroffaith.com

23

Going for the Gold

OMAR REYES

Kelly's Heroes, a WWII movie about soldiers in search of Nazi gold, exemplifies leadership in an open and relational view of God.

"A generous person will prosper; whoever refreshes others will be refreshed" (Prov. 11:25), says the wise writer. And that's how I feel about open and relational theology. It refreshes those it touches. That's also how I feel about the movie, *Kelly's Heroes*. I'd like to take this movie as my way of exploring leadership from an open and relational perspective.

Unlike many theologies, open and relational thinking takes as true the reality of creaturely randomness and regularity, freedom and necessity, good and evil. Other theological traditions have dismissed randomness, for instance, thinking nothing is random in a God-controlled world. Others denied the reality of evil, thinking all pain and suffering must be caused or allowed by God for some greater purpose.

Open and relational theology views God as acting in and responding to the world. God does not control the universe, as we are lead to believe by traditional ways of looking at God. God influences others and is affected by them.

At first glance, some wonder whether we're even talking about *God* if this being cannot control. Or some wonder if God can be anything other than timeless, unchanging, unaffected, and more. In other words, some start with a conventional view of God and assume any other perspective is wrong.

It is precisely this conventional view that's the problem, however. And this problem is evident in how the view influences common views of leadership, especially in church circles. If God is a top-down leader who controls others, we're easily tempted to think the best leaders are top-down controllers.

I saw this in my own family. My Dominican father acted like the God of conventional theology, not much interested in relating to his family. Like a distant God who knows everything and only gives information on a "need to know basis," my father was often aloof and disconnected.

And this brings me to *Kelly's Heroes*.

The movie is based on the adventures of Private Kelly, a former World War II lieutenant demoted for a failed infantry assault. But Kelly captures a German colonel of intelligence. After interrogating his prisoner, Kelly notices the officer has several gold bars disguised under lead plating. Kelly eventually gets the colonel to divulge the location of $16m worth of gold bars stored behind German lines.

Kelly decides to risk going after the gold. He gets enough supplies and ammunition for the venture, including some tanks. He recruits several fellow soldiers as well. Their plan involves splitting into two divisions: one with tanks and the other with infantry.

Few things go according to plan thereafter. The crew loses tanks, jeeps, and human lives. The Germans respond in unexpected ways. When the two divisions link back up, they battle toward the goal, but only attract more attention. They eventually find the gold, despite overwhelming odds against them. The whole escapade has unpredicted positive and negative results.

I think this movie tells us something about the God who acts without a fixed and predetermined plan. In terms of leadership, Kelly took a risk for something of value. He acted not according to a predetermined script. And when obstacles presented themselves, he worked creatively with his men to change directions to do what must be done to complete the mission.

The story of Moses points to a God who acts with a goal but no predetermined script. Here's the story from Exodus 32:

The Lord said to Moses, 'Go down at once! Your people, whom you brought up out of the land of Egypt, have acted perversely; they have been quick to turn aside from the way that I commanded them; they have cast for themselves an image of a calf, and have worshipped it and sacrificed to it, and said, 'These are your gods, O Israel, who brought you up out of the land of Egypt!'

The Lord said to Moses, 'I have seen this people, how stiff-necked they are. Now let me alone, so that my wrath may burn hot against them and I may consume them; and of you I will make a great nation.'

But Moses implored the Lord his God, and said, 'O Lord, why does your wrath burn hot against your people, whom you brought out of the land of Egypt with great power and with a mighty hand? Why should the Egyptians say, 'It was with evil intent that he brought them out to kill them in the mountains, and to consume them from the face of the earth?' Turn from your fierce wrath; change your mind and do not bring disaster on your people. Remember Abraham, Isaac, and Israel, your servants, how you swore to them by your own self, saying to them, "I will multiply your descendants like the stars of heaven, and all this land that I have promised I will give to your descendants, and they shall inherit it forever.'

And the Lord changed his mind about the disaster that he planned to bring on his people (7-14).

In this story, God has a plan. But this plan changes, because Moses reminds God of the greater goal. Moses asks God to reconsider the plan in light of the larger goal for Israel. Killing his people would undermine the overall goal and reflect badly on God's character. And Moses convinces God to scrap the plan!

God's overall goal is outlined in Genesis 1:26-27: "Then God said, 'Let us make humankind in our image, according to our likeness; and let them have dominion over the fish of the sea, and over the birds of the air, and over the cattle, and over all the wild animals of the earth, and over every creeping thing that creeps upon the earth. 'So God created humankind in his image, in the image of God he created them; male and female he created them."

God wanted a loving relationship with humans. And when they disobeyed, God took the initiative to restore relationship. We see this divine initiative most clearly in Jesus, whose life, death, and resurrection aims at healing the breach. God keeps the overall goal in mind but changes specific strategies along the way.

Open and relational leadership modeled after God's way of relating offers insights to leaders today. It admits that creatures are flawed, they fail, and sometimes they disobey. But they are made in God's image, and it's worth the trouble of trying to restore the relationship and get it back on track.

Nearly every success starts with an initial idea. But getting to that success takes time and patience. God will go to any length that love will go to save us. Saving does not mean becoming detached. Nor does it mean we are pawns in a master plan. Such uncaring leadership leads to mistreating followers.

OPEN AND RELATIONAL LEADERSHIP

Great leaders care as much for the welfare of those they lead as they do about any bottom line. Great leaders are neither distant nor uncaring. They seek the well-being of those they lead. They join with others to work together toward solutions and success.

Rev. Omar Reyes is an ordained Episcopal priest with more than six years of diverse ministry experience. After graduating from Gordon Conwell, he served four years in Western Newfoundland, with six churches under his care. He now serves Christ church Albertville, Alabama and is a student at the School of Theology of the University of the South (Sewanee), working on his Masters of Sacred Theology. His wife Jennifer has been on this journey with him for 22 years and they have three lovely boys, Azriel, Tennyson, and Vadim. He was born in Brooklyn to immigrants from the Dominican Republic and tweets from @trueanglican.

Leading Through the Contention: Guidance from Open and Relational Theology in Navigating Conflict

KYLE ROBERTS

Open and relational theology is well positioned as a resource for leaders to navigate tensions and leverage them for good in everyday decision-making.

What is contradictory can produce new life through the contention, if the differences are accepted as challenges.[4]

Life is full of conflict. Leaders encounter conflicts on a regular basis. Conflicts are often caused by tensions and oppositional factors that are inherent to the dynamics of social life and are persistent within organizations.

We can think of these tensions and oppositional factors as *polarities;* poles that reside on opposite sides of a tension, of a seemingly impossible choice, or of a persistent conflict. The tension created by these polarities creates *contention* for leaders and their organizations.

Leaders are often called upon to make decisions, to write and enact policies, and to adjudicate between seemingly competing sides of a conflict. For this essay, I'm indebted to Peter Krembs for articulating a compelling thesis about polarities in the context of leadership development. He argues that

---

[4] Jürgen Moltmann, Experiences in Theology: Ways and Forms of Christian Theology (SCM Press, 2000), pp. 171-72.

polarities should be treated not as problems to solve, but as tensions to navigate and ideally to leverage for the greater good of an organization.[5] When leaders prematurely try to eliminate the contention created by the polarities, consequences follow: They create more conflict. Or, they truncate depth, expunge diversity, or result in a hasty decision with negative consequences.

What leaders often assume to be problems in need of an immediate or imminent solution are actually persistent and potentially constructive tensions. They require managing, negotiation, and navigation--not the implementation of a clear-cut decision.

When I was invited to contribute to this volume on leadership through the frame of open and relational theologies, I thought right away of this connection to this notion of polarities. Open and relational theologies provide a theological basis for recognizing and engaging polarities. They provide a basis for deconstructing the either/or thinking that plagues so much of our modern ways of operating and of leading.

Thinking about Polarities

It is easy to think of common polarities we experience in life and in organizations, for example: hierarchy/democracy, control/organic flow, freedom/limitation, dependence/ independence, power/vulnerability, part/whole. Neither of the poles are *wrong* in and of themselves. Rather, they are phenomena of human and social life. One does not necessarily decide between these poles—rather, one recognizes their power and influence within a field of reference. Differing personalities and organizational styles will gravitate to one of these poles or to the other. The nature of the circumstance may also determine which of the poles has more gravitational pull.

When leaders are faced with decisions or are confronted by conflicts emerging from polarities, our temptation is to decide between options that we sense cannot reside together Leaders often rush to eliminate one pole or the other, thereby reducing anxiety and the persistence of conflict, rather than letting the tension remain and seeking ways to utilize the tension in productive and constructive ways.

---

[5] Peter Krembs lecture was presented during a course on Executive Leadership at the University of St. Thomas' Opus School of Business, 2019.

In a broader context of organizational leadership, other polarities easily come to mind: external growth/inward maintenance, innovation/preservation, collaborative leadership/authoritative decision-making, adaptive evolution/strategic planning.

Again, the leader may find herself oscillating between the poles or choosing one over the other. Imagine a leader of an organization, for example, declaring, "From now on we will only focus on innovation—preservation of things that we've valued up to this point will no longer be our concern!" Or, "Now we will only be planful and strategic; no extemporaneous developments will change the course of our actions!" These are caricatures, but we can likely think of real-life examples where leaders make intentional choices between opposite poles.

Take the context of academic administrative leadership (my context as a seminary dean). In the higher education world, there are common polarities: academic freedom/fidelity to traditions; faculty governance/administrative leadership; student as consumer/faculty as expert; practical and vocational training/humanities and liberal arts; education for vocational preparation/education for inherent value; wider access/greater rigor.

Poles shift from one to the other within the educational arena, reflective of internal trends and external pressures. As educational institutions, colleges, universities, and graduate schools face the pressures caused by enrollment declines, decreasing revenue, and other challenges, leaders are tempted to dismiss academic freedom and to short-circuit faculty governance. When institutions focus on the student as consumer, attention to educational integrity may get short shrift.

In the face of these pressures and the pragmatic response by leaders concerned about economics and declining numbers, faculty may double down on traditions of academic freedom and faculty governance—and in so doing may circumvent innovation and undermine efforts toward growth and change— even in the face of a challenging present and an increasingly ominous future.

Guidance from Open and Relational Theology

Our western inheritance, which relies so heavily on dualistic constructs (body/soul, spirit/matter, right/wrong, individual/communal, competition/collaboration) and in which dualism undergirds so much classical theism and theologies framed by classical theological models, forms leaders to think of conflict and tension as "problems to solve, rather than tensions to navigate." They rush to make decisions—with suboptimal or even destructive consequences.

The rush to decision, thereby eliminating one pole in favor of the other, reflects a theological underpinning based on a classical model of God and God's relation to the world, which also tends toward prioritizing one end of any number of polarities: spirit/matter, power/dependence, justice/forgiveness, holiness/love, sin/salvation, divinity/creation, and so on.

A relational and open theology model more readily allows for the recognition that the poles are interconnected and it is best to acknowledge their interconnection and persistence.

The divine reality involves both spirit and matter, both prescience and learning, both power and dependence upon others. God can be both vulnerable and powerful—perhaps vulnerable in power—or powerful in and through vulnerability. This "both-and" rather than "either-or" theology means that the persistence of oppositional poles creates tension, even in Godself, but that—as with Moltmann's quote earlier—the tension or *contention* can be constructive and life-giving if accepted as a challenge.

Creation itself can be imagined as a spirituality of polarities in which dualities are not stark and inter-connections are infinite. Material reality is connected to and with the realm of spirit. Justice can be interspersed with lavish forgiveness and love. Beauty is found within the midst of ugliness and terror. Order and chaos mingle. Freedom and limitation cohabitate, and in that cohabitation produce life.

For the leader who leads through contention that springs forth from polarities, decisions cannot always be held at bay. Leaders eventually need to decide between options, ruling out some in favor of others. Leaders certainly cannot please everyone, and leaders cannot indefinitely linger between polarities.

But to recognize the polarities of life and those that work within our organizations and perhaps even between ourselves provides a basis for letting the tensions reside within the whole, rather than eliminating one pole to reduce the tension. Maintaining and even leveraging the tensions for a greater, common good means that diversity is encouraged rather than discouraged, healthy pluralism is embraced rather than suspected, and relationships are deepened rather than reduced to an algebraic economic exchange, all based on a perception of a need to choose and to choose *right now*.

Leading through the contention is not a simple way to lead. It will not always be possible or even optimal. It will take the cultivation of wisdom and of contextual application to know when a polarity must be managed rather than eliminated and how it can be leveraged for a constructive end. It will call for leaders and co-leaders patient and thoughtful enough to discern the difference between polarities and decisions, and patient enough to leverage those polarities *through the contention* toward a constructive end.

That's the nature of leadership within our complex fields of life—but it's also the nature of life and of God under an open and relational framework of the divine being and of our human and created life.

Dr. Kyle Roberts is Academic Dean and Schilling Professor of Public Theology and Church and Economic Life at United Theological Seminary of the Twin Cities. He has been a professor and theologian for over a decade, publishing several books and numerous essays, and has served full-time in academic leadership since 2018.

25

We Can't

PETE SHAW

Open and relational theology requires a change in our language, and this shapes our beliefs and practices.

"How are we going to get people to tithe without using fear?"

My fellow-pastor-friend was only sort of kidding when he asked the question. As like-minded pastors leading churches that operate from an open and relational theological perspective, his was not really a hypothetical question. Neither was it just related to financial contributions. Might as well add serving to the list (*especially nursery duty*). And small group involvement. And worship attendance. And even conversion. When fear of God's judgment is off the table, a lot of our comfortable rhetoric is, too. We can't say things the way we used to.

I grew up in the Baptist tradition. We are a tribe who take pride in the freedom to interpret the Bible as we see fit. Ironically, while this might cause one to assume there would be greater openness to varying biblical interpretations, Baptists have become associated with being rigid and closed-minded, even judgmental toward those who disagree with the established position. The certitude about doctrinal positions and whom God will surely judge has created great passion for evangelism yet brought with it some unintended consequences that became too much for me to live and lead with. My personal faith journey was motivated by what Thomas Jay Oord calls the uncontrolling love of God that has room for an open approach to understanding the faith and assumes that God's love means relationship between the Creator and created is paramount. Was my language and leadership reflective of such love?

I was never very extreme in this regard thanks to my more moderate upbringing, yet I am certain that in my earlier years of ministry I used a degree of the fear of God's retribution in my rhetoric to motivate people to make faith-related decisions about conversion, worship attendance, discipleship program participation, service, devotional life, and personal evangelism. The boiled down message was, *"God loves you, but if you don't do 'X', there will be hell to pay."* It's not that there aren't consequences to choosing not to follow God – of course there are. Jesus came to lead the way toward an abundant life built on love and grace that leads to all the fruits of the spirit available in every season. Not following in Jesus' footsteps at least minimizes such a harvest, and at worst can result in a very self-and-other-destructive rendition of living that nobody wants.

There is surely FOMO (fear of missing out) that is worth lifting up related to the Christian life and its message. But when we, with great certainty, tell our audiences that God's love is conditioned upon our allegiance, that God's "control" means our life script is pretty much set, and that our eternity may be in the balance if we're not careful to toe the line, I think we're adding an element that does not reflect Jesus well. This articulation of Good News may be well meaning, but it doesn't quite come off as "good" as we might think. If we really, really, really believe that God is love and is lovely, we can't use fear in our rhetoric or leadership strategy.

Easier said than done. Language is powerful. It not only communicates what we believe, it shapes it. We might get into trouble as we change our language and strategy, because it will challenge the held beliefs it seeks to articulate. When we shift one, it can have a domino effect on the other. Open and relational theology is messy.

This reality reminds me of Peter, Jesus' disciple and apostle. His humanity seemed always on display. Peter was a person in process. He identified Jesus as the Christ, and then told him how to be Christ. He proclaimed unshakable loyalty, and then denied knowing him three times. He assured Jesus of his love, then, after being restored (!), whined about whether or not he was being treated fairly given the grim news of his distant-future death. He refused to call edible the forbidden foods God was calling "clean" in the thrice-experienced lunch buffet vision, followed God's instructions to go to Cornelius' house, but then in good klutz fashion treated his Gentile audience rudely (*I shouldn't be talking to you people...*). God bless, him, though – after seeing the Holy Spirit welcoming them into the fold, Peter authorized their baptism, giving them a rite of passage that had not yet been granted to non-Jews. Peter would eventually have to explain his actions to the other Christian leaders where he essentially said, *"We can't say and do things like we used to because they are no longer true."* His was an open theology! Three steps forward, two steps back, one foot in mouth is how it seemed to go for him.

Like Peter after baptizing Cornelius' household, when he had some explaining to do with the Jerusalem Council, so I have moved forward in leadership, building on a foundation of grace, and sometimes facing unpleasant consequences in response, because the *new* challenges the *established*, and we generally like things to remain the same. Yet the beautiful example Peter offered was rooted in an open theology that allowed for ongoing discovery and change, fostered by love from God that would not let him go. Peter's language shifted along with his theology, which then opened the door of grace to the non-Jewish world.

Refusing this kind of fear a place in my teaching and at the leadership table required the development of a different skillset, especially given the fact that the larger culture around us uses fear in its myriad forms of communication all the time. Fear is effective and efficient, after all. In very specific situations, using fear to motivate may be prudent (*e.g., telling your young child not to play near the street*). But leading a community for the long haul in the way of Jesus necessitates something more akin to Jesus' approach. After all, he spent three years developing the disciples so that they would not depart from it once he was no longer physically with them. If all he offered was fear avoidance, he could have done that in ten minutes (with a tract?) and get back to heaven. The way of love and grace, however, was and will always be counter-cultural and counter-lizard-brain-intuitive. As was the case for Peter, for me, and for every human being (I think), the Micah 6:8 way of life modeled by Jesus takes time to work in and work out. Our hearts are changed, and so is our language. There are things we just can't say and do anymore.

We don't talk about fear in my church. Instead, we speak of opportunity, possibility, responsibility, and maturity as better motivation centers. We stretch in our thinking because God is bigger than any box and discovering more about God is really amazing and freeing. We kneel in service to others because we get to make a meaningful difference in the lives of others and, at the same time, grow from the experience as well. We offer words and expression of grace to others as a holy privilege, and find that when we do, we become more graceful and grace filled. We open ourselves to be the incarnate presence of God in the highs and lows of those around us and find ourselves more filled with the presence of God. We choose to connect with God to foster an ever-deepening relationship with God, and find God doing the same right back, which serves to strengthen our love for the lover of our souls. We choose to offer ourselves and resources for local and global service in ways that promote the larger vision of healing people and communities instead of trying to get them signed up for heaven.

Interestingly, all of these choices serve to create a greater confidence that we are a part of something eternal at work in us and through us, and therefore our hope for life after the grave increases. All of these choices are made without the fear of what God might do to us should we ignore God. All of these choices are made with an eye on the possibility of renewed, restored, resurrected life now. An open-ended script written with the help of a relationally driven God. Our invitation to follow Jesus, therefore, is given without a hint of fear. It relies instead on the genuine love of God. We can't and don't use fear rhetoric or gimmicks. For the love of God and God's love for us, we simply can't.

Pete Shaw has been the Senior Pastor of CrossWalk Community Church in Napa, CA, since late 1999. He earned his M.Div. (1995) and D.Min. (2006) from Northern Seminary and has consulted many churches seeking transformation. Pete and Lynne have been married since 1992, their two kids are their greatest joy and pride, and U2 his favorite band since 1984.

26

Power-less Leadership

JEFFERY D SKINNER

Since God's leadership is power-less, the best leaders are also power-less.

*L*eadership is hard. Yet, even if people remain skeptical, leadership has never been more popular. Universities are offering degrees in leadership, bloggers are writing about leadership, companies are studying leadership, and the world is searching for the perfect leader. Ironically, it seems the more we study it and the harder we try to be better leaders or identify the perfect model, the more it eludes us. Some might argue there is a crisis of world leadership and that is the reason it seems to be on the minds of so many people.

In his most recent book, "Ring of Fire," Leonard Sweet uses the metaphor of a "global ring of fire…Moving fault lines that generate earthquakes and volcanic eruptions multiple times a day." These "seismic" events are constantly reshaping the landscape and making the atmosphere toxic. No wonder leadership today is so difficult.

When asked, most people have very little trouble identifying experiences they have had with poor leaders or identifying poor leadership. "Lead. Follow. Or get out of the way." "If you want something done right, do it yourself." "Leadership is the art of convincing people to go and do things they would not otherwise do." Maybe you recall a leader who asked you to do a job and then was constantly looking over your shoulder to be sure you did it "right." The opposite of such a leader is the one who asks you to a do a job, is then unavailable to review progress, and seemingly abandons all interest in the entire project. Volumes could be written telling stories of poor leadership. Even if finding the perfect leader is elusive, everyone recognizes poor leadership when confronted with a bad leader. No one desires to serve under such toxic leaders.

No one desires to serve a leader who is controlling, does not give clear direction, has double standards, has a lack of presence, or is an unclear communicator.

Ironically, such qualities are often identified as characteristics of God. Traditionally, God has been characterized as being an unclear communicator, distant, controlling, power hungry, and even angry. Popular scriptures are cited such as Isaiah 55:8, "For my thoughts are not your thoughts, neither are your ways my ways, declares the LORD" (God is mystery) or Isaiah 43:13, "Even from eternity I am He, and there is none who can deliver out of My hand; I act and who can reverse it?" (God is all-powerful and all controlling). The typical views of God tend to cast God as a benevolent dictator who acts upon the whims of God's divine mood. If we do not accept such characteristics in our leaders, why should God get a pass? No one can be certain whether we have experienced such poor leadership and as poor leaders unintentionally project those views on to God, or whether our views of God shape how we lead? Is that the reason many tolerate bad leaders? Is that why we *are* sometimes such bad leaders? Perhaps we are resentful? Maybe we are in agreement with Johnathan Edwards who said we are "Sinners in the Hands of an Angry God" and so we take it out on everyone else?

Maybe, if people were offered an alternative to an all controlling, all powerful, all knowing God, there could be more widespread agreement on the definition of leadership and thus better leaders? Perhaps if people did not believe God had one standard for God's conduct and another standard for God's creation, leaders wouldn't have double standards? Maybe if people did not believe God micromanaged their lives, they wouldn't accept a leader who micromanages? What if God is not all controlling, all powerful, or even a mystery? What if we held God to the same standards as we hold leaders? What if God wasn't a benevolent dictator? What if God is not the divine hypocrite who has a different standard operating procedure for God's creation than God does for God's self? What if we do not have to make exceptions for God's leadership in our lives?

The good news is there is an alternative.

Scripture tells us God is love! God is not just a loving God, God's nature is love. God has no choice except to love. God could no more not love than a fish could not swim. Love does not control. God's nature does not flow from a divine need for power. God's power source is God's love. Since God is like no other God, God's love is like no other love. God's love is self-giving, other-empowering, non-coercive love. In other words, because God empowers others,

God is power-less. God cannot force creation to do anything. God requires the co-operation of God's creation. This theory of "uncontrolling love" or power-less leadership is an interpretation that Thomas Jay Oord published in a book called *God Can't* as well as other books that explain God's "uncontrolling love" in detail.

If God's love is uncontrolling and God's people are supposed to mirror God's love toward others, how should Godly leadership look? Having already discussed some images of leaders that are not healthy or inspirational, let us turn our attention to some leaders and characteristics of leaders that could be considered in the vein of uncontrolling love. History seems to be filled with leaders who at least embody some of these characteristics.

Few people would disagree that Gandhi was an inspirational leader. His fight for Indian nationalism against British rule did not include violence. He sought to inspire his enemies; not coerce them. Martin Luther King, Jr.'s weapons of choice were the words of letters he wrote while sitting in jail, in sermons preached from pulpits in the "projects" and speeches in the streets. King ultimately gave his life for his cause—the cross upon which he gave his life for the freedom of his people was a hotel balcony in Memphis.

Other great leaders from history, for whom there is widespread agreement on their embodiment of great leadership qualities, include George Washington, Harriet Tubman, Abraham Lincoln, Hellen Keller, Alexander Hamilton, Mother Teresa, Nelson Mandela, and Pope John Paul II. The followers of Pope John Paul II credit him with giving Catholics a clear understanding of Catholic identity and its beliefs. Emmeline Pankhurst led the women's suffragette movement and ultimately opened the door for women to have the right to vote. The problem has been that once these leaders pass, their stories become exaggerated; their mistakes are overlooked. It is easier to be gracious after death. This process of mythologizing does not suggest that they did not exist or that their accomplishments never happened. However, one problem with mythologizing a leader or his or her legacy is that it becomes an idealized standard that is impossible to attain. The result is many refuse to attempt to attain it at all.

Perhaps Oord's power-less view of God is a view of leadership that is simultaneously attractive and attainable. Robert Greenleaf coined the phrase "servant leader" in an essay first published in 1970. In that essay, "The Servant Leader," Greenleaf said, "the servant-leader is servant first." The servant leader is "sharply different from one who is leader first, perhaps because of the need to assuage an unusual power drive or to acquire material possessions...The leader-first and the servant-first are two extreme types." The servant leader seeks the interest and the needs of the people first and the needs of the organization last. The theory suggests that if the leader serves the people, they will be inspired to work to meet the needs of the organization. The servant leader works as a part of a team where "coercion", "intimidation", and "boss" are considered dirty words and are never on the table as options. For the servant leader, leadership is not about the accumulation of power and control; it is about empowering others and allowing them to be in control. The servant leader trusts the team to work together, cooperate with each other, and to work with the leader to fulfill the mission. In fact, the servant leader is not always leading. At any given point in the process of fulfilling the mission, the leader simply becomes another member of the team, trusting the expertise of another.

Greenleaf believed that servant leader organizations could and would radically transform the known world. In his second essay, "The Institution as Servant," he wrote:

This is my thesis: caring for persons, the more able and the less able serving each other, is the rock upon which a good society is built. Whereas, until recently, caring was largely person to person, now most of it is mediated through institutions—often large, complex, powerful, impersonal; not always competent; sometimes corrupt. If a better society is to be built, one that is more just and more loving, one that provides greater creative opportunity for its people, then the most open course is to raise both the capacity to serve and the very performance as servant of existing major institutions by new regenerative forces operating within them.

Perhaps in a world suffering from the trauma of volcanic personalities, seismic shifts, and a toxic atmosphere, power-less leadership is the answer? Perhaps the answer has been under our collective noses the entire time. Matthew 20:25-28 finds Jesus facing a hostile context as well. People were searching for a leader then too. The Roman soldiers lined their streets and occupied their villages. The Caesar of Rome ruled with an iron fist and the religious elite watched for and interpreted every action in the spirit of an oppressive law to empower themselves. Anyone who dared to step out of line or failed to recognize his/her place in the pecking order was quickly punished. It was to these people that Jesus said:

You know that the rulers of the nations lord it over them, and their great ones play the tyrant over them. It shall not be this way among you. But whoever wants to be great among you shall be your servant, and whoever wants to be first among you shall be your slave—just as the Son of Man did not come to be served, but to serve, and to give His life as a ransom for many.

If God entrusts God's creation with the power of choice and believes in their capacity to do good, cooperate to the completion of God's mission for the world, and become power-less for the sake of us, perhaps we too should consider power-lessness. Imagine such a leader.

Jeffery D. Skinner is a business leader and serves as the communications pastor at Gainesville First Church of the Nazarene in the Greater Atlanta area. He earned his Doctorate in Organizational Leadership and Professional Practice from Trevecca University in Nashville, Tennessee. Skinner is the author of the essay, "Miracle Quotas," in the book Uncontrolling Love: Essays Exploring the Love of God with introductions by Thomas Jay Oord and other articles on God's love. He and his wife, Lisa, have two adopted children, Blaine (16) and Hayden (13). Jeffery loves nature and technology.

27

Are Some of the Best Leaders the Most Reluctant?

IAN TODD

God cannot achieve God's aims alone. We must respond to God's call to leadership, despite the reluctance we may feel.

When Moses came upon the burning bush on Mount Horeb, he was just a lowly shepherd working for his father-in-law (Exodus, Ch. 3). And yet, he'd previously known a life of great privilege and luxury, as the adopted son of an Egyptian princess. Of course, that had all gone horribly wrong on the day that he murdered an Egyptian who was beating up a Hebrew slave. So, when God spoke to Moses from the burning bush, offering to make him "Leader of the Israelites," you'd think he'd seize the chance. Here was a (literally!) God-given opportunity to re-establish himself as someone important, someone prestigious, someone to be looked up to, someone with REAL POWER! Forget herding sheep, he was going to lead a whole nation!

You might have expected that to be his reaction, but you'd be wrong. What Moses did was come up with a whole load of excuses about why he wasn't the one for the job:

"Who am I that I should do this?" said Moses. "I will be with you," replied God.

"What shall I say is Your name?" asked Moses. "I AM WHO I AM," said God.

"But suppose they don't believe me or won't listen—what shall I do then?" argued Moses. God had equipped Moses with miraculous signs to convince even the most hardened sceptic.

Moses tried a different tack: "I'm not a good speaker; I'll get tongue-tied!" God replied with some exasperation, "I'll give you the words to speak."

Moses had run out of excuses and bleated, "Oh my Lord, please send someone else!"

By this time, even God had lost patience: "Okay, okay!" said God, "Your brother Aaron is an eloquent speaker. I'll tell you what needs to be said, and Aaron can say it!" (Exodus, Ch. 4).

Not a very auspicious start to one of the most momentous events in the Old Testament, you might think. Or, on the other hand, maybe this was exactly the sort of start needed to ensure the eventual success of the Exodus. If Moses' response to God's call had been, "Righty-ho God, leave it with me, I know exactly what to," it might all have been a disaster and the Israelites would have disappeared into obscurity as a footnote of ancient history. If Moses had been full of himself and buoyed up with his own importance, he could have ended up as one of the best examples of the old adage, "Pride goes before a fall." It was, in fact, Moses' insecurity and lack of self-confidence that enabled God to say, "I will be with you" and "I will tell you what to say." In other words, Moses became a great leader because he was fully open to being led by God.

We see this repeatedly through the Bible—those with the greatest influence for good often seemed the least likely to make great leaders and role models at the outset. And the repeating pattern is that their lack of *self-assurance* meant that they were open to—and therefore had—*assurance* of God's guidance. For example, the disciples were vulnerable and uncertain until the Holy Spirit came upon them at Pentecost. They were then able to speak openly and boldly (in multiple languages!) to any and all who would listen (Acts, Ch. 2). Saul (Paul) provides another example: he was driven by his own conviction to persecute the followers of Jesus until he was struck down and faced with Christ on the road to Damascus. While in that state of vulnerability, he three days later was filled with the Holy Spirit. This enabled him to become one of the greatest leaders of the early Church (Acts, Ch. 9).

Turning from a great Christian writer of the first century A.D. to one of the twentieth century, this is how C.S. Lewis described how reluctantly he turned to God: "You must picture me alone in that room in Magdalen, night after night, feeling, whenever my mind lifted even for a second from my work, the steady, unrelenting approach of [God] whom I so earnestly desired not to meet. That which I greatly feared had at last come upon me. In the Trinity Term of 1929 I gave in, and admitted that God was God, and knelt and prayed:

perhaps, that night, the most dejected and reluctant convert in all England. I did not then see what is now the most shining and obvious thing; the Divine humility which will accept a convert even on such terms" (Lewis, C.S. *Surprised by Joy: The Shape of my Early Life*).

Jesus of Nazareth, our consummate leader and role model, is the one person in history whose relationship with God is so complete that the two are indistinguishable. Yet even Jesus didn't burst onto the scene in a blaze of glory, or with a fanfare of self-promotion. He sought baptism by his cousin John before spending weeks of soul-searching alone in the desert (Matthew chs. 3-4). And one of his final acts before his execution was to wash the feet of his disciples— the ultimate expression of perfect leadership being synonymous with perfect service (John, ch.13).

Jesus' understanding of how a person's vulnerability provides the fertile ground necessary for a meaningful and constructive relationship with God is considered in some detail by Roger Bretherton in his book *The GOD Lab: 8 Spiritual Experiments You Can Try at Home* (River Publishing & Media Ltd.). In this book, Roger explains the human conditions necessary for a full relationship with God in the context of the first beatitude that Jesus pronounced during The Sermon on the Mount: "Blessed are the poor in spirit, for theirs is the kingdom of heaven." As Roger says, this is the most difficult of the eight beatitudes for us to understand these days. What is "poor in spirit" supposed to mean? In this context, Roger interprets "spirit" as meaning *what we're like*. In other words, the essence of everything that we are and how we regard our being in relation to ourselves, to others and to God. He therefore goes on to question why "Jesus blesses *poverty* of spirit" rather than "*richness* of spirit". The answer, in Roger's words, goes as follows:

Richness of spirit, taken to its logical conclusion, is to be full of ourselves. To be certain, ruthless and unyielding. To be rich in spirit is to believe we have a lock on the truth and no longer need to consider other points of view—so entrenched in defending our position that we no longer tolerate questions or disagreement. We are rich in spirit whenever we feel full of our own ideas and ambitions to the exclusion of everything else. To be rich in spirit is to be closed, rigid and proud...

By contrast, Roger goes on to say that Jesus,

Commends the virtue of openness as the gateway to knowing God. It's in an attitude of openness and hospitality that we can find [God]. Poverty of spirit isn't low self-esteem or lack of backbone, but a simple acknowledgement that we don't have it all nailed down and can therefore hear the needs and opinions of others. Poverty of spirit, among other things means being available to others and responsive to the world. A recognition that we're not totally self-sufficient.

And Roger further asks, "Could it be that God isn't looking for people who can offer him a seamless performance?"

Putting this into the context of leadership comes back to the point that the best leaders are those who are themselves led by God and are therefore fully open to, and accepting of, God's guidance. Having said that, there may be those who would argue that, if the best leadership requires a good dose of modesty, and possibly reluctance, in order to be fully open to God's influence and guidance, perhaps we should not take up the call to leadership at all. Perhaps the best policy is to leave things entirely to God to sort out because, at the end of the day, God knows best! We may hinder rather than help!

"Not so" is the response to such an argument by Thomas Jay Oord in his book *God Can't: How to Believe in God and Love after Tragedy, Abuse, and Other Evils*. (SacraSage Press)—a response with which I agree. The reason for this is that Tom believes that God doesn't just *invite* our cooperation, but absolutely *requires* it for the best possible outcomes to be achieved—or, as Tom puts it, "for love to win." Tom calls this cooperation between God and creation "indispensable love synergy." This means that God's aims are achieved (which are always loving) by working with creation (synergy) and that the part played by creation is essential (indispensable). In other words, God's aims for the created Universe cannot be achieved by God acting alone. This puts responsibility squarely on our shoulders to respond to God's call to leadership, despite the reluctance we may feel. Indeed, as with Moses, initial reluctance may actually turn out to be an advantage!

Ian Todd is a retired immunologist and Honorary Assistant Professor at the University of Nottingham, UK. His main research interests are in autoimmune and respiratory diseases. He lives in the town of Wirksworth in the Derbyshire Peak District, where he helps with a thirteenth century church (and its twenty-first century congregation!).

28

Waking up with Truman Burbank: Leadership alongside Spiritual Refugees

JASON TRIPP

The movie The Truman Show serves as an allegory for those in the process of awakening to a God who is uncontrolling and unrelenting love.

*"We accept the reality of the world with which we are presented." –
Christof, The Truman Show*
"When I was a child, I spoke like a child, I thought like a child, I reasoned like a child; when I became an adult, I put an end to childish ways." – 1 Corinthians 13:11 (NRSV)

*I*n the description of his excellent book, *Movies are Prayers: How Films Voice Our Deepest Longings*, popular film critic Josh Larsen writes, "Movies do more than tell a good story. They are expressions of raw emotion, naked vulnerability, and unbridled rage. They often function in the same way as prayers, communicating our deepest longings and joys to a God who hears each and every one."

I deeply resonate with these sentiments from Larsen. As a self-professing cinephile, one of the most meaningful and regular ways in which I experience the love of God, while contemplating the journey of life and faith, is in my local movie theater. When the lights go dim and the big screen lights up, my soul sings.

To this day, one of my favorite movies is *The Truman Show*, the 1998 comedy drama starring fellow Canadian Jim Carrey as Truman Burbank. The film, which can rightly be called a classic, portrays the life of Truman who, at birth was legally adopted by a major television studio and whose entire life (unbeknownst to him) has been broadcast to the entire world as a sort of reality television show. Everything and everyone in Seahaven Island, the town in which Truman lives, is carefully constructed and meticulously controlled by Christof (played by Ed Harris in a performance garnering him an Academy Award nomination) the architect and designer of the fabricated reality in which Truman lives.

Through a series of bizarre events and experiences, Truman begins to suspect that something is amiss and pieces together the truth that his world is a façade filled with cameras, props, and actors (including his best friend Marlon and wife Meryl). This series of "woke" moments propel Truman into an agonizing and enthralling search for truth and an attempt to escape the world he once naïvely thought to be good, true and beautiful.

As Truman begins to wake up to the truth of his fictitious world, Christof and his personnel are forced to go to great lengths to ensure Truman remains content and contained in the faux-paradise world of Seahaven Island, as millions around the world remain glued to their television screens to see *how it ends*.

As things begin to unravel, Christof, in an unprecedented move, gives a rare and exclusive live television interview. In responding to the question of why Truman has never come close to discovering the true nature of his world until now, Christof stoically states, *"We accept the reality of the world with which we are presented. It's as simple as that."*

As a pastor and university chaplain, I continually have the privilege of listening to and walking alongside men, women, and children of all ages, who, like Truman, are discovering that the worldview with which they were presented is somewhat illusionary and problematic.

Day after day, I rub shoulders with many of the "Trumans" of my world. Whether in coffee shops, pubs, churches, or through social media, I hear many stories of life experiences which have led to confusion, disillusionment, and despair. While each of these stories is unique, the common thread that binds them together is the way they highlight how lived experiences can bump up against one's inherited worldview and accompanying theological presumptions, leading to a sense of doubt, disorientation, and discouragement.

Recently the Pew Research Center released updated statistics of America's changing religious landscape. The results highlight both the continued decline of those identifying as Christians, while those who identify as religiously unaffiliated (religious "nones") continue to be on the rise, now comprising more than one quarter of the American population. In Canada, and to a greater degree most European nations, the trends parallel those of America where percentages of religious nones grow even higher.

While there is undoubtedly some truth to Christof's claim that the worldview a person is given is typically accepted as truth, the current massively shifting cultural and religious North American landscape suggests an alternate and competing truth—many, like Truman, are waking up to the reality that the spiritual/theological worldview they inherited is faulty. This cognitive dissonance has and continues to lead many to walk away from the church and/or the Christian faith, essentially throwing out the baby with the bathwater.

I empathize deeply with those undergoing a season of spiritual disorientation and disillusionment. It can be extremely fearful and unsettling to have one's theological house of cards come crashing down. The more isolated and sheltered from the world a person remains, the easier it is to naïvely live, work and worship in the neat and tidy confines of a small and sheltered existence. Ignorance is indeed bliss—until life happens.

It didn't take long for doubts, questions, and fears about aspects of the worldview I inherited to arise in my life. I vividly recall being in junior high when my family received word that my mother, a woman of great faith, was diagnosed with breast cancer. Growing up in a religious environment espousing a God of meticulous control very much like that of Christof, my world was rocked. Why would a God of love give a faithful God-fearing woman like my mother a terminal illness? How can a perfectly loving God co-exist with so much senseless evil and suffering?

My doubts, questions and curiosities led me into a lengthy period of disillusionment and spiritual unravelling which in many respects paralleled the painful disorientation of Truman Burbank as he awakened to—and attempted to break free from—the confines of his fabricated, and ultimately toxic world.

Whether it be questions related to inconsistencies and violence in the Bible, science and faith, human sexuality, the problem of evil or a host of other issues, countless masses of people are wrestling with the increasing divergence between one's lived experiences and rational thinking and one's inherited worldview and theological system. Essentially, many—like Truman Burbank, and unlike Christof—are adamantly no longer willing (nor able) to accept the reality of the world in which they were presented.

These courageous, yet fragile spiritual refugees need the safety and comfort of authentic communities where they can have a place to wrestle, heal, and reorient their lives and worldview. It is essential that Christian leadership in North America include the recognition, inclusion, and embrace of the "Trumans" among us. The God revealed fully and finally in the incarnation of Jesus is nothing like Christof, nor is the world a product of a meticulous controlling architect. As I reflect upon my own *"woke moments"* and the joy of leading and being led by fellow pilgrims on the journey towards a more beautiful Gospel and a God of unrelenting love, I humbly offer three observations related to effective leadership for and with those undergoing a season of spiritual disorientation and detox.

Staying in the Ring and Going to the Mat with God

One of my favorite stories in the Old Testament is the story of Jacob's all-night wrestling match with God. (Gen. 32:22-32) What I find so fascinating about this strange and epic story is how Jacob's divine wrestling partner doesn't overpower Jacob, but seemingly invites such wrestling which eventually leads to a blessing and a new name for Jacob. The new name given to Jacob is Israel, which means to contend or wrestle. Much like my home wrestling matches with my two children, rather than overpowering them as I could, I invite and enjoy these shared experiences. Healthy Christian leadership involves cultivating communities in which authentic questions, doubts and wrestling with God within the ring of faith is not only permitted, but is encouraged and embraced. In contrast to the rigidity and uniformity that is mandated in many faith communities, to go to the mat with God within the ring of faith is to embrace and embody the heart of a "true Israelite."

A Time to Carry and A Time to Be Carried

For the last few years, every second Wednesday evening is spent in a living room with a group of fellow pilgrims on the journey of life and faith. I consider this "Band of Brothers" group to be a part of my family—a vulnerable community where those present can share both their victories and struggles and process their pain and shame together. One common thread that binds us together is our desire to listen, learn, and heal together in a spirit of love absent of judgment. As I reflect fondly upon the importance of this community, I'm reminded of the story recorded in both Mark and Luke's Gospels where another "Band of Brothers," in their desperation and determination to have their friend healed, rip off a portion of the roof of the house where Jesus was teaching (Mark 2:1-12, Luke 5:17-26). Those of us waking up to a more beautiful Gospel and a relentlessly loving and uncontrolling God bear the wounds and scars of holding onto toxic theologies and traumatic church experiences. Healthy leadership acknowledges the need for vulnerability and authenticity in community. The reality is that everyone, including leaders, goes through paralyzing life experiences that leave us wounded on the mat and needing to be carried to Jesus. Other times we carry our wounded brothers and sisters to Jesus in an effort to find healing and wholeness.

Opening the Door to the Great Wide Open

The final scene of *The Truman Show* is one of my favorites in cinema history. Having pushed through the fear and trauma accompanying his "waking up" and surviving the fear mongering attempts by Christof and his cronies to stifle and contain Truman within his fabricated world, Truman literally reaches the end of the world as he knows it. As he stands before an open door to an unexplored world, Christof makes one final appeal to Truman from his control studio perched high above: "You can't leave Truman. You belong here with me. Talk to me. Say something."

Truman responds by turning his gaze skyward, smiling and responding with the words he has mindlessly and monotonously uttered to his neighbors throughout his life: "In case I don't see ya, good afternoon, good evening and goodnight." After taking a bow to those watching around the world, he walks through the door into the great wide-open future awaiting him.

The story of Truman Burbank serves as an allegory for those who are in the process of awakening to the reality that the God of uncontrolling and unrelenting love bears no resemblance to the distant, micromanaging character of Christof. In contrast to Christof, it is Christ who reveals to us a God who is not a distant controlling architect, but rather an authentic loving friend (John 15:12-17).

Leadership that gives permission to wrestle with God, humbly recognizes the necessity of both carrying and being carried by others. It encourages others to leave behind toxic pictures of God to step out into the beautiful and open future together is essential in a culture increasingly and rightfully unwilling to accept the reality of the world. Let's stay awake to the "Trumans" around us and the God who is faithfully present with us all moment by moment.

Jason Tripp lives in Sudbury, Ontario where he serves as the Lead Pastor at Valleyview Community Church (The Free Methodist Church in Canada) and Assistant Chaplain at Thorneloe University. He earned his M. Div. from Tyndale Seminary in Toronto. He is an occasional contributor to The New Leaf Network, a collaborative missional organization that supports and equips church planters, spiritual entrepreneurs, and missional practitioners in post-Christian Canada. (newleafnetwork.ca)

Application: Leadership in Church and Society

29

Loving and Relational

DONNAMIE K. ALI

Compared to Jesus' servant leadership, leadership in the church is often more concerned with power than demonstrating love for the marginalized.

The internet and many book collections are littered with articles and books on leadership. John Maxwell, a leadership guru, penned the well-known saying that "Everything rises and falls on leadership." From a pastoral viewpoint, it seems that if a person is not a strong leader with great measurable results, numbers of congregants, and money raised, one is not successful. However, the pages of the New Testament reveal that, while on earth Jesus only had a few genuine disciples among the many that followed him. Within Christian congregations are numerous examples of both domination and the lack of real care for persons.

People become part of a church fellowship for a variety of reasons: to draw closer to God, to find comfort when hurting, to find a shelter in the figurative storms, to receive help in navigating the maze-like corridors of life, or simply to have caring people to run to when the pressures of life are overwhelming.

A leader who embraces an open and relational God seeks to connect with the people of the congregation and community in loving non-judgmental ways. The God revealed in the bible is uncontrolling; therefore, those who lead the church of Jesus Christ must not seek to control those who come into the sanctuaries with great needs. What does an uncontrolling pastoral servant look like?

Parishioners must never be made to feel that they have to buy God's pardon for sins committed or favors needed. The poor must be treated as well as the rich. The black as well as the white. The educated as well as the uneducated. The immigrant as well as the citizen. God loves all and sent Jesus into the world to die for all. He forgave the woman taken in adultery and all he asked was that she go and sin no more. He healed the Canaanite woman's daughter who was persistent in her appeals for his intervention. Jesus, who demonstrated what God was like, embraced the rich Nicodemus, the children seeking him, the scorned lepers and the despised prostitutes.

God deliberately chose a position of vulnerability by taking on human form in the person of Jesus Christ. Jesus demonstrated his willingness to mingle with, to touch, and to empathize with the common people. He touched the lepers, raised the widow's son, and stayed at the house of the tax collector Zacchaeus, who, by virtue of his profession, was a social outcast.

In each of these instances, Jesus demonstrated God's empowering love: the lepers were cleansed, the widow's son was brought back to life, and Zacchaeus's life was revolutionized by the intervention of love. There was never any hint that Jesus considered himself to be above the common people for he was one of them, though King of Kings and Lord of Lords.

Some religious leaders cultivate an aura of aloofness and are even accompanied by unofficial foot soldiers! How this must sadden our Lord! Those who know the New Testament portrayal of Jesus and have been touched and transformed by the Holy Spirit as they meditate on his example, strive to be humble amidst impulses to be prideful. Success in ministry leading to elevation is often accompanied by the belief that one is somehow superior to others. While this would hardly be spoken of in Christian circles, the old adage that action speaks louder than words is often true in these instances. The very one that they serve is relational while they confine themselves to mingling only with those they consider to be equals.

It is reasonable to wonder if seating arrangements in the practice of table fellowship do not contribute to this. While people of similar interests may have more to say to each other, surely it would be more Christlike to foster mingling between the spiritual leaders and the general membership as often as possible? When ministers reach the position where they become untouchable, the relational Jesus is no longer exemplified in their Christian walk.

The questioning mind will observe that church leaders of large congregations sometimes do not attend to the spiritual needs of poorer congregants, except for sermons that all hear. These needs are left to the associate or lay ministers. The wealthy, on the other hand, gain the full attention of their spiritual leaders. What would Jesus do in these situations? The relational and humble Jesus had dinner at the wealthy Simon's home and broke bread with his lowly disciples. In fact, the recorded gospels, in particular Luke, cited many instances of his interaction with society's marginalized people.

Open theology identifies a God of relational love. God gives and receives love. Christian devotion and willingness to be conformed to what God expects speaks of love. Interaction with all of God's created beings proclaims such relational love because the essential characteristic of God is love. To be elected or appointed to serve God's church in a leadership position is a sacred privilege. It is not for self-aggrandizement nor is it for using one's privilege to fatten one's material coffers. Sadly, there are too many examples of selfishness among Christian leaders who at times seem to be more concerned with pomp, ceremony, and fine clothing than with reaching out to those they are called to serve.

Leadership that is open and relational will be servant leadership. Christ came to serve not to be served. That is loudly proclaimed when he washed his disciples' feet. How far leaders sometimes fall from this ideal! People may be simple but they will not be fooled for long. Many walk away from the church because of leaders who exploit people's ignorance. Leaders at times use the very bible that they draw their sermons from to browbeat the congregation rather than using it to preach grace for their sinfulness. N. Graham Standish in his book *Humble Leadership,* when talking about choosing leaders, mentioned, "We need to put much more emphasis on assessing their openness to God—and their readiness to let go of their own pride."

Open and relational leaders will stay tuned to Jesus Christ. It is my opinion that the gospels need to be read regularly and preached from regularly so that both pulpit and pew will be reminded of a loving and relational God whose son Jesus Christ, came into the world. Preachers are leaders of their congregations and loving grace must be evident in their words and actions. When love is present, it is more likely to produce the desired change when rebukes need to be applied. Those who have the authority over pastors must also be servant leaders encouraging and demonstrating what John C. Bowling calls *Grace-full Leadership.*

Donnamie K. Ali is a devoted Christian who has been actively serving the Lord for the past 42 years. She is an ordained elder in the Church of the Nazarene on the Trinidad and Tobago district and earned a M.Div. from Northwest Nazarene University in 2017. She is married and has been blessed with three children and four grandchildren.

30

Listening Together: Vision-Casting in Community

CHRIS S. BAKER

Casting vision should be shared among leaders rather than done by one in top-down fashion.

"There has to be more than this."

That was the impression I was left with after one specific session in a class about pastoral leadership. We were reading books with titles like "37 Lengthy Laws of Leadership for the Lonely Latecomer" and "The Pastor as President of the Church". The advice and instruction given seemed like decent, common-sense leadership direction. It's not that the information was bad; it just seemed like something was missing. If Jesus was actually the unique, revolutionary person most Christians think he is, shouldn't leadership taken from his example be unique too? There had to be more than what I was reading in these leadership manuals.

Fast-forward a number of years to the time when I became familiar with Thomas Jay Oord's work on God's nature as uncontrolling love. I soaked in all I could and found it very helpful in many areas of thought and life. As I read, I realized there are two major characteristics of God that run through Oord's work: God is self-giving and God is others-empowering. Those two characteristics are at the core of who God is and what uncontrolling love looks like. If we are created in the image of God and God is self-giving and others-empowering, what might that mean for leadership? What might it look like for Christian leaders to be self-giving and others-empowering?

OPEN AND RELATIONAL LEADERSHIP

I co-pastor a small Nazarene church with my wife Teresa. For a number of reasons our church is going through a time of turning the page. We're experiencing redefinition and transformation in many ways. Because of the needs of the church, we find ourselves in a time of heavy vision casting. Quite naturally, then, we have been considering what it might look like to cast vision in a way that is self-giving and others-empowering.

In the contexts that Teresa and I grew up in and serve in, it is common to think of the pastor as the sole vision-caster. Though it is not usually spelled out quite this plainly, the model most people have in their minds is that as the pastor spends time in prayer, God gives the pastor a vision for a local church. It is then the pastor's job to express or share that vision in a way that excites or inspires the local church enough to go accomplish the work of the vision. It is common to hear people pray that God would give vision to the pastor for the church.

With this model of vision casting, there can be great pressure on the pastor to hear something new from God. Everything relies on the pastor and her reception of the vision God is giving. How long should it take to receive God's vision? How much time is too much time? As the pastor, should I have heard a clear vision from God yet? Did God already speak, and I missed it? Then, when the pastor receives the vision from God, there is pressure to communicate that vision to the church board, council or congregation in a way that inspires action and dedication to the vision. If the dedication and inspiration aren't there, is it because the pastor misheard the vision? Or maybe the pastor just didn't communicate the vision well. This method of vision casting can lead to great anxiety, pressure and doubt about the process itself.

What if there are other models of vision casting?

As we listen for God's voice leading our church, we have taken a few steps that don't fall neatly into the vision-casting model summarized above. First, as we met with the church board, we encouraged them to take a full month to pray consistently that all of us—the pastors, church board and whole church—might hear where God is leading us. We asked them to pray not just for us as pastors, that we might hear from God, but also for themselves as the church board and the whole church body. This was important because it affirmed to them that as pastors, we believe God speaks not only to us but also to the whole body of Christ. In addition, it made them aware that not only should they be praying for us as their pastors (which we greatly appreciate!), but they also should be listening for what God might be saying to them about the vision and future of the church.

OPEN AND RELATIONAL LEADERSHIP

The second step in vision casting happened over a period of time. The next few months as the leadership of the church gathered in different settings, Teresa and I opened the conversation by asking a number of different questions: How has God made this local body of believers unique? How is this local body different from other local bodies of believers? What do we do well? What gifts has God created us with that God might be leading us to use both for the benefit of the local church and for the benefit of our community?

As we began to ask these questions, ideas began to flood out. People began to affirm gifts in one another. As we thought about the history of the church, specific events and ministries were affirmed as beneficial and helpful. We began to see a few key gifts that were common to the ministries and events that were brought up. Recognizing the gifts that were common in those ministries and events helps us to be intentional about using those gifts in the future. For our particular church, those gifts were hospitality/sharing meals and music.

The last step we've taken is to put the theory into practice. We ask the question "How might we use these gifts for the benefit of our church body and our community? How might we use these gifts to love God and love others?" For our particular local church, the question was "How might we use hospitality/sharing meals and music to fill the needs of our church and community?" Once again, as the leadership of the church began to ask this question, ideas flowed. (How different churches decide on which ideas to implement will likely depend on the polity of the church. For our church board, it was a simple majority vote when needed; although in most cases, these were agreed upon unanimously.)

In our context, we prepared meals for a recent widower. We had a gathering in a local park open to the public with the purpose of celebrating music in the community. It's likely this music gathering will become an annual event. We have regular events when we welcome people not associated with the church for a meal. We have had other ideas that we are still in the process of putting into practice.

It is my belief that this model of vision casting reflects a more others-empowering, self-giving model than I have typically encountered. It is intentionally designed to be others-empowering. All three steps have an element that empowers others. Others are empowered to listen to God themselves, because God is giving vision not only to the pastor, but to them too. Others are empowered as gifts are recognized and affirmed. Others are empowered as they give ideas of how we can practically use our gifts together. Overall, others are empowered because the process continually draws ideas out of the group, rather than just one leader.

This model of vision casting will also be self-giving or self-sacrificial, especially for the leader who likes to be in charge. This model is the polar opposite of controlling. The leader is constantly asking for input from others and taking that input seriously. Rather than being the sole person receiving the vision, the pastor becomes the person who helps other leaders to hear where God might be leading the body. The pastor is no longer in the center as the one who has the "inside word" from God. This may take some sacrifice on the part of the pastor who is used to the more traditional view of vision casting.

There are other benefits to this model as well. Excitement is almost built-in automatically, as it is the leaders themselves who are coming up with the ideas. There isn't much convincing needed. They're already excited because the ideas were theirs in the first place. Or more precisely, they don't need to be convinced of the ideas because they have been listening to God's leading voice from the very beginning. Another benefit is that pressure is relieved from the pastor, since vision casting becomes less centered on one person.

When we empower one another to follow God's voice and when we as leaders are willing to give up our power in order to empower others, we grow closer to one another and closer to God. As we have used this model, a unity has developed that I didn't anticipate. That unity feeds further vision casting as we grow even closer to God and others. Empowering others and giving of oneself brings people together like little else. That alone is reason enough to practice leadership that is love-centered and uncontrolling.

Chris S. Baker is a co-pastor at Columbus Community Church of the Nazarene in Columbus, WI, alongside his wife Teresa. He previously served as Associate Pastor involved in worship and discipleship in Upstate New York. Chris enjoys reading, a wide variety of music and camping.

Creating Open and Relational Communities

PETER BENEDICT AND MIRIAM CHICKERING

Leaders can create open and relational cultures of trust where self-determining communities flourish and participation and empowering is normative.

Peter Benedict and Miriam Chickering met at Theology Pub, a monthly book club hosted by River Heights Vineyard Church (RHVC) at a local bar. This essay shares key concepts and practices that have created open and relational culture in service organizations. We'll share examples from RHVC and Nurses International (NI, a non-profit organization). We define open and relational culture as a self-determining organization where people practice listening to God and to each other; where people share the pursuit of faith, hope, and love; and where everyone's voice matters. In this culture the leader's goal is to create the conditions for flourishing in the community, and in each member, through shared relationship and discernment. Tasks are important, but secondary to people; it turns out that this can be surprisingly efficient in accomplishing the actual work of the organization.

The Benefits of Open and Relational Community

Open and relational community has driven growth, drawn volunteers, and increased our budgets. Our services reach a broader cross-section of our cities (RHVC) and the world (NI). We have found our model successful across generations, from Boomers through Gen Z. We believe this model can be useful in any organization, empowering leaders to grow in diversity and effectiveness.

At RHVC and NI, we ask people to give away time, money, and resources to create good in the world. At NI volunteers often do what they do at their day jobs, but for free. At RHVC, people watch kids, clean, cook, and welcome all kinds of people (addicts, people with mental health challenges, etc.). If open and relational leadership and community have inspired a growing number of people to give away their time and money to our organizations, how much more could this model empower for-profit organizations?

Models for Effective Dialogue

Open and relational dialogue depends on members that can speak and listen well. River Heights teaches a prayer model that grows these skills, emphasizing listening to God and listening to the person before praying aloud. Nurses International uses an operational framework called *Listen, Learn, Serve, Share* that works similarly. These tools emphasize dialogue that empowers service. Martin Buber's "I/Thou" relationship of equals, perceiving one another rightly in the presence of the Other, is the foundation for these models.

Shared Values

Open and relational culture depends on shared values that permeate the organization's relationships. At River Heights Vineyard Church our values are: the presence of God, loving relationships, diversity, and service. Nurses International values faith, hope, and love, emphasizing diversity and sustainability as reflections of these values. Emphasizing and revisiting these values regularly helps us keep our cultures open and relational through growth.

We Pray with Hope

At RHVC, we pray "Holy Spirit, come." Over time we grow in seeing and hearing what God is doing, because the Spirit does come! This builds hope within the community, helping us approach our work and prayers with expectation.

At Nurses International we're trying to make sure that every nurse in the world has access to the educational materials needed to provide excellent patient care. We hope together in a God who can help us accomplish our task. Team members who are comfortable with prayer pray together, and we can all hope together in the mystery of goodness and beauty in the world.

We Engage Everyone

We tell our members that everyone can participate, and then consistently teach and model that "Everyone gets to play." As leaders we're responsible for the structures that empower members to share leadership, and we leave space for the community to discern and direct its steps.

We Do Stuff Together

The quality of our relationships determines the openness of our culture, so we create structures that grow the connections among our members.

At Nurses International we have "Open Sky" meetings. We ask team members to share their hopes and dreams for the work that we do together. We ask, "If we could do anything, what would it be?" or "If resources weren't an obstacle, what would we do?" We also have annual retreats where we spend several days at a camp dreaming and playing together. Playing together is crucial to building understanding and care.

River Heights has a monthly meeting that includes extended worship, a short message, and prayer ministry among those who attend. During prayer ministry we start with the community waiting on God together and offer everyone the chance to share what God might be saying. God's guidance comes through community members ranging from servant leaders to members with mental health issues, addictions, etc. When someone shares a prayer or vision that starts with "I think...," that is treated as an opinion, but when someone shares "I believe God is saying" or "I hear God saying," it is treated more seriously.

Self-determining Communities: A Three-Step Process

We follow a three-step process during times of critical community discernment. This process has been used for leadership transitions, considerations of potential mergers, building campaigns, and expansion plans.

Step 1: The core leadership team discuss, pray, meditate, and reflect on the issue individually and together.

Step 2: We present the results of our discernment to our wider leadership teams. Sometimes the results include a sense of a clear path forward, but often we're not sure which way is best. At River Heights, volunteer leaders pray together around tables, with each table recording what people are hearing or sharing. At Nurses International, several people meet in person while the majority join from locations around the world through video conference. Written feedback is compiled for sharing with the wider community.

Step 3: We then invite our entire network into community discernment. We share the results of the first steps, invite everyone to pray, and open the microphone or group chat to anyone willing. A leader will facilitate, helping people to finish or get back on track if needed, but this rarely happens. This has worked with people who are located in different countries and time zones, with people from vastly different cultures and socioeconomic classes.

Community Discernment can be Slow and Scary

We have also found that the use of community discernment creates the high levels of engagement and investment that have produced a thriving church and growing non-profit. This model is also less nimble than a top down leadership structure. Decisions can take months. This model often feels scary as well!

Peter: I've opened the microphone numerous times to people who I thought were going to wreck what we were doing. I've always been wrong so far, but the moments leading up to those times of sharing can be challenging.

Miriam: Though the model is less nimble, the decisions are shared with the entire community which creates a sturdiness and a shared buy-in. I was facing significant financial pressure when I declined a recent merger, but the team came together, and donations were made to ease those pressures.

The Benefits

This practice of everyone engaging in community has consistently produced better outcomes than the best strategies we could have devised. It has served well through seasons of leadership transition, expansion, and increasing diversity. Both our organizations have experienced numerical growth throughout.

Community discernment allows us to value our differences rather than mistrust them, even when those differences could be painful. I (Peter) serve with an older friend who's a Tea Party conservative, and he often remarks about how amazing it is that he and I get along so well. I see this across our church: people may not be sure about the value of one another's differences, but they don't care as much when we're doing the work God has given us. Over time, common work leads to trust.

OPEN AND RELATIONAL LEADERSHIP

We Reflect

Miriam: One of the challenges at Nurses International is that our work is so big, no one person can do this work alone. Even a growing network can't do all the work. This means that we have to grow leaders who can continue the work independently. Open and relational communities give everyone a chance to play and invite everyone to shared responsibility. This really means that each person is given the opportunity to grow in their ability to lead and create positive change. Many of our team members have started and completed degrees, pivoted in their careers, begun businesses, and grown tremendously during their time with us. Part of the way that I evaluate Nurses International is by asking myself, "How well are we doing as an incubator for educators and leaders?" "How well are we loving the people who are giving so much of themselves to make the world a better place?" When people are loved, they grow, and this growth results in their greater empowerment.

Peter: It's possible my church has been riding a wave of good luck and/or unspoken processes that have manipulated us into a place where the results of our community discernment are more due to luck or human interactions than God's guidance. It's possible I've overlooked a bunch of challenges or drawbacks to this model that would cause it to fail anywhere else, and eventually will cause us to fail too. But so far, this model has been joyous, helpful beyond our hopes, and fruitful. So, I offer you this model as a testimony of God's faithfulness, and encourage you to try it as God leads, modifying whatever you like to fit your community and culture. In the end, this depends on a God who speaks and cares where we go. We trust that everybody gets to hear and share what God is saying. We continue to pursue and grow in willingness to let go of the kind of power that often accrues as we lead. I think it's worth it.

Peter Benedict is the lead pastor at River Heights Vineyard Church in Inver Grove Heights, Minnesota. He earned his undergraduate degrees at Grand Canyon University and is planning to attend seminary next year. His hobbies include home brewing, recreational and theological reading, cooking for friends, and motorcycle rides on beautiful days.

Miriam Chickering is the CEO of Nurses International, an organization that provides free curriculum to healthcare educators in 86 countries. Chickering is a co-author of two books and of academic research articles related to work in global education. Her hobbies include interdisciplinary creative endeavors—most recently the creation of a Modern Midrash workshop and a new modality to assist therapists and clients called Implicity.

32

What We Know that Just Ain't So

DONNA BOWMAN

Leadership requires the humility to face an uncertain future and the courage to seek discomfort.

I became a university instructor with zero training in leadership. It was the turn of the millennium, and as far as I knew, leadership was something you had or did, not something you could learn or think about. At a division of General Electric where my husband and I worked during my doctoral studies, leadership was a word on the cover of the business-guru books that littered our supervisor's desks, and a graphic on the Six Sigma training PowerPoint slides. I figured nobody could teach you leadership. You found out if you were a leader by trying to lead people.

My students and I come from similar backgrounds and had many of the same formative experiences. High-ability students change in some ways from generation to generation, but some things you can count on. We were identified as academically talented early and tracked into advanced placement classes and a college prep curriculum. Our schools emphasized standardized test scores, and we probably got the chance to take those tests multiple times to improve our outcomes. Competing for limited spots in elite settings—class rank, college admissions, scholarship offers—defined success for us, and colored our relationships with our peers.

I was a loner, an introvert, happiest when reading on my own. I was emphatically not a joiner. Not only was I not running for elected office or volunteering for positions of responsibility in organizations, I wasn't even interested in being a part of them. While that doesn't describe the majority of my students these days, they are united in their distaste for that most dreaded form of academic assignment, the group project. Even the most involved, gregarious, or organizationally inclined students hate group work. And that's because of the competitive, zero-sum definition of academic accomplishment in which we were immersed as smart kids. Our world keeps score through GPA, ACT, and GRE. In those arenas, you go it alone. Any time you're forced to drag someone else behind you, it can only hurt—never help.

Now my university has a Leadership Studies department (where my dean is tenured). And the undergraduate honors program where I teach has leadership as one of its three major goals for students (along with scholarship and citizenship). Suddenly it's something we're all talking and thinking about, on a regular cycle.

Early in our discussions about the student goal of leadership, we wrangled about how we could expect that of every student in our program. Can they all go occupy leadership positions in campus organizations? Could we possibly create enough group activities in classes for each of them to practice this skill of leading an endeavor?

We decided to interpret this goal through the more focused idea of *self-authorship*. By this, we mean that students come to an understanding of their own freedom and responsibility to choose the values, principles, and trajectory of their lives. Making these decisions authentically requires awareness of the many possibilities (and so we bring them into conversation with diverse examples of flourishing lives founded on a variety of values, representing divergent choices). Students also need to recognize that they will never have enough information to make a choice they can confidently defend with plenty of evidence. They'll have to choose—like all of us must—while we're on the way, before the results are all in, without knowing for sure how it will turn out.

I see a clear connection between this goal and my process worldview. One of the many ways process theology saved my life was by showing me that Christianity need not be founded on *eschatological triumphalism*. We are not moving along the grooves in a vinyl record, on our way inexorably to an end already recorded and determined in God's timeless perspective. And that means that the struggle against the evils of our epoch is not an empty exercise, ultimately meaningless in the light of the final inevitable victory (of our side). What will happen is not knowable because it is *not yet*, not actual until we get there. So, we cannot dismiss the possibility of setbacks or even defeat, nor deny the reality of the evil that results. What we do to affect the future matters, and we are responsible for our choices.

My upbringing in the church was marked by smug certainty. "God is in control" can be a comforting expression of hope for those who lack control over their own lives, but when spoken by the wealthy white majority in whose privilege I partake, it is a door slammed in the face of the changes needed for true justice. "God is in control" means "everything is just as it should be." "God is in control" means "I don't care what the scoreboard says; my team's victory is assured."

The self-authorship I had to learn, haltingly and unsystematically, was that my tradition did not have a monopoly on truth-bearing perspectives. My meaningful choices were not limited to saying the sinner's prayer and assuring myself a mansion in heaven. I needed to shift from dogged certainty to *epistemological humility*—holding my views firmly enough to act on them, yet lightly enough to change them in the face of new information or altered perspective. For our students, that's the beginning of leadership: knowing what you do not know, recognizing that you are still obligated to act, and accepting that your actions will create a future marked by the values they express.

It's a lot to ask of people in their early twenties. I don't think I really started to grasp it until I was in graduate school, closer to thirty. On the other hand, I didn't have anyone trying to teach it to me. I didn't have any community where we could talk about what we were going through together, as we learned it. As far as self-authorship goes, I was a product of the school of hard knocks. I wasted a lot of time, made many costly mistakes, and most critically, I thought I was all alone.

Leadership does involve others, both necessarily and optimally, and that requires the interactions my students would rather avoid. The next step of leadership, the part that I'm now trying to teach more actively and intentionally, is the value of *discomfort*. A smoothly running process is pleasant, but we can skate through it without engagement. Friction—an intentional gumming-up of the gears, a situation that needs work to make it work—teaches us how to problem-solve, and this is especially valuable but least frequently applied in the social arena. Students are used to having problems put to them as exercises to be tackled individually, as practice. They hate group work because it adds problems of personal interaction on top of that. Yet this despised process demands exactly the kind of attention and effort that builds leadership beyond the individual, in the interpersonal dimension.

The opposite of triumphalism is fatalism—if the future is already determined, then I am doomed to be a follower of a path already laid out for me.

Any attempt to set my own course merely kicks against the pricks. And those smoothly running processes that students love, those exercises devoid of frustration that can be completed on autopilot, encourage fatalism—as does, I would argue, all systems set up in higher education to disempower students. Put your head down and endure; there's nothing you can do about it; that's just the way it is, and we all have to deal with it. Process thought reminds us that nothing is set in stone, and therefore everything can be changed.

I spent the first ten years of my teaching career learning that I needed to give my students way more information, guidance, and support than I received in order to create an environment where there were minimal barriers to the learning I wanted them to do. Then I spent the next ten years learning that I needed to create barriers so that they couldn't get away with not expending effort. It was the effort, the friction, the discomfort, that created the conditions for real learning, the kind that can be transformative.

An open future requires not only our humility about what we know and what path we forge into it, but also our willingness to endure the discomfort of this uncertainty. If we are honest with ourselves about this, we might also be honest with each other. And that paves the way for the kind of solidarity that empowers everyone in the community to step up, leading when it is their turn and when their abilities can make the biggest difference.

Donna Bowman is a theologian and professor of interdisciplinary studies at the Norbert O. Schedler Honors College, University of Central Arkansas. Her books include Prayer Shawl Ministries and Women's Theological Imagination *(Lexington Books 2015) and* The Homebrewed Christianity Guide to Being Human *(Fortress Press 2018). When not knitting or teaching, she's watching and writing about television.*

Leading From the God-Shaped Pole

TIM BURNETTE

Authorial and authoritarian leadership styles are different. How does God lead, and how can we lead lovingly?

Since this is a book about leadership and open and relational *theology*, I'm gonna assume you, the reader, are cool with me beginning with God as a model for leadership. In essence, the central question for this exploration will be, "How does God lead?"

For process theologians like myself ("process" coming from philosopher Alfred North Whitehead's vision of an open and relational universe always moving), God is often referred to as a "lure." And, yes, that is meant to evoke exactly the kind of image you think it is.

Think of what happens when you cast a fishing pole out into a body of water — the purpose of the lure on the end of the line is to draw fish toward it for a bite. The same goes for God. Part of God's activity in the universe is to draw all things like a lure toward their most intensely beautiful expressions in every moment of becoming. And yes, all means all — even you.

Whitehead remarked, God "is the poet of the world, *leading* it by God's vision of truth, beauty, and goodness." In short, what Whitehead is saying here is that God is a leader — and a leader who leads by *casting* a vision, not *implementing* a vision.

For those of us wondering how we might emulate God in our own leadership situations, it's also important not only to note the positive values associated with God's vision, but also the *nature of how* God's vision leads the cosmos forward. Whitehead winks and nods at the nature of God's leadership style just before the aforementioned quote in saying, "God's role is not the combat of productive force with productive force, or destructive force with destructive force."

So, what does that even mean then? Basically, it means that if God does not operate in the universe like a productive or destructive force — or what we in philosophy often call an "efficient cause" — think a pool stick striking a billiard ball to make it move — like one force crashing in to another thing — then, God must operate in a different way altogether.

If Whitehead gives us a hard 'no' to a God who acts by using some kind of coercive force, then instead, he must conjure up for us the image of God acting as a poet for a very specific reason. It's clear that he is using the image of the poet to create an altogether alternative form of power or force.

Think of the power of poetry. It doesn't lie in its communicating a proposition to be asserted as true or untrue. Its real power lies in the aesthetic allure of the words and ideas themselves in the sense that they evoke something in the reader. To be moved by a poem is not the same as being moved by pool stick. The moving element in a poem moves us in a fundamentally different way than a coercive force. Its power (which could also be a grand meditation on the nature of true power) lies in its evocative, alluring, and value-saturated invitation to the reader.

This is the way that God deepens Beauty in and actually, in Whitehead's words, saves the universe — as a poet. It's simultaneously both God's activity and God's leadership style — and it should be our leadership style too if we care to lead like God and be in the flow of life.

At different times in our lives, each of us is tempted to lead from places of power. It may be climbing an institutional ladder to reach the top and have the most influence, achieving the top performance in an organization to prove our value, or getting the highest degree in our field so everyone in our leadership context will know how powerful we really are. We've all likely played those kinds of leadership power games in some form or another.

But friends, this is simply not the heart of God. It's not that success, achievement, or accolades are bad, per se. It's just that they're not the place from which divine leading comes. Leadership flows not from the top-down, but from emphasizing a kind of leadership that flows from "the tender elements in the world, which slowly and in quietness operate by love." Notice the profound change in source here — namely that God's force is not productive or destructive — meaning, God does not ever lead like an all-powerful leader from the top, but rather, God's leading is power-giving in its immanent tenderness and love.

What a different world we would live in if our organizations, churches, governments, etc., did not see power or domination as fundamental to successful leadership, but rather tenderness and love. This process understanding of God offers us such a radically alternative vision for leadership than we often observe in our world. In a time where religious and political leaders almost unconsciously put their powerful and loud personas (which are really just their public-facing masks of ego) on display, God offers us an entirely opposite vision of a leadership that operates by love.

In this distinction about power lies the secret of God's leadership of the universe itself, and our invitation to lead as well. God acts in a way that is empowering rather than power-ful. And, what ends up happening if we embrace this shift of perspective is that we too will find ourselves as leaders having the real potential within us to lure and change systems as we align with God's loving lure.

The name of the way God leads the universe, which includes our everyday lives, in this alternative manner *actually is love,* plain and simple. In 1 John 4, the Bible goes as far as to say that *God is Love*, but as many of us in Western Christian contexts know, the biblical definition of love is often distorted and defined in ways that don't really reflect the heart of the tender love of the process God at all. Some people employ what I like to call 'love, and' or 'love, but' theologies. Love is patient, love is kind…*and* will send you to hell if you aren't a believer. Love the sinner, *but* hate the sin. You know what I mean.

This kind of love is not really love at all. It's really just the result of the western-moving Christian movement of love getting in bed with imperial power — yes, the very same power that we are countering in this essay. When love becomes associated with power in any sort of domineering or colonizing way, we can be sure that it is not love…at least not the love displayed by God, or the love seen in the life of Jesus of Nazareth. Authentic love is self-giving, and in this kind of giving is true allure and true 'power.'

So the challenge for those of us longing to lead like God in our leadership contexts is to lead by love — which is always non-coercive, always tender, caring, and quiet, and always casts a vision that invites the most Beauty possible in a given context or season of organizational life. Where the rubber hits the road with this highly theoretical approach to leadership is here, in a simple (and hopefully as profound for you as it was for me) charge. In every leadership situation, pay attention to which power is luring you: Is it *authoritarian* power or *authorial* power?

Authoritarian leadership is always quick to coerce others to conform to their agendas. Authorial leadership is the power of giving away a generous invitation to the world to participate together in a more collective expression of creaturely cooperation. And that's what leadership environments usually are, creatures learning to cooperate to make something beautiful in the world. Monitoring our internal motivations can help us to stay in the flow of love as we lead. Are we grasping for power and affirmation? Or, are we giving out of the surplus of the very loving lure of God within us?

The true power of leadership flows from finding an authorial place within you where you, responding to God, can draw others tenderly toward a more beautiful togetherness. When we do this, we can be sure that we are leading from the God-shaped pole. If we can be continually mindful of our hearts' motivation and lead from this place of love, then we can proactively work for a more beautiful future rooted in a source that promotes harmony in every leadership endeavor.

Tim Burnette is a contemplative philosopher, theologian, writer, and teacher. He earned his doctorate from Claremont School of Theology, where he studied process cosmology, philosophy, theology, contemplative practice, and compassion. His professional interests are in philosophical beauty/aesthetics, communal formation, and spirituality. He curates the Way Collective, a spiritually rooted and theologically fluid contemplative Christian community of shared practices and values in Santa Barbara, CA. He is also a partner, father, and musician who tries to keep his head in the cloud of unknowing as much as possible so his heart can remain open to the Manifold's polyphilic embrace.

Open Leadership as Creative, Loving, and Just

JOSHUA CANADA

Christian higher education leaders should seek to co-create loving and justice-seeking institutions.

𝓗igher education in the U.S. is in transition. Hardly can one turn on the television, read a newspaper, or go on social media without coming across a piece about the challenges faced by leaders in higher education: tuition costs continue to rise while federal and state grant funding stagnates, the intentions and limits of free speech are being challenged by polarizing campus speakers, mental health concerns are overwhelming counseling centers, and dominantly-White institutions are finding themselves unprepared to educate a racially and culturally diverse student body. These industry stressors contribute to a high turnover rate for middle and senior leadership. In turn, this unrelenting change in leadership creates organizational instability and ambiguity about the identity and purpose of these colleges and universities.

What does open theology have to say to these challenges? How can an approach to leadership, rooted in a theology in which humanity co-creates the future with God, bring clarity during this era of transition? I propose that a view of God that has not fully determined the future requires leadership to take responsibility for these efforts and not displace that responsibility solely on the divine actions. Moreover, leadership in an open theological framework necessitates that higher education leaders actively create educational organizations that are lovingly engaged with people and communities and invested in creating a just future. This article posits that open leadership is creative, loving, and justice seeking.

Leadership as Loving

Leadership is a posture of love. This love comes as a response to an outflowing of God's love given to us as individuals and corporately. Love is not passive; it pursues, it seeks, and it continually motivates us to know others better. Poor or oppressive leadership often occurs within a context in which a positional leader has power but does not truly know those whom they have power over. In scripture, knowing and loving are entangled. God's love for creation is inseparable from engagement in knowing creation. The Christ is the paramount example; God's love for creation was expressed by God becoming human and thus engaged in knowing humanity and creation in an intimate way.

This knowing-love requires leaders to carry the responsibility for the impact of their decisions on others. Leaders are not simply pawns in a cosmic chess game, leaders have agency to act and respond to others—including God. The decisions of leaders have real consequences. Decisions that have negatively impacted historically marginalized persons, groups, and communities do not fall upon God, but rather on those humans who made—or remained complicit with—those decisions. Often such decisions are made because the perceived "other" is not truly known by those with power.

The priorities of higher education institutions are not always the same priorities of the local community. Yet colleges are embedded within communities, cities, and regions. Although studies show that colleges contribute to the economic welfare of a region, they also strain public resources and utilities, can drive-up the cost of living, and college students often occupy important housing stock. Moreover, as non-profits, institutions of higher education are not directly contributing to the taxes in the city or region. Open and relational leadership requires the leader to develop values and make decisions that foster deepening relationships with the local community.

What might this mean in practice? I argue that leaders should learn the assets and needs of the local community and those assets and needs should become important to university leadership. The welfare of the community should become integrated into the institution's posture toward the community and its own welfare. Academic divisions can cultivate *engaged scholarship*— scholarship linked with local community development—and *action-based research* as a fully respected track of research (that benefits faculty promotion).

University expertise can combine with community expertise to cultivate flourishing.

Moreover, institutional decisions should be made with the involvement of local leadership and the community. New building or annexation projects should be subject to public forums about the impact of such projects. More significantly, institutions should be willing to delay or even cancel projects that are likely to impact the local community adversely, even if those impacts were not foreseen during planning. A loving relationship between the college and community pursues commonality and mutuality even if at the cost of perceived progress for the institution.

Leadership as Creative

In times of chaos or confusion, people often retreat to a theology of God's ultimate providence: when a key leader suddenly departs, when finances are tight and cutbacks occur, or when campus issues become a public relations problem. In these times, it is common to try to calm the chaos within ourselves and within our organizations by claiming, "God is in control" or even suggesting that God intentionally brought about the crisis for some expression of God's will which we are simply not privy to. Conversely, when things are operating well and there is little anxiety for the future there is little talk about God's plans. Perceived organizational stability often leads people to assume that all is well with God, but chaos sends us searching for God.

An open and relational view of God runs counter to either posture. God's engagement is always present and active, but that presence is not deterministic of the future. We engage with God and God engages with (and for) us as we make decisions about our reality. We co-labor and co-create with God to bring about restoration and wholeness in the world. Higher education leaders embracing creative leadership will not simply double-down on the past or attempt to revive historical organizational mythos. Rather, they will take stock of what is present, good, and life giving about their institution and be critical about what is unjust and detrimental. From that posture of being present, they then will work to co-create with God and others.

It is common to read commentary on the status of higher education and the diminishing of the liberal arts or humanities. Professors and commenters argue for a revival of classic literature that undergirds much of the curriculum of early liberal arts colleges and curricula in the United States. Yet, our culture has changed and our students are no longer predominantly White and financially privileged as was the case for those "classical" liberal arts programs. Open leadership assesses what is present in the here-and-now and asks, "How will today's curriculum cultivate the future?" as opposed to looking backward. This may mean creative intersections of the sciences and humanities, expanding the core courses beyond White and Eurocentric curricula, or building experiential programs based on diverse learning styles that prioritize experiential learning. Students do not thrive in a systemized, unresponsive, education machine. In contrast, students thrive by being in culturally relevant and responsive academic communities that are inherently relational and in which students can partner with others, take responsibility for their learning, develop a sense of ownership of their education, and experience belonging and membership (Museus, 2014, Schreiner, 2006).

Leadership as Justice Seeking

Leadership in the context of an open view requires partnership with God's restorative, redemptive, and reconciliatory mission—God's mission of justice. Paramount to the pursuit of justice is addressing racism and racial inequity in higher education. Organizational studies literature reminds us that simply changing the composition of an organization does not guarantee an equitable and inclusive culture for people of color. Leaders must actively pursue changes to practices, policies, cultures, and the systems that prevent equity. This means confronting white supremacy and the white norms of their institution's culture.

Colorblind approaches to race are common for white people and dominantly-white organizations. However, this colorblindness in which people "do not see color" attempts to minimize and delegitimize the experience of people and communities of color. Overwhelmingly, research in higher education shows that race matters for faculty, staff, and students and that people and communities of color have more complicated, less satisfactory, and more inequitable experiences as compared to white people.

Open leadership must unabashedly be race conscious, anti-racist, and actively pursue justice. White leaders should avoid taking on the label or posture of an ally or justice warrior—both of which often benefit that white individual rather than people of color—and relinquish power so that people of color can influence and shape the culture and values of the institution. Moreover, leaders need to ask exploratory questions of their institutional culture and thus the future that culture is constructing.

- Does the faculty and staff composition represent the racial diversity of the students?
- Is the Board of Trustees predominantly white? And what cultures are represented and expressed on the Board?
- Are faculty and staff of color experiencing racism in the tenure or promotion process?
- What external relationships are the institution informed and formed by? Are these relationships racially and culturally diverse?
- Are there racial differences between measurable student outcomes of graduation rate, GPA, campus climate rating, debt, job placement, etc.?

These questions are not rhetorical. The answers should change the way institutions fund programs, recruit, and hire faculty and staff, develop a board, and apply financial aid. The answers to these questions should lead leaders into a deeper "knowing" of their campus. A knowing that is racially conscious and critical of the status quo. Christian justice occurs within God continually knowing and wanting to know of those struggling against injustice. Likewise, racial justice in higher education cannot happen without a deep rootedness in the experiences and cultures of people of color.

Conclusion

As beings created in the image of God, we are to mirror God's essential characteristic—Love. Proceeding from this open view of God requires responsibility on the part of leaders. For those in higher education this responsibility requires a disposition that transcends contemporary challenges and seeks to create new, more relational and more just institutions of learning.

Museus, S. D. (2014). The Culturally Engaging Campus Environments (CECE) Model: A new theory of college success among racially diverse student populations. In M. B. Paulsen (Ed.), *Higher education: Handbook of theory and* research (pp. 189–227). New York, NY: Springer.

Schreiner, L. (2006). [Psychological sense of community on campus index]. Unpublished raw data.

Joshua Canada, M.A., serves as the Director of Strategic Partnerships for the College of Liberal Arts and Sciences at Azusa Pacific University. He is currently pursuing a

Ph.D. in Higher Education at Azusa Pacific University. His research focuses on organizational theory, culture, and religion as they relate to higher education. In addition to his professional work, Joshua serves as a lay leader in the Free Methodist Church. He and his family reside in the San Gabriel region of Los Angeles County.

35

To the Ends of the Earth and Beyond in the Spirit

ROBERT D. CORNWALL

A Spirit-empowered church requires spiritually gifted leaders who take us to the ends of the earth and beyond.

$\mathcal{W}$hen Jesus's disciples gathered in an upper room in Jerusalem, they were waiting for the Holy Spirit to come and empower them for a ministry of witness that would take them from Jerusalem to the ends of the earth (Acts 1-2). As 21st century Christians, this remains our calling. We engage in this mission rooted in a community in which, according to Paul, "there are different spiritual gifts, but the same Spirit; and there are different ministries and the same Lord; and there are different activities but the same God who produces all of them in everyone" (1 Cor. 12:4-5 CEB). Paul speaks of these gifts, ministries, and activities in organic terms. There are many members, but one body of Christ. Each member of this body has their own purpose and calling.

I have written in some depth about spiritual gifts and the role they play in the life and mission of the church, including gifts of leadership. I have suggested, "Leaders are called to equip, guide, and build up the community of faith so that the community or congregation may live out its own calling to love God and the world."[6] While Scripture doesn't prescribe a particular form of leadership, most of the models we find there are dynamic and relational. These

---

6 Robert D. Cornwall, Unfettered Spirit: Spiritual Gifts for the New Great Awakening, (Gonzalez, FL: Energion Publications, 2013), p. 99.

models stand in contrast with the patterns of leadership presented to the church by the business/corporate world, which tend to be institutional and hierarchical. Yes, there is the priesthood and the monarchy, and Paul pulls rank on occasion, but even Paul's leadership is more relational than institutional.

The models of leadership present in the New Testament depend on the Spirit, whom no one can control. We have tried to bottle up the Holy Spirit with our institutions, but history shows that the Spirit moves as the Spirit desires. If we're open to the Spirit, then no matter the format the church takes, whether episcopal, presbyterial, or congregational, the Spirit can engage with it. The key is being sensitive to the Spirit's lead. If we understand the way God works in our midst non-coercively, then to be led by the Spirit requires our cooperation. To lead in the Spirit is to provide a context where the people of God can discern their gifts, and then work together as members of the body, toward the end that is the reign of God.

What might this look like? The analogy that comes to mind is the call and response hymn. The Spirit calls and we respond. It is in the midst of this call and response experience that we discern our gifts, our callings, and our pathways of service, including ministries of leadership.[7]

As I read about spiritual gifts in Scripture, I have concluded that we can understand that some gifts seem to be innate and others do not. There are gifts that are context-specific and emerge when needed. Other gifts are present from birth and reflect God's creative presence in our origins. We might think of this as a matter of genetics or DNA. I'm not a scientist, so I can't make any pronouncements on this matter. It's just a feeling and an observation. Looking at the question of relational leadership biblically and theologically, I start with the premise that while we're not robots who are programmed for a particular job, God plays a role in the creation of our identity. Consider the call of Jeremiah. The word of the Lord came to Jeremiah declaring: "Before I created you in the womb I knew you; before you were born I set you apart; I made you a prophet to the nations" (Jer. 1:4-5 CEB). While I don't want to press this too far, this call story is illuminating.

Looking at myself, I can see aspects of my personality and abilities that seem innate and lend themselves to certain callings. That being said, how we discover them and use them isn't predetermined. We discover these gifts and their uses as we flow in the Spirit. Jürgen Moltmann puts it this way: "the person

---

7 Cornwall, Unfettered Spirit, p. 102ff.

who believes becomes a person full of possibilities. People like this do not restrict themselves to the social roles laid down for them, and do not allow themselves to be tied to these roles. They believe they are capable of more."[8]

Moltmann's vision of spiritual potential is helpful in thinking about ministry in the Spirit in an open and relational context. Society or culture can impose barriers, but they do not limit the Spirit. One of the barriers/boundaries that the church has imposed down through the ages concerns the role of women in the church. Even today, the majority of Christians live within religious systems that do not allow women to join in the leadership of the church. This is true despite the fact that women play leadership roles in Scripture. Deborah is a Judge. Mary Magdalene is numbered among the first witnesses of the resurrection. Priscilla was an important teacher, while Phoebe was one of Paul's most trusted associates. Then there is Junia, who together with Andronicus (likely her husband), was counted among the Apostles. While the institutions of the church have long placed limits on the role of women in leadership, making ministry a male domain, the Spirit has called, and women have responded. Consider Margaret Fell, an early Quaker leader, who heard the call and wrote defenses of women taking up the role of a preacher. As Amanda Benckhuysen writes of Fell's argument for the inclusion of women, preaching "was the task of all Christians who shared in the indwelling of the Holy Spirit, in whom the Inner Light was present. In other words, all on whom the Spirit had been poured out were called to share in the prophetic ministry of announcing the good news of God's love and grace, including women."[9] I believe we can say the same about the inclusion of LGBTQ Christians, who have sensed the call of the Spirit to lead and have said yes.

While the church plays a role in recognizing and affirming our gifts, as well as equipping and credentialing persons for ministry, ultimately the Spirit gifts and calls. Since I affirm the premise that God does not coerce us, which means God will wait for our response, I believe that it's the Spirit who first issues the call, and generally does so from within the community. From there, in the company of the Spirit and the other members of the body of Christ, we can exercise our gifts, including gifts of leadership, in ministry within and beyond the body of Christ.

---

8 Jürgen Moltmann, The Spirit of Life: A Universal Affirmation, Margaret Kohl, trans., (Minneapolis: Fortress Press, 1992), p. 187.
9 Amanda W. Benckhuysen, The Gospel According to Eve: A History of Women's Interpretation, (Downers Grove, IL: IVP Academic, 2019), p. 113.

One question has arisen for me since writing *Unfettered Spirit* (2013). It concerns the way we are called to engage with those outside the church and the broader Christian community. How might the Spirit empower us to engage in conversation with and in ministry with those living outside the Christian context? As I've contemplated this question, in the context of my own interfaith engagements, I have been influenced by Amos Yong's work. Like Yong, I remain strongly rooted in my own Christian faith, but in my cross-religious work, I have discerned the work of the Spirit. Yong has written that when we start our conversations Christologically, we tend to end up at an impasse over the role that Jesus plays in the relationship.

If, however, we start with the Spirit, many of those barriers begin to fall. If we start with Jesus' commission in Acts 1, which speaks of sending Spirit-empowered persons outward, bearing witness to the gospel, reaching to the ends of the earth, does that mission require conversion as the end game? There was a time when I thought it did. In the course of my own journey, I am no longer certain this is God's desire. As one who embraces an open and relational understanding of God and God's people, we can ask the question: where is the Spirit leading? The second question concerns how we might engage in Spirit-led leadership that crosses previously sacrosanct boundaries.

Robert D. Cornwall is Pastor of Central Woodward Christian Church (Disciples of Christ) in Troy, Michigan. He holds a Ph.D. in historical theology from Fuller Theological Seminary and edits the journal Sharing the Practice for the Academy of Parish Clergy. He is a blogger and author of nearly twenty books.

36

America: The Un-United States

RANDALL E. DAVEY

Those in whom God lovingly dwells stand for the possibility of a new heaven and new earth.

With the stench of the Civil War, still burning in the nostrils of a bitterly divided nation, Captain George Thatcher Balch, a Union Army veteran, crafted the first iteration of The Pledge of Allegiance. His 1885 draft was soon modified by fellow northerner, Rev. Francis Bellamy, a Christian socialist minister of Baptist stock. Both patriots believed in the power of liturgy in creating a vision for the future, quite unlike the present or past; a future of "one nation, indivisible, with liberty and justice for all."

While Balch and Bellamy saw the pledge as a way of teaching children "true Americanism" while reigning in immigrants, the Dixie flag (the Southern Cross), a symbolic reminder of the deep divide, didn't die with Lincoln. It still flies indiscreetly today.

Though the end of the Civil War aborted secessionist objectives, America was far from united or re-united. Admittedly, slaves were freed and males granted the right to vote but African American women, Asian Americans, Hispanic Americans, and Native Americans wouldn't realize the same liberties for nearly a century

God made it into the pledge by 1948. Illinois attorney Louis Albert Bowman offered the addition "under God," a suggestion that later got real traction with the onset of the Cold War. Those who wanted to distinguish America from the state atheism advocated by Marxist-Leninist countries roundly endorsed it. On Flag Day, June 14, 1954, President Eisenhower, a newly minted Presbyterian, signed a bill making the edits official.

OPEN AND RELATIONAL LEADERSHIP

Most public schools in America require students to recite the pledge daily, an expression of the belief that recitation can be a means of incarnation, breeding loyalty to God and country. Ironically, President Richard Nixon, throat-deep in the Watergate Scandal, was the first president to conclude an official speech with "God bless America," linking patriotism, nationalism and God. His April 30, 1973 benediction included a blessing for "the American people." "May God bless America, and may God bless each and every one of you," a request that God *surely* couldn't grant.

Far from being united, America was then and is now, a country where women rarely get equal pay for equal work, are regularly excluded from places of leadership, are routinely unwelcomed in pulpits—with notable exceptions. The "me too" movement exposed a dark and malevolent attitude and practice in which women were treated as objects to be "grabbed," versus a gender to be esteemed and honored. America was then and is now a country where the color of one's skin may ensure discrimination, substandard education, suboptimal opportunity, and compromised human rights. America was then and is now, a country where justice for all is inconceivable. Clearly, persons of wealth and persons of power can navigate the halls of justice where the poor and marginalized can't manage the freight to make it through the front doors.

In the waning days of 2019, anti-Semitism coupled with violence against Jews is on the upswing in America, as is white-on-white terrorism. School, church and synagogue shootings undoubtedly reflect the pervasive and malignant presence of hate groups, a hallmark of white supremacy, the Ku-Klux-Klan, neo-Nazis, white nationalists, racist skinheads, black separatists, neo-confederates, anti-LGBT, anti-immigrant, holocaust denial, male supremacy, and anti-Muslim groups. These factions show no signs of dissipating.

Still, politicians regularly speak for and of the "American people," as though the country is philosophically, theologically, sociologically, and pragmatically monolithic. The American people are no closer to constituting "one nation, under God, indivisible with liberty and justice for all," than at the inception of the pledge. God cannot honor the late Richard Nixon's request then or now, and ecumenism has done little to help.

Pausing to reminisce may be helpful. Balch, Bellamy, and Bowman were not the first with a Utopic view of the future. According to Scripture, God trumped this trio—envisioning a new Eden characterized by love and unity. (The church, as a microcosm of the world, and the church in America—as a microcosm of the church global—are characterized by many things but loving one another is not one of them). The mere existence of denominations or "independent, non-denominational" churches is evidence of a history of schisms.

Self-confessing Christ followers are no less likely to use uncomely narratives when squaring off on theological, social, and political issues. For proof-positive, scour Facebook and other social media platforms. There, one can see a person who objects to a president's dishonesty or where hate speech is automatically lumped in with "baby killers," and all things liberal.

The United States of America is no closer, and perhaps farther away, from God's "Kingdom on earth," or from being Eisenhower's "one nation under God," in 2019 than it was in 1885. That assessment isn't intended to rain on America's parade. It does suggest that the means by which Americans have attempted to achieve "peace on earth," or peace in the neighborhood have failed to meet expectations.

For the bulk of 2020, Americans will be offered a steady diet of plans, policies and programs, the proponents of which aspire to the office of president. Offering their resumes, awards and achievements, candidates will crisscross America, promising a better America contingent on their election to the office of president. While some of the candidates give a tacit nod to Rome, others to Jerusalem and a few to the Christian right, none of them advance their platform with the Bible in one hand and the newspaper in the other. Rather, they point to the ways their leadership held sway in their respective parties with respect to jobs, health care, and education. Their election, they imply, will yield more of the same: more jobs, better health care and broad-based educational opportunities—ushering in an idyllic America.

Here, one wonders. Imagine a leader who has sufficient intellectual acumen, commendable character, exemplary integrity, physical and emotional tenacity, and political panache. Could a candidate of this ilk enjoy a leg up on the competition if this same leader lived in submission to the Trinity? Is this possibility the stuff of fantasy?

Maybe there is a better question with a broader application. Can leaders of any stripe who live in submission to the Trinity show up differently in the world? Is it reasonable to think that a loving God living in a God-loving leader could bring a different twist to her or his constituency and maybe foster a semblance of unity where division currently exists? Imagine.

Imagine a leader committed to both truth and grace and quick to confess and make amends when failing on either front. Imagine.

Imagine a leader who acknowledged and respected every individual, regardless of race, religion, age, gender, nationality, language group, political persuasion, or sexual preference as an image bearer of God. Imagine.

Imagine a leader who treated everyone with dignity or who refused to impugn the character of others or diminish anyone's value. Imagine.

Imagine a leader who esteemed others more highly then her or himself. Imagine.

Imagine a leader who listened to learn versus listening to react. Imagine.

Imagine a leader committed to building her opponents up versus tearing them down. Imagine.

Imagine a leader who forgave without an apology from an offending opponent? Imagine.

Imagine a leader who was compassionate and especially sensitive to the mentally ill or physically disabled. Imagine.

Imagine a leader who was committed to pursuing peace and understood that to be more than the absence of conflict. Imagine.

Imagine a leader sensitive to the poor, concerned for the hungry, alert to the sick, and not indifferent to the imprisoned. Imagine.

Imagine a leader who saw migrant children as the least of these and advocated for their health and welfare. Imagine.

Imagine a humble leader. Imagine.

Imagine a leader who sought and respected the counsel of others. Imagine.

Imagine one nation, under God, indivisible, with liberty and justice for all. Imagine.

Imagine a leader, a follower, a community of persons committed to lavishing love by "acting justly, loving mercy and walking humbly" with Creator God. Imagine.

Is all of this—the one nation under God, the Kingdom on earth as it is in heaven, a nation united—the stuff of dreams or myths? Is the notion that a leader who serves redemptively with a God who loves uncompromisingly the business of fanciful thinking? Is the dream Martin Luther King, Jr. advanced in 1963 a nice but unachievable idea? It remains to be realized and remains to be seen.

May it be so.

Randall E. Davey earned the M. Div. from Nazarene Theological Seminary and is A.B.D. from Lutheran Theological Seminary of Philadelphia. Davey, a chartered advisor in philanthropy, is an investor advisor representative with Geer Financial Group. In this capacity, he consults with foundations, charities, and major donors. He and his wife of 49 years live in Phoenix, Arizona.

37

The Home of the Brave

BETH ANN ESTOCK

We are called to open our hearts to the holy discomfort of the unknown so we can bravely lead communities toward faithful futures.

*H*ave you ever walked into a room and immediately felt like you did not belong?

Have you sat in a meeting and wondered if it was safe enough to share your thoughts and ideas?

Do you find yourself checking to see where or with whom is it safe enough to let your guard down and be fully yourself?

If you have answered "yes" to any of these questions, welcome to the human race! You are not alone. Our need to feel safe is hard-wired into our very survival. We would not be here today if it had not been for our ancestors who knew how to fight, play dead, or run away when they sensed danger. Neurologists call this primal area found at the base of our head the reptilian brain stem. This part of our brain controls our body functions like breathing and heart rate as well as our survival instincts. When we sense potential danger, adrenaline is released, and our heart begins to beat faster so that we can be ready to respond instantly to what threatens our survival. Unfortunately, when our blood is being directed into our reptilian brain stem, the neo-cortex in our frontal lobe shuts down, preventing us from accessing our creativity and playfulness.

In our modern world, we may no longer have to fight off lions, tigers and bears, but our brains are still hardwired to sense danger and be ready to respond. This is the unconscious current running underneath all of our encounters as we determine, in various ways, whether we are safe. As leaders in community, it is important to understand this phenomenon, especially if we want to be a part of the unfolding of the Holy Spirit's creativity in our communal lives.

We are told that in the beginning God created humans in God's image and proclaimed all of creation as very good. If God is the creator, then we, made in God's image, are partners in creativity. This creative process requires us, just as God did, to create out of the void, the unknown, the space between the now and the not yet.

This liminal space can be as scary as walking into the wilderness without a compass or trail map. It is unknown territory filled with potential danger. We believe that if we step out into that unknown, something bad will happen. If we examine these beliefs further, we might find that those "bad things" involve our sense of self-worth and security. After all, who wants to risk sharing a new idea if we fear potential judgment from others? However, this is exactly where the Holy Spirit encourages us to go—feeling into that place of holy discomfort. For God is constantly inviting us into this co-creative process!

The Book of Acts is filled with stories of the early apostles partnering with the movement of the Holy Spirit in highly unusual ways. Ananias was asked to find Saul, the killer of the followers of Jesus, and heal him of his blindness. Phillip was asked to hitchhike on a dangerous road and climb into a passing chariot. Peter, a devout Jew, was led to baptize a Gentile family and to eat all kinds of non-kosher food. To an outside observer none of this makes logical sense, but this is exactly how we are formed into a life of faith, by trusting in the grace of the unknown.

Interesting, isn't it that anytime an angel shows up in the Bible, the first words spoken have to do with addressing our needs for safety and security? "Do not be afraid, for I bring you good tidings..." I could imagine in those instances it was easier said than done because it is difficult to trust when we feel vulnerable stepping into the unknown. But the very essence of faith is having a sure trust that God loves even us. As Psalm 23 assures, it is the capacity to know deep within that, even through the darkest valleys of life, God is with us as a comforter and guide. The very word, "faith", is correlated to the word "trust." Both have their roots in the Latin word, *fides*. To have faith is to trust in something that we have no control over. If we are unable to trust in our divine belovedness then fear can easily have its way in our lives.

In the 21st century we have much to fear—global warming, pandemics, polarized politics, failed democracies, terrorism, weapons of mass destruction in the hands of despots, and the lack of affordable housing, healthcare, and living wage jobs, to name a few. Churches fear their own decline as worship attendance atrophies and with it, financial solvency. In the face of all this fear, how are we going to lead?

Our set point has been to unconsciously play out our fight, flight or freeze reptilian brain responses. We see this in fighting over issues of doctrine, trying to make the church great again by trying harder at what no longer works, or simply repeating our favorite mantra, "We already tried that…Don't rock the boat!" at the hint of some potential new way forward.

Jesus reminds us that the world will not accept the advocate that God has given us in the Holy Spirit. But when we open our hearts and find our home in love, we can step out in courage just as our ancestors of the faith in the early church.

As leaders, we can practice this by creating what Brian Arao and Kristi Clemens call Brave Spaces in our communities. Brave Space, as opposed to safe space, acknowledges that we come together with different histories, customs, gifts and ideas. In this space, we are invited to listen to each other's stories with curiosity, trusting that we are together for a divine purpose that is ours to figure out. It is a space where failure and uncomfortable emotions are expected as we hold one another in compassion.

As leaders, this requires us to develop robust self-reflective skills, discerning the difference between our personal preferences, based in our fears and unchecked assumptions, and the guidance of the Spirit in the ways of holy discomfort, resilience and grace. That means allowing curiosity to have its way with us as we seek to discover God's grace with our everyday encounters. Researchers are finding evidence that curiosity is correlated with creativity, intelligence, improved learning, memory, and problem solving. We can begin by asking questions such as these that pique our curiosity on a regular basis:

What does God want me to learn or discover about myself, the other, our context, our world?

What conditional beliefs or assumptions might be holding me back?

What is that new thing that longs to spring forth?

What is one step I could take into the unknown, where creativity and playfulness await?

Brené Brown, a research professor studying courage, vulnerability and shame, discovered that we cannot be brave without having the courage to feel into our vulnerabilities. The origin of the word *courage* is from the Latin root, *cor*, meaning *heart*. The word, *courage*, originally meant, "To speak one's mind by telling all of one's heart." When we are willing to risk sharing from our hearts, we grow our capacity to be courageous. We begin to see all of life as a sacrament of God's grace.

As leaders, we can help our communities by modeling this. One effective way is to create a culture of Brave Space. We can begin to invite teams or any groups in our communities to create covenants of how we will relate to each other. When we gather, our first ritual can be creating a list of how we want to hold each other accountable as a group by asking the following questions:

How do we want to show up to each other in this meeting, project, or group?

What do we need in order to show up in authentic ways that honor each one of our community and us?

During each meeting, we can refer back to the covenant that the group created, setting the stage for openhearted conversations where trust is nurtured. The safer people feel with one another, the more likely they are to admit mistakes, to partner, and to take on new roles. When we feel a sense of safety then our souls can come out and play! One sure sign of this is when light-hearted laughter is present in our gatherings.

We can also begin to build a culture in which failure is viewed as a wonderful learning opportunity through a simple assessment process that encourages spending five minutes at the end of any project, event, or meeting to ask the following questions:

What worked well?

What could be improved?

Brené Brown's research on vulnerability found that the level of collective courage in an organization is the absolute best predictor of its members' ability to be successful in developing healthy leaders and meeting their mission. These practices build resiliency to weather any storms of passing fear in the midst of constant change. What the world desperately needs today are brave leaders with open hearts. Are you willing to take that next courageous step?

Beth Ann Estock is an ordained United Methodist minister, leadership coach and author of two books, Weird Church: Welcome to the 21st Century *and* Holy Living: Discernment: Spiritual Practices for Building a Life of Faith. *She enjoys the wilds of Portland, Oregon and can be found at bethestock.com.*

38

Democracy and the Divine

PATRICIA ADAMS FARMER

Our image of God affects the choices me make in our leaders.

What if an eleven-year old refugee to the United States grew up to become Secretary of State? It happened, of course. Her name is Madeleine Albright, the first female Secretary of State (1997-2001), and she knows a thing or two about tyranny and its consequences. Her family was forced to leave their homeland of Czechoslovakia twice, first because of Hitler, and then because of Stalin. It is no wonder that Albright has dedicated her life of service to the tenets of American democracy, guarding against fascism and political bullies of all stripes.

Albright, also a distinguished professor and author of the noteworthy book *Fascism: A Warning*, recently spoke to a large crowd of admirers at a college in my town. I was entranced by her strong and gracious presence. At 82, she possesses the voice and energy of a much younger woman, and I think it is because she lives with such purpose. Listening to Albright's historical perspectives made me keenly aware that what we thought was solid as a rock—our democracy—is much more fragile than we ever imagined. That's because democracy demands constant care: voting, thinking, working together, sharing ideas, and even sacrificing for the sake of the common good. But when our primitive fears are stoked by charismatic leaders, we lose all sense of what democracy means. The so-called "strong man" suddenly looks good, as if we forgot the whole Twentieth Century and its wars and horrors.

This, I believe, is where theology comes in. Why theology? Isn't it irrelevant to politics, leadership, and democracy? On the contrary, it matters more than we know. I believe that good theology can help reignite our love and responsibility toward democracy, while bad theology exacerbates authoritarian tendencies. Of course, religion itself needs to stay out of politics, as democracy needs a strong separation of church and state in order to celebrate diversity. Still, God is in our psyches, whether we are believers or not. We are either acting or reacting in relation to some image of God or the Ultimate. During one of the 2019 Democratic debates, a commercial ran with atheist Ron Reagan promoting the "Freedom from Religion" movement. Such passionate atheists are reacting to a particular view of God (a distasteful view of God, in my opinion), and rightly wanting this ogre of a God to quit playing with politics. But democracy deals with values, and our values are often tied to our beliefs about ultimate matters. We cannot escape theology, even as we react against horrific notions of the Supreme Being.

Theology matters because we will be drawn, even on a subconscious level, to those leaders who exhibit what we imagine to be God-like traits—or at least traits that we consider elevated and noble. We will follow them; we will rally with them. Good or bad, it's what we do. So, we'd better be sure we have thought this through.

If our view of God is that of an omnipotent deity who wields unilateral power in the world, a God who resembles kings and emperors of old—or even a grumpy old white man in the sky—we're in trouble. We're in trouble any time we ascribe unilateral, all-controlling power to a deity because, sure enough, that is the image we will find and crown and worship here on earth.

The word "omnipotent" is not found in the Bible. It is found in the past, in philosophy and theology that fit the worlds of the past—worlds where power was concentrated in the hands of a few with one shining autocrat at the helm. We confuse God with monarchs when we need to make a clear distinction: "Give to the emperor the things that are the emperor's," says Jesus, "and to God, the things that are God's" (Mark 12:17).

All the Abrahamic traditions are saddled with histories dominated by images of an all-controlling God, but each tradition also offers open and relational alternatives. A beautiful expression of this relational God from the Jewish perspective is found in Rabbi Bradley Shavit Artson's book: *God of Becoming and Relationship*. Two of the best Christian discussions of the nature of God's power are found in Thomas jay Oord's *The Uncontrolling Love of God* and David Polk's *God of Empowering Love*. For a Muslim perspective, Muhammad Iqbal's open and relational approach in *The Reconstruction of Religious Thought in Islam* has profoundly influenced some young Islamic scholars like Farhan Shah at the University of Oslo. For these open and relational thinkers, it's all about the power of love over the love of power.

Love is at the heart of everything meaningful and true and worthy of sacrifice. It insists on shared power, relational power—power that lifts up the "least of these" in our communities as well as every last bee that pollinates our food sources. This view of relational power galvanized the leadership of the Rev. Martin Luther King, Jr., and the Civil Rights Movement.

For King, theology mattered, faith mattered; but his kind of faith sought justice for the sake of love with a capital "L". King understood the underpinnings of the Universe: Love seeking to be embodied in forms of social justice, Love seeking incarnation in a radically relational world, Love seeking hands and feet and voices "to do justice, to love kindness, and to walk humbly with thy God" (Micah 6:8). We live in a universe of radical relationality, and that includes a radically relational God who is here, now, sharing our sorrows and our joys, and inspiring our "better angels" to bring forth justice and goodness and relational beauty. This means that everyone counts, that power is shared, that democracy is a better model for what God's power is like than any form of authoritarianism.

Yes, a refugee should be able to thrive in our country and grow up to be a great leader like Madeline Albright. While her theology is unknown to me, her words and actions exhibit a core belief in a relational view of power, which serves as the foundation for any version of democracy in the world. If our view of God is counter to this—that is, if we cling to the omnipotent autocratic image—we're going to have a huge psychic struggle on our hands, and authoritarianism will be always be a threat. So, until our view of God evolves from the love of power to the power of love, we are lost.

And maybe we are lost. At least for the moment. Maybe our psyches are too fearful of change, too threatened by the "Other," too enmeshed in the charismatic influence of cult-like figures to get back home to love and justice. But this we must do and quickly, especially in the face of the existential threat of climate change.

One thing is for sure: Love is relentless. No matter how many bullies wreak havoc on the world, Love will never give up or give in. Yes, leaders drunk on their own power can drench the world in blood and suffering for a very long time, but Love doesn't go away. It pursues us, lures us, and beckons us toward a better way. As egoistic autocrats continue to rise in these times of change and fear, we must choose which kind of power we believe is divine or of ultimate value: shared power or all-controlling power. Which will it be? Which way will we go from here?

Theology matters.

Patricia Adams Farmer (patriciaadamsfarmer.com) is a minister and author of several books including Embracing a Beautiful God and Fat Soul: A Philosophy of S-I-Z-E. She blogs and teaches online courses for Spirituality & Practice and is a featured writer for Open Horizons. Her work has also been featured at A Network for Grateful Living and The Interfaith Observer.

39

An Open Pulpit

JR. FORASTEROS

Preaching offers an occasion for the inclusive nature of God's activity to be revealed when the church includes laity rather thinking it the exclusive activity of trained clergy.

*I*n maybe my second year as a youth pastor, our church staff had the chance to spend about an hour with an older pastor I really admired. Our senior pastor asked him, "How do you decide when to hire staff?" The answer he gave changed the course of my ministry career.

He said, "We don't hire people to do ministry. We hire people when we need someone to equip our members for ministry." Their church didn't expect their children's minster to do children's ministry alone—they expected them to recruit and lead a team of volunteer members who did the ministry. Same with the hospitality ministry, the teen ministry and nearly every other aspect of their church. The pastor cited Ephesians 4:12, which describes the role of spiritual gifts as given, "to equip the saints for the work of ministry, for building up the body of Christ."

"We don't hire ministers, because every Christian is a minister," he insisted. "We hire equippers."

Years later, after I had moved into a full-time preaching position at a large church, his words haunted me. My role was not to do ministry, but rather, as one called to vocational ministry, to dedicate myself to helping those to whom I am called to discern and live into their gifts.

It was during this same period of pastoring and continuing to study and grow I became captivated by the open and relational nature of God. When God created the man and woman, in the Hebrew creation story, God invited them to join in God's work. God planted a garden; the man and woman were to "till and keep"—gardening commands. God is a gardener in Genesis 2, so God invited us to join God's gardening work. Jesus later insisted the Son of Man did not come to be served, but to serve.

This is the way of God: to give away power (because in God's upside-down economy, power is an infinite resource, not something to be hoarded).

But even in churches with large staffs and a wide volunteer base, there's one position of power still reserved for a chosen few: the pulpit. I understood this before I began preaching full-time, but once I was preaching week after week, the weight really set in. Was I, like some latter-day Moses, meant to ascend the Sinai of solitude—my church office or a hip little coffee shop—, divine God's rightly-divided Word for the week and return, tablet in hand (just one—our contemporary scroll fits all ten commandments on one screen), to deliver those sacred musings to a congregation gathered for their weekly manna? There's a lot of power there.

I wondered how a church might open its pulpit. There's not a list of spiritual gifts in the New Testament, after all, that highlights preaching or teaching as special gifts bequeathed only to a chosen few in each congregation. And there's nothing about a call to vocational ministry that necessitates the gifts of preaching or teaching.

When I interviewed at my current Dallas-based church, Catalyst, I told the board about my dream—to build a lay preaching team with the explicit goal of opening the pulpit and decentering power in the church. They were open to the idea, so I got started soon after I was hired.

As I was still getting to know the congregation, I began with educators—people who had skill and training in teaching. Might they be expressing a gift their church had not equipped them to employ for the benefit of their spiritual body?

Within a year, I had a handful of lay preachers. Most of them did not have formal theological training. So, contrary to the models I had seen, I didn't simply hand them a text and wish them luck. Instead, we meet together. I tell each of my lay preachers that our goal is to discern three things:

What the Spirit is doing in the text (Ancient interpretation)

What the Spirit is doing in the life of the Church (contemporary interpretation)

What the Spirit is doing in the life of the preacher (spiritual formation)

OPEN AND RELATIONAL LEADERSHIP

Once we've identified the intersection of those three trajectories, we've found the heart of their sermon.

Next, we work through an extensive outlining process that incorporates a number of minds from Andy Stanley to Nancy Duarte. This outline provides a familiar structure and helps them think through their message—it provides the dry bones of a skeleton they can flesh out and bring to life.

In the last year, a couple of my lay preachers have begun to chafe at the strictures of my outlining process. This is an exciting sign that signals they've internalized the process to the degree it feels like a baseline. They have begun to experiment, injecting even more of their own personality and style into their sermons.

This model takes a lot of coaching of the congregation. I must constantly field complaints—"Pastor, I don't like it when so-and-so preaches."

I always assure them by pointing them back to the community of the Church. "That's okay!" I insist. "Did you know that persons D, E and F all find so-and-so to be their favorite Preacher?"

"Really, Pastor?"

"It's true. In fact, F likes so-and-so more than me." I say it with a smile to show I'm not offended by this idea.

"So it's okay if they're not your favorite. When they're preaching, enjoy the fact that your brothers and sisters are having their best Sunday—and your favorite preacher will be up there soon enough!"

I designed my responses to teach unity that's not uniformity. I don't *have to* like every single sermon or every single preacher to be a part of this congregation. And we have to get used to hearing God speak from every place and every person—not just our pastors.

The net result has been overwhelmingly positive. Our preaching team has a strong sense of ownership in the direction of the congregation. And we have a plurality of voices preaching and shaping the theological imagination of our church. Our congregation has learned to see the sermon as a conversation, not a lecture. The most important question isn't, "What did the pastor say today?" but rather, "What is God saying to us today?"

JR. Forasteros is the author of Empathy for the Devil and pastors at Catalyst Church in Dallas, Texas. He has been in full-time ministry for nearly two decades. He holds a Master of Arts in Religious Studies from the University of Missouri-Columbia, where he specialized in New Testament and Early Christian Communities. He hosts the

Fascinating Podcast and *In All Things Charity*. On Saturdays, he announces for Assassination City Roller Derby, where his wife Amanda skates as Mother Terrorista.

God and Doctors

WILLIAM HASKER AND JONATHAN KOPEL

Through relational leadership, a physician reflects God's relational nature to heal the emotional and physical needs of patients and themselves.

The physician-patient relationship is an intimate relationship fostering open communication while respecting patient autonomy. Without this therapeutic alliance, patient confidence and compliance with treatment goals would be impossible to maintain. Traditionally, the leadership role in the physician-patient relationship rested primarily on the physician. This model, known as medical paternalism, placed responsibility on the physician to determine what treatments or choices a patient should take with respect to their illness. In this model, the physician-patient relationship is the ship; the physician is its captain.

Although this may be helpful in complex medical situations, patients prefer having shared decision making in understanding their diagnosis and treatment options. As a result, medical paternalism can cause ineffective communication between the physicians and patients, leading to poor management and coordination in a patient's treatment. Furthermore, a patient's satisfaction and treatment outcomes improve when leadership in the physician-patient relationship is understood to be a partnership whereby each member contributes towards a common goal. This relational leadership between patients and physicians requires an openness and mutual participation between both parties. Such a relationship resembles aspects of open theism, which challenges the theological doctrines of divine impassability and of God's complete, perfect and unchangeable plan for our lives.

Relational Leadership

Yet, what exactly is a relation? We may initially draw metaphors from marriage or friendships to gain some intuitive feel of a relation. In a marriage, the interactions of love and unity between two individuals provides the foundation for the relationship. As within the relationship of friends, physician and patient exist in deeply intertwined relations. The physician-patient relationship requires both individuals to have unique personalities embodying their identities, worldviews, and interactions. The physician-patient relationship is subject to change and may grow or diminish. In medical practice this often occurs through patient hand-offs or referrals to other clinical departments or institutions.

A patient also exists independently whether he or she has formed a therapeutic alliance with a physician or other caregiver. Given this complexity, a *relational leadership* model is necessary to balance the intrinsic and extrinsic relations within the physician-patient relationship. In this model, a physician seeks to cultivate an authentic relationship with patients and healthcare workers towards achieving a common vision, connection, and interdependent action. A physician trained in relational leadership seeks to understand people's motivations, how they acquire and utilize information, and how they influence the physician-patient relationship. An effective relational leader seeks to foster teamwork, to coach and develop, to improve self-management, and to accelerate change in an organization. Furthermore, a relational leader embraces and encourages the relations inherent within the healthcare system to foster and encourage cooperation and unity towards a common goal.

God's Perfect Plan

But what does all this have to do with God? Of course, God is seen in the Bible as our healer and comforter, one who is very much present with us in time of illness. But how does this relate to the doctor-patient interaction? The doctor is not God, and the doctor's role is specific and limited. All the same, ideas about the doctor's role say something about the part patients are expected to play in their own healing, and this in turn says something about the way we should think about God's care for us. It would be troubling if our best understanding of God and our relationship with God should urge us to adopt a stance that does not fit with our best understanding of the doctor-patient relationship.

One common, but flawed, way of thinking about this is the idea of *God's perfect plan*—a plan God has for your life that will work out exactly right, so that everything turns out exactly the way God intended. But what if things don't go so well for you? There is a saying among Presbyterians that a Presbyterian is a man who, after he has fallen down a flight of stairs, says "Thank goodness that's over!" The fall was obviously part of God's plan for him, so there is no use complaining about it; he is only glad it wasn't worse!

This suggests that our approach to things that happen in our lives should be one of passive acceptance—this is just the way things were meant to be. And this resembles the paternalistic model of the patient-doctor relationship in which the doctor is completely in control and makes all the decisions. But as we have seen, it may yield better results if the patient is seen as an active participant in the relationship, using her own judgment in combination with the doctor's superior knowledge—in other words, relational leadership. And it may be better if the Christian's life is seen as a journey together with God, using a person's own judgment together with the wisdom God provides. (God rather seldom issues explicit instructions as if they were written out on a sheet of paper!) So maybe God's plan for us is best seen as open-ended, allowing for Plan B or Plan C in case Plan A doesn't work out.

Can God Suffer?

Another point worth noticing is the traditional doctrine of *divine impassibility*. This means God can never be caused to suffer or to feel any negative emotion. It is meant to underscore God's invulnerability; nothing that ever happens can diminish God's happiness in any respect. But in relating to a doctor, we very much want the doctor to care how our treatment comes out. Even more, we expect our friends and loved ones to be happy or saddened depending on the result. Excluding God from this "circle of care," as is done by the doctrine of impassibility, does not have a good feel about it. It's as though we must push God away from us, lest God be compromised by being affected by our troubles! But God can't be compromised; God is the Greatest One, who has compassion on us and suffers when we suffer, without being diminished by this in any way. Once again, there is a parallel between how we think of our relationship to a doctor, and of our relationship to God, the Great Physician.

Conclusion

Overall, the physician-patient relationship and personality exist as rich relational entities producing profound impacts on communication and patient outcomes. A relational leadership model provides physicians with a framework to apply a relational or open theist theology—a theology in which God interacts with human beings, sympathizes with their joys and sorrows, and maintains a flexible plan that can adjust to events as they occur—to their practice and their relationships with patients. This framework fosters deep relationships between physicians and patients by acknowledging their numerous and rich qualities. A relational understanding of physician-patient relations presupposes a relational universe, and a relational universe requires physicians to be relational in their approach to patients, in service to the Hippocratic Oath, an oath of respect for human life. This oath is itself an invitation to relationality. Through a relational leadership model, a physician reflects God's relational nature in order to heal the emotional and physical needs of patients and themselves.

William Hasker is the Distinguished Professor Emeritus of Philosophy at Huntington University. He is the author of several books, including The Emergent Self and The Triumph of God over Evil. He is a former editor of the journal, Faith and Philosophy.

Jonathan Kopel is an M.D.Ph.D. student at Texas Tech University Health Sciences Center in Lubbock, Texas.

41

Pump, Pause, Release, Repeat

BETH HAYWARD

Creativity and beauty are born when we lead from a place of grounded pause.

In the place where I began, or more accurately the place where the possibility of me began, in the place where my parents met, there's a swing. It's quite possibly my favorite swing, though I've never met a swing I didn't like. This particular swing is located on the property of a rural, residential retreat center. I had the privilege of swinging there both as a child and young adult. The view from the top of the swing's arch—rolling hills, derelict train tracks, and marshy waters—connects me to my dreams. The ruddy wooden seat grounds me in my roots.

I love to swing. I love the soothing rhythm of back and forth, up and down; the exhilarating breeze as it washes over your face, and that unsettling feeling as your tummy suddenly drops. It's a beautiful coming together of science and faith. The simple design coupled with the right coordination of muscles and mind brings you higher and higher. And though science may well explain how it is that you reach the top only to come back down again; I think the dissent is all about faith. *Is this the time the swing will buckle and fail me? How is it that it feels like I'm one with the sky by just tilting my head back? Could I really fly?*

There's a moment in swinging that is at once exhilarating and utterly filled with angst: that moment when you reach your full height either backward or forward and you are about to come back down. It's the pause between the pump and release. In that instant it's as if you are neither here nor there, not heading back or moving forward. Suspended as if beyond time, it's the briefest of moments, but the most important. It's the pause between inhale and exhale. It's like that elusive moment in meditation when you aren't telling your thoughts to take a hike.

Good leaders, effective leaders are the ones who can attune others to that time-between-time, to that place of pause from which clarity arises.

We live in a time when people are less likely to trust institutions and their leaders. Have you ever noticed how everyone is an expert these days? Part of my work is to officiate at funerals. It's a learned art to create a ceremony that is individually appropriate and sensitive. There's way more to consider than most people might know. As I sit down to plan the service of a loved one with the family, more and more, I find that they are sure they know how to plan the service better than me with my twenty years of experience. I have at least two choices in those moments: I can set them straight, let them know who's boss. I can go deep with my ego by insisting that I am the expert *or* I can pause. I can lean in closer, metaphorically speaking. I can choose curiosity over defensiveness. I can in that suspended, beyond-time moment, make room for more creativity to emerge. I still bring my leadership, my expertise but from a posture of calm and curiosity; from the swing's timeless moment. My brain often tells me to stand my ground and insist on the victory of my rightness. It's an open posture, however, that allows for so much more beauty to emerge. That's what it is to lead from the pause.

I'm more and more convinced that we need less strategy and more intuition. Less push and more swing. I've participated in the creation of enough strategic planning reports over the years to fell a few trees. Yet if you were you to ask me what the one-, three-, or five-year goal was for any one of those plans I'm afraid I'd come up short. Think about it, did Moses have a plan? No, his successes, when he had them, were because he stopped long enough to pay attention to burning bushes and holy ground. Jesus noticed those right in plain sight. He attended to the need before him, keeping in mind the bigger picture of what was coming to life. He was fully present to the moment, and those were the times when amazing stuff happened.

A number of years ago the church I serve did away with committees. Except for the one or two mandated by our governing body, we have no endless conversations that go in circles; no committees. It's been absolutely liberating to no longer meet for meeting's sake. It's also had the unanticipated but much appreciated side effect of diminishing the entrenched power of special interest groups. It's no longer about outreach in a tug of war with choir, it's more about us now. We wanted to lift the burden from people of filling vacant spots on committees and liberate them to offer their time to the organization in ways that are life-giving for both them and the congregation.

Around the same time, we began offering a program called *Living Your Spiritual Gifts*. Participants engage in group and individual discernment leading to an articulating of three spiritual gifts that they possess and claim. From there they begin to match those gifts with opportunities available to serve in our community. We've learned over the years to build two important things into the process: first, there is always room for you to name a spiritual gift that has never made it onto our list before and, second, you can define a new opportunity in the church to match your gifts rather than slot yourself into an already existing ministry. These two things have provided the creative, mid-air swing energy that enables the program to grow and shift as needed.

These times we live in are marked with angst and uncertainty. Things are changing quickly and what we once knew for sure can no longer be counted on as solid ground. Changing times call for changing leaders. We need leaders who are authentically attuned to this moment, this place, and this time. Our job is not to scribe a well thought out plan in pen but rather to intuit our next best move and that of the people we serve. We do this best in our top-of-the-swing moments because that's the place where anything is possible. This moment in time demands that we evolve in our leadership, beyond the quick fix to-do list, the consumerist tendencies, the just-give-me-the-goods pressure.

An open, relational way is more long-haul, not as glamourous, not prescribed. It will give you a kick in the shins (or worse) every single time you slip back into claiming you have all the answers from your wealth of experience, every time you start checking off the "best leader" boxes. Open and relational leadership is not bland or passive. It's about holding that space between dreams and roots. It's about noticing the pause, so that you can shift things ever so slightly, as needed, in the mid-air moment. It isn't easy. There is no simple five-step way of making decisions, or a one-size-fits-all approach to take your organization to the next level. It's more about intuition than instruction, more about swinging movement than structured assent. It's about you as a leader radiating beauty all the while being open to how your contribution comes back to you.

It is the task of the leader to point to that place. To hop on the swing and call others to join in. To gently, persuasively even, draw the attention of others to the moment at the top of the swing, the moment of still possibility and endless creativity.

OPEN AND RELATIONAL LEADERSHIP

Beth Hayward is Lead Minister at Canadian Memorial United Church in Vancouver, Canada. A storyteller, pastor and preacher; she finds rest and renewal in knitting, belly dancing and beach walking. You can watch her preach what she practices here: www.canadianmemorial.org/sermons

42

The Missing Finger: An Analogy of Love

ROLAND HEARN

When the church focuses primarily upon its own needs, it drifts from its God-given mandate.

Many years ago I worked in the morally questionable environment of the Australian used car industry of the early '80s. At that time only sales mattered. People were seen as "marks" to be separated from their money. Many car yards would open, operate, and close within 12 months to avoid having to respond to customer needs. In that world, lies to clients were nothing more than punch lines in jokes to be told in the lunchroom. To cheat someone with a plausible fabrication was highly lauded.

In one of the yards in which I worked I came across an individual that was quite remarkable. A man with integrity. He owned and operated that yard. I liked him. He spoke words of wisdom, encouragement, and affirmation. It seemed he liked me too. Enough that when he was forced to sell his yard and take on the role of sales manager of a much larger business, he invited me to go with him. Almost anytime I was with him I felt better about myself. He spoke to me with concern about the negative influences within the trade impacting me. He taught me how to sell a car honestly, and he gave me tasks of responsibility to perform. I enjoyed being with him. We laughed easily together, even though I was just out of my teen years. He spoke to me as if I was an adult, as if I was someone that mattered. I had no doubt that to Bill Muir I mattered, and it did not have anything to do with my performance. Whether I sold cars or not, he was the same. I was surprised by how much he seemed to value me.

As I worked with him, I developed a very peculiar habit. A long time before I had known him, he had lost the little finger from his right hand in an accident. He was a man that spoke using lots of hand gestures, and the missing digit was clearly apparent whenever he spoke. I found myself, without awareness, copying his many gestures. As I did, I rolled my little finger into the palm of my hand when I spoke so that it was not visible. I was talking to a customer one day and I happened to notice my hand as it waved in the air. It was the first time I was aware of how much I was imitating my employer. To my surprise I saw the little finger of my right hand tucked discretely away and I knew instantly that act was a representation of how much he meant to me because of how much I meant to him.

In scripture we are called to be "imitators of Christ" (Eph. 5:1). We are charged to "act justly and to love mercy" (Micah 6:8). This is what God requires of us. Ultimately, we are to be ambassadors in the ministry of reconciliation (2 Cor. 5:19-20), reflecting those clarion words of Christ: "Therefore go and make disciples of all nations" (Matthew 28:19). These statements, and many others, blend together to create our understanding of what it is to "serve God." Captured within them are hints on how to evaluate our performance in each of these areas. When we evaluate our performance, we can determine if we are fulfilling those charges given to us. So, as a result, we can consider the number of disciples we have made, the number of times we speak forth "the word"—be it in a sermon or in a "witnessing" event. We can evaluate our influence on the laws of the church, and, dare we believe, the laws of the nation. We can ultimately determine if we are truly "being the church," "being faithful," "committed," and "honoring the sacrifice of Christ."

The whole of our faith journey, as a result of these perceptions, can, in one way or another, be understood in terms of things we do and the methods we use to evaluate those activities. This is often a subtle process because it is the opposite of how we construct our understanding of faith and grace. But the evidence of that reality is that we discover our freedom is gone, the burden becomes heavy, and the church takes on the role of an institution with institutional demands. In this reality, leaders—pastors and lay people—move ever more toward feelings of inadequacy and isolation, and ultimately, for many, the result is burnout.

This shift from a focus on the centrality of grace to an overwhelming burden of performance reveals the truth that among the things we need is a transformation in the way we perceive leadership. That is evidenced by our apparent obsession with results. Be it the local church pastor, lay leaders, ministry coordinators, and denominational leaders, the way we talk and think about the church effectively being the church, reveals something to us. It is almost always expressed in terms of results that can be measured numerically. We become results focused because we have trained ourselves to believe that reaching certain goals is akin to advancing the Kingdom of God. Those goals are usually framed with regards to membership, attendance, finances, or education. None of those things are inherently bad and measuring them does make sense. But a shift occurs in our understanding of the role of the church in the world when these measures become measures of our personal worth or acceptability.

Two significant representations point to this shift. Firstly, the leader begins to connect her or his sense of worth, and therefore identity, with the achievement of those goals. Secondly, the leader creates an environment that increases the sense of inadequacy for those they are leading by linking the worth of those being led to the leader's expectation. That is, because of the first issue—an environment where a leader's sense of worth relates to results—a dominating awareness exists that participants in any project believe they must achieve certain expectations, communicated by the leader, to validate their own sense of worth. They are subsequently uncertain that they can achieve the perceived expectations in a way that will remotely positively impact their own sense of worth. An overwhelming sense of shame over their sense of inadequacy can quickly follow. Simply put, individuals don't feel "good enough" to adequately achieve the results required. Even when expectations are reached there can be a constant sense that new expectations will quickly emerge that will negate the achievement of the existing ones.

Worth and identity are profoundly and inextricably linked. A leader that is results focused can believe that they are wisely balancing capacities and resources, when first and foremost they are fulfilling a vital role in identity formation—or at least they should be. The delusion is played out in a thousand contexts where a leader is pushing people to achieve certain ends. On the achievement of those results they may then be found patting themselves, and even their team, on the back for achieving such results, blissfully unaware that resentments or dysfunctional relational dynamics may eventually develop. The ultimate failure of the organization or the team is already being established without their knowledge, even while they are applauded for reaching certain targets. This reality exists as much in the church as it does in secular contexts. It is the dominance of a results focus, and the subsequent inevitable sense of shame, that is crippling the church in its desire to represent the grace of God to a hurting world.

That is not the representation of grace in scripture. We find in scripture a genuine confidence that transformation of an individual's life empowers a lifestyle of transformation. That transformation will, in and of itself, produce the Kingdom of God. The focus is love changing lives. The transformation is an inevitable consequence of the reception of grace as love. Like my finger inevitably curling under as I spent increasingly more time with an individual that valued me, our lives take on the imitation of Christ. This is the result of becoming vulnerable to grace, love, and the subsequent identity and worth that flows in relationship to Christ. This imitation is not an activity, but a reality of relationship. The "result" for which we aim is becoming like Christ in love with the absolute confidence that such a reality reproduces the values of the Kingdom of God. The primary value of the Kingdom of God is love transforming humanity into the likeness (love) of God.

There is a certain self-obsession with the idea of achieving expectations in terms of results and goals. On the other hand, it is *love-obsession* that focuses on transformation. However, such a love focus reduces a leaders' capacity to control and push in the direction of numerical results. This then can be perceived as "failing to lead adequately." It is a brave and transformed leader that has confidence in love alone and allows the people for whom she is responsible the freedom to explore what it means to be transformed in love. Numbers do matter, but they are the consequence of grace not the focus of effort.

Roland Hearn has been married to his wonderful wife, Emmy, for more than 30 years. They have been in ministry together for most of that time. He currently serves as the Chairman of the board of trustees for Nazarene Theological College, the primary coordinator for ministry within the Church of the Nazarene in Australia and New Zealand and the district superintendent of the Australia North and West district of the church of the Nazarene. His research passion is the healing and transforming power of divine love.

Leadership after the Funeral of the Church

GEORGE HERMANSON

A word of warning to the church: be aware that things are changing.

We are in a time of asking hard questions of what it means to be a congregation. It does not stop there, for individual Christians are asking what does it mean to be a follower of Jesus? We are trying to navigate these questions in a time of unrest.

Most American adults now say it is not necessary to believe in God to be moral and have good values (56%). This reflects the continued growth in the share of the population that has no religious affiliation. The demise is continuing among young people who see Christianity as irrelevant to issues of climate change, inclusion and justice. This decrease is also happening in white evangelical circles.

In response, many churches seek out those who will help them, as if there is a technique that provides a simple solution, a magic bullet for what ails us.

Using the image of *funeral* suggests beginning to let go of some of the ties that bind us. Funerals celebrate memory. They invite us to move on.

We need imagination to create our life together, one that is worthy of us. We know that faith calls us to world care. It is not always easy to discern what is worthy of us, or how to make reality better.

Leadership

The future is radically open even as we go about the job of creating it. We live in open, not closed, systems. So, we must say goodbye to the way the church was in order to open a space to what must imaginatively emerge. One image comes from ice hockey: skate to where the puck is going to be, not where it is. Great hockey players see the ice as open space. This requires an understanding of leadership that affirms open space, or living without plans.

The image that grounds leadership is open space. The role of the leader is to keep the space open. It is not to determine the outcome, but to hold open whatever space the group is in, letting the group determine what they want to achieve by sharing their hopes and dreams there in that collective space. Open space is a communal task.

First, a topic or issue is named. Then group members are invited to offer responses. Each names a way forward. Participants are invited to enlist in those ideas that capture them. The job of the leader is to send those groups off and hold the space open for their responses. The leader is comfortable with the letting go. Leadership is thus shared and the direction is determined by the feedback from the groups.

Premise of Leadership

A basic feature of open space is that we live in a relational world, context, or group. Identity as individuals and groups emerge through mimesis. In the context of religious reality, the leader is grounded by commitment to the following theological ideas: It is based on imitating a loving God, and affirming that God is relational and uncontrolling love. It begins with the reality that this world does not have a straight path, that God has not decided the future, and that we live in randomness and chance. It is committed to developing leadership that will guide us without guarantees. By beginning without a safety net, we can have confidence in our actions, and agency.

The type of leadership is clear: persons who are open to the prompting of the Spirit of God—who always transgresses boundaries—find creative ways to bear witness to uncontrolling love. It is the sacral act of being present, to hold the space open. It is an understanding of the Spirit as located in many religious and secular forms. It is to have a pluralistic understanding of the Spirit.

The distant God of conventional religions is gone, having given way to a more intimate sense of the sacred in the world. The shift has many causes, but one I like is what my wife Suzanne said: "May 25, 1977, was the cultural shift, the coming of the Star Wars." This shift, from a vertical understanding of God to a God found on the horizons of nature and human community, is at the heart of a spiritual revolution. Using the idea of the uncontrolling love of God gives us a way of leadership and living that the community can mimic—setting one's face toward the future, being spiritually alive, and taking our faith seriously.

This type of leadership is to be comfortable with Christianity as no longer privileged: it's one among many options. Pluralism is now the defining metaphor. And pluralism seeks common cause among all religious traditions.

Open-space leadership is being present and listening. Such leadership creates space for listening that affirms the world and for letting go of former constructions of faith.

Leadership is holding space open so we can rage and find compassion. Sometimes the only way to express compassion in the face of dangerous times is to practice truth telling by declaring our faith in our capital for solidarity to commit to building a different world. "Compassion is relentless effort, compassion is humility, compassion is listening as practice—listening as a deepening that enriches one's empathy"." (Conrad Tao in his album American Rage.)

Listening is crucially important to the creation of jazz. It is full of a listening that creates music that moves the body and the soul. In jazz, space is held open so the musicians can listen to one another and move to the creation of a new piece, even if you can hear the traces of the old.

Every jazz group illustrates that at the base of all creative acts, a new reality was created through intentional listening. We could say the same of God, and generalize this to how all things become. Becoming a piece of music is more than notes added to notes; it is creating some new intensity and harmony out of what has been given, and now made new by the players.

One vivid experience of this for me was a group whose leader is a bass player who provided a grounding of free jazz that is sonically rich, relaxed and almost cinematic; her whole body was involved. Both feet stomping, embracing the bass, kinetically visual, the group lifted us, and transported us in new reaches of the music. This process invited other group members to build on what she offered and push the music into new realms. It was clear that in order to be able to this, the players watched and listened to one another, looking for clues in the music and in their eyes and bodies. Listening and space allowed them to improvise.

There is a call-and-response pattern built into our relational world and the world becomes through it. This means that what we do and how we respond determines what the world will become.

OPEN AND RELATIONAL LEADERSHIP

Jay McDaniel suggests uncontrolling Love Supreme (God) as a listener. This is the importance of listening in leadership. God is a listening God. Before God speaks, God has had to receive. Even God must begin with listening. After all, God cannot respond to the cries of the world, or share in its joys, unless God first hears those cries and feels those joys. In the beginning, even for God, there had to be a listening. This is true of all of life. This is the meaning of open space leadership.

Coda

In British Columbia (as elsewhere) outdoor recreation is an enjoyed experience. In Squamish there was tension with the indigenous community about the use of a mountain area for hikers and mountain bikes.

To deal with the issue of use, a gathering was called with those involved. In an open space context, new understandings emerged. By holding a space open for Chief Planes, listening and considering the story of the T'Sou-ke people, an opportunity was created for the community to rethink its relationship with the land, recognizing it as one that requires ongoing care and renewal. An insight was to recognize that we must work with First Nations.

Following the event, people bustled about the conference hall preparing to go riding. One person asked, "Are we riding Broom Hill?"

"No," came the response. "It's Sacred Mountain. We're riding on T'Sou-ke land. Show some respect."

"We recognize that we live on the lands of the Squamish Nation. We unequivocally support the Squamish Nation's right to self-determinacy on its lands, and we are grateful to share in the spirit and beauty of this place."

The community has a long way to go to realize fully the vision of reconciliation. This was only the beginning. Chief Planes' people will take the time they needed to decide what was best for Sacred Mountain and the T'Sou-ke Nation.

Leadership, after the funeral of the church—noticing where God is in the world—requires discernment. Leadership is keeping the space open and practicing discernment by being open to the presence of the Spirit of God sliding in, unexpectedly.

George Hermanson is a retired United Church of Canada clergy living in Nanaimo, BC. He studied anthropology at the University British Columbia, studied theology at Chicago Theology Seminary, and earned his doctorate at Claremont School of Theology. He has been a parish minister, campus minister, Director of a retreat and education centre, and Director of Madawaska institute for Religion and Culture.

Passion, Authenticity, and Commitment: A Reflection on Theological Education

SHERYL A. KUJAWA-HOLBROOK

If we believe all are called to use their agency for the good of the world, we must vigorously advocate for theological education.

One of my formative influences was the late Marianne Micks, a professor at Virginia Theological Seminary, who published widely on ministry when few women were on theological school faculties. She believed that one of the limitations of theological education, and by extension the Christian church, was that we ascribe to a God "who is too small and too tame."

In my experience, much of the focus of theological education is too small and too tame. Theological education focused on educating pastors the way we did a generation ago is inadequate. Theological education today is in-between times, and as some would say, has lost its prophetic voice. That is, many of the old operating assumptions have slipped away, but we have yet to reach a new equilibrium. The smaller, freestanding schools are the most vulnerable, but even large institutions with large endowments are dealing with shifting resources.

A recent study on "pastoral imagination" funded by the Lilly Endowment, Inc., suggests that capacities for pastoral leadership are sparked early in life, and take years of daily practice before they come to fruition. If we truly believe that all are called to use their agency for the good of the world, we must then vigorously advocate for theological education that transforms both individuals and communities through evoking giftedness, healing painful pasts, practicing peace with justice, and serving all creation—the kind of theological education relevant to all who minister: preachers, teachers, workers, parents, children, youth, elders, citizens, activists, and yes, even professors!

The theological education that is needed is a dynamic and embodied process whereby our hearts and minds are turned toward God in the expectation of transformation on every level of our being. Theological education is about both theory and practice: the integration of academic content, practical skills, and ritual practice, along with a deepening knowledge of the self, relationships, contexts, and commitment to peace with justice.

Such theological education integrates intersectional identities into theology and ministry; race, gender identity and expression, sexual identity, social class, ability, language, immigration status, addiction status, etc. While it is not always comfortable, it is sacred space, and for many a rare opportunity to be part of a community that welcomes differences, while always continuing to push the boundaries, and re-examine systemic biases. This capacity to claim intersectional identities as integral to ministry is at the core of discipleship today.

Interestingly, very little of Jesus' public ministry took place within traditional religious spaces, except for a few instances that did not turn out very well. Mostly, Jesus taught on the road, among the people. His focus was on expanding the boundaries of his community to include those most feared—Samaritans, Gentiles, sex workers, tax collectors, sinners in general—rather than teaching about who should be excluded. There is a school of opinion in the Christian world that argues the church is going down because we continue to bring up controversial issues and hang out with the wrong people. But the idea that moderation contributes to growing membership is reminiscent of a time in the mid-20th century when the church was much more accepted as part of the dominant culture. Today what is attractive in religious movements is *not* conformity *but* passion, authenticity, and commitment, and the ability to form community across differences with our neighbors from other religions (and no religion) who share in a vision of the common good. In a climate of growing intolerance, we should not forget that genuine welcome fills a deep human need these days. Perhaps we need to begin to see the church in expansive terms inclusive of the many ways we live together and work with our neighbors for peace with justice?

A spirituality of resistance is embedded deep within the Christian faith, for those of us who choose to recognize it. Just as Jesus of Nazareth called out those in his own tradition who were too comfortable with the empire, so too, his followers in this age are challenged to resist. Scripture is filled with stories when humanity fails to resist the forces of domination and death. On the one hand, our failure to resist could result in death by irrelevance. On the other hand, and a more deeply troubling scenario, is to become identified as a people comfortable with the status quo, thereby losing our moral agency and connection with our prophetic past.

It is integral to theological education today to teach theology in ways that acknowledge the value of context and individual stories; appreciate that there is not one truth, but multiple centers of truth; and, to cultivate activist-theologians who thrive on pluralism, while standing deeply within their own traditions. This style of leadership is found in the prophets, who both loved and challenged their own traditions.

In my experience, part of what theological education gives to the world is a framework within which we practice formation from the perspective of the transformation of whole persons in community. Ironically, the best way we can witness to the importance of theological education, is to give the world *more* than churches.

The cultivation of wisdom depends upon theological education that prioritizes integration over fragmentation and stratification. We need to invent ways going forward to cultivate opportunities for the kind of theological education where the boundaries between the classroom and "real life" are porous and where the gifts and life experiences of students are highly valued in the educational process. We need to cultivate "courageous spaces" where we can build solidarity across divisions.

In a world where the majority are in some way marginalized, religion easily becomes a tool of oppression when limited to correct belief, or focused on internal squabbles, when most people are deprived of basic human needs, and the fate of the planet is in jeopardy. Those of us who are teachers, preachers, activists, citizens, parents, workers, must be equipped to engage in prophetic responses to injustice for the rest of our lives.

In my own formation, I learned if I first transformed my understanding of myself as powerless, then everything changed, and I was then empowered to expand my vision of how I am called to live in the world, as a theological educator, as a priest, as a partner, parent, citizen. Open and relational formation builds agency and moral integrity. All around us, we have examples of negative formation, whereby religious identities are formed in opposition to others, rather than in the spirit of the commandment to love our neighbors as ourselves. My ongoing formation at home, church, and school have shaped my vision of the reign of God in a palpable way. As a theological educator, not only am I concerned with my own formation, and my students', but that of the communities we serve now and in the future.

The Prophet Mohammed, *pbh*, says that those who search for wisdom walk in the path of God. I first came to theological education in my early-20s and the experience was transformative. I learned that theology is an academic discipline, but also that it is about embodied practice, and about the lives of people who suffer, and hope, and search for meaning. There is always a need to re-imagine how best to theologically educate emergent generations. Religion is not considered the only source of meaning anymore. Many ethical humanists live fulfilling and generous lives. If, however, we believe that spirituality is a source for liberation, we need to reveal that truth through the quality of our communities, and how we embody our values every day.

One of the great Talmudic sages, Maimonides, taught that while it is not our responsibility to complete the task of healing the world, we cannot refrain from engaged participation. In Christian contexts, we have been talking about the need to re-imagine theological education for the last generation. Yet true learning is not limited to schooling, after all, but a recognition of the truths revealed most plainly in relationship. What lies ahead is the ongoing work of the transformation of humanity (and our planet) in which each one of us shares a part. Theological education is about strengthening hearts and challenging minds. At its most basic, it is about creating intentional communities of transformation.

This work is yet to be fully realized; there is much ahead to do.

Sheryl A. Kujawa-Holbrook is vice president for academic affairs, dean of the faculty, and professor of practical theology at Claremont School of Theology. She has gratefully been active in theological education for 40 years!

45

Do Your Best to Present Yourself as One Trusted by God

WM. CURTIS HOLTZEN

Church leadership involves trust between fellow Christians and mutual trust between God and the leader.

*I*t is difficult to think about leadership without considering the idea of trust. Leaders who do not have the trust of their followers must lead by means of threat or unspoken fear. We all have likely had bosses or managers we did not trust but followed their lead out of apprehension of being reprimanded or fired. Others attempt to lead by promise of reward or personal gain. Think about the promises presidential candidates make in order to secure your vote so they can be your leader. Many promise financial gain in the form of lower taxes, a higher stock market, or, in general, a better economy. But in the absence of such tactics of fear, reward, or some combination, a leader will lead by securing the trust of his or her followers.

Search any article, sermon, or blog on the topic of Christian leadership and it will become clear that discussions of trust are ubiquitous. There are discussions of followers trusting leaders, leaders trusting followers, leaders trusting one another, and of course, everyone's need to trust God. But there is an important avenue of trust not being discussed—God's trust. God trusts the church's leaders or, minimally, God desires to trust those in leadership. God trusts these leaders to care for the wellbeing of their followers, to manifest justice, to encourage both spiritual and moral virtues; in short, to be and to model authenticity as a follower of Christ.

The Bible is not shy in speaking about divine trust, especially trust in God's leaders. In Numbers 12:6-8 God, speaking to Moses, Aaron, and Miriam, says, "When there are prophets among you, I the Lord make myself known to them in visions; I speak to them in dreams. Not so with my servant Moses; he is entrusted with all my house." In several of his letters, Paul speaks of God's trust. For example, in Romans 3:2 Paul says the Jews were entrusted with the oracles of God. In Galatians 2:7 Paul says he was entrusted with the gospel to the uncircumcised just as Peter had been entrusted with the gospel for the circumcised. It is not just prophets and apostles who were trusted by God since Paul also includes Silvanus and Timothy when he says, "we have been approved by God to be entrusted with the message of the gospel" (I Thes 2:4). The message of divine trust is extended to the entire church when Paul writes, "in Christ God was reconciling the world to himself, not counting their trespasses against them, and entrusting the message of reconciliation to us" (II Cor 5:19).

In order to make sense of these declarations of divine trust it might be helpful to discuss just what trust is or entails. I have a lengthy treatment of trust (as well as faith, hope, and love) in my book *The God Who Trusts* (IVP Academic), but I think a brief statement can work here. The most succinct description of trust I have found is from philosopher Annette Baier, who says that to trust someone is to give them discretionary power over something you value. If I loan you my car, I trust you to care for it. But I also trust you to use it as you see fit given unforeseen circumstances. For example, it may become necessary to drive a friend, who cannot fly, to an important medical procedure hundreds of miles away. I believe this understanding of trust as giving one discretionary power may go a long way in helping us better understand the parable of the talents (Matt 25).

To trust someone is to become vulnerable. You risk something you value in the hope that something even more valuable might be gained. I entrust my car to a friend to help them, but also further the friendship. I trust my young daughter so that she might grow into maturity but also to strengthen our family bond. I trust my wife because that is what it means to be in a loving relationship. I am not saying trust is merely a means to an end, but I am saying that trust is the means *and* end. The difference between a casual and an intimate relationship is the depth of mutual trust.

From an open and relational perspective, the idea of God trusting those in leadership should hardly be controversial. Open and relational theists affirm that humans are sufficiently free to make genuine choices—choices that cannot be known prior to their being chosen, even by our omniscient God. Add to this, God has certain desires related to what we do, think, believe, and value. That is, God desires we become mature trustworthy covenant partners in the ministry of reconciliation. God does not control what we do and cannot know what a free being will do, and yet God deeply cares about what we do and become; God chooses to trust us. And because leaders are in place to work with God in making all mature in Christ, God has even greater trust in Christian leaders.

To borrow imagery from the business world—even though there are those who may not like this assessment—Christian leaders are essentially middle management. They are unquestionably not the CEO but they are also not the rank and file. And remember, all are valuable in the body of Christ (1 Cor 12:15-20.) Middle managers are semi-executives who need to be mindful that to do their job properly they need to procure the trust of not only their subordinates but also their own leaders. Likewise, Christian leaders need to gain and keep the trust of their fellow Christians who are under their leadership. These same Christian leaders need to earn and affirm the trust God has in them or the trust God desires to have in them. To worry only about the trust of one's followers is to ignore the one whose trust is most important. Isn't what we long to hear most, "Well done, good and trustworthy slave; you have been trustworthy in a few things, I will put you in charge of many things; enter into the joy of your master" (Matt 25:23 NRSV)?

We must not confuse obedience for trust. Obedience is good. It means submission. God surely wants church leaders to obey. But if that were all God desired, they would not be leaders, they would merely be those following a different set of rules or commands. This is not bad, but it is not leadership. Christian leadership is more than obedience; it means the leader has a say in the direction and execution of a plan. Leaders influence. To be in leadership is to have the capacity to influence another's beliefs, behaviors, values, ideals, and hopes. This is a lot of power and with great power comes great responsibility but also great trust.

Does this mean God trusts every leader? Of course not! Christian leaders can disappoint and lose God's trust just as they can lose our trust. Furthermore, God's trust is not merely in the leader but also in the people who place leaders in their position. God trusts communities to raise up those into leadership who are wise, resolute, and most of all trustworthy. Again, communities fail, they can be imprudent or self-seeking. So, while God loves all, this does not mean God trusts all. But, I believe, it means God desires to trust all, especially those in leadership. Partnership is simply not possible without mutual trust. Trust is the ground of mutuality; it is the means of real partnership.

What does this mean for Christian leaders? Christian leaders need to remember that they do not work *for* God but *with* God. God desires our partnership and when we fulfill our role well God is well pleased, for we have shown ourselves trustworthy. Divine trust also means that when Christian leaders fail, the repercussions are not that God is angry, but that God is disappointed. I care much more about not letting down or betraying the trust of a friend, spouse, parent, or coworker than I do about angering a boss. My motivation in my vocation is to show that God's faith in me has not been in vain. 2 Tim 2:15 says, "Do your best to present yourself to God as one approved by him, a worker who has no need to be ashamed, rightly explaining the word of truth" (NRSV). What higher approval is there than to have ones full and complete trust?

Wm. Curtis Holtzen, D.Th., is Professor of Philosophy and Theology at Hope International University. He holds graduate degrees in theology and philosophy from Unisa, Pepperdine University, and Loyola Marymount University. Holtzen is the author of The God Who Trusts: A Relational Theology of Divine Faith, Hope, and Love (IVP Academic). He has contributed chapters to books on The Simpsons, The Peanuts, as well as open and relational theology.

Creativity, Community, and Transformation: Treasures Discovered through Dreams

SHERI D. KLING

A practice of group dream work holds treasures for individuals; might it hold treasures for leaders and organizations as well?

*C*reativity. Community. Transformation.
These treasures can be discovered in doing dream work as a spiritual practice within groups. As I write this, individuals are gathering regularly all around the United States and beyond, sharing their nightly dreams and mining their content in community to find treasures within. *What kind of treasures do dreams reveal?*

Not long ago, in my role as director of a program center within an institution of higher learning, I hit a snag with one of my employees. Actions we had both taken while at a distance from each other had resulted in miscommunication and frustration. I was aware that we shared certain tender spots left by early life wounds, and I could see that our emailed communications were inadequate. I was left feeling hurt and angry, and I knew those feelings were mutually held.

The night before we next met, I had the following dream:

I am at my desk and circumstances at the University have required a public event to be held in my office within a matter of minutes. I am anxious about this, because my desktop is a mess, and I try to clean things up. The main presenter is a foreign leader from Europe. I realize at one point that someone has left a paper bag full of dog poop under the table where he is sitting! I feel like someone there has tried to sabotage me. I am very unnerved and call security to report the transgression, even though I don't know who is to blame. Despite my feeling vulnerable and embarrassed, the event proceeds and all ends well.

The next day, I began our meeting by sharing openly the anxious feelings the employee's actions had triggered in me and connected those feelings to my early life experience. I wondered if our similar histories might have left us prone to jumping to unwarranted conclusions and said that I'd like us to assume that we were both seeking for the best. In other words, I led with vulnerability rather than anger or frustration. The employee followed suit, and we had a very healthy conversation. Though I had not reflected on my dream prior to the meeting, I later wondered if it hadn't shown me unconsciously that being willing to be vulnerable and imperfect without blaming might lead to positive results.

In 2014, I conducted a pilot study in which I interviewed five Christians who use Jungian dream work in a spiritual way and who frequently attend the Haden Institute Summer Dream and Spirituality Conference in Hendersonville, North Carolina to find out more about their experiences. As I describe in my upcoming book, *A Process Spirituality: Christian and Transreligious Resources for Transformation*, five themes emerged:

All described experiences that we might call mystical, such as feeling God's presence;

All claimed dream work to be significant in their spiritual lives and dreams to be carriers of valuable meaning;

All saw dreams as divine communication that provides insights, guidance, support, and healing;

All believed dream work positively changed their experiences of self, often increasing self-acceptance and personal growth; and,

All believed dream work positively changed their relationships with God and others, allowing them to broaden their spiritual perspectives, deepen their friendships, and heal past hurts.

The rise of psychology has introduced many to the value of dreams. Carl Jung saw dreams as natural expressions of the unconscious psyche that carried purpose and higher wisdom. In the 1970s, psychiatrist Montague Ullman, Unitarian minister Jeremy Taylor, and others began teaching and writing about the power of dream sharing groups, leading to the formation of many such groups around the United States.

A method they pioneered called Group Projective Dream work is still used widely today. In this method, group members "project" their own associations onto the images a dreamer shares, saying, "if it were my dream…" or "in my dream…" In this way, boundaries are respected, and psychological safety is maintained while possible meanings of dream images are brought forth and connected to group members' waking life concerns. Dreams can even reflect job concerns, as researcher Robert Hoss has discovered in his work with people who have dreamt of new career opportunities in times of crisis.

While psychologically, dreams are primarily seen as a window to the individual psyche, many cultures understand that dreams sometimes speak to entire communities. This is true because dreams tap into our collective lives as well as our personal lives. For example, just prior to the outbreak of World War I, Jung had three dreams of rivers of blood and frozen wastelands blanketing Europe.

How does this relate to open and relational theology?
What can this possibly mean for people in leadership roles?

Here we must weave together the threads of leadership, open and relational theology, and dream work. Let's begin with three ideas at the heart of open and relational theology: 1) The present is always in process, change is inevitable; 2) Creative possibilities for new futures are always available; and 3) We are not independent agents but live in a web of relationship. Each of these ideas are important for organizations. And while most business leaders are acutely aware of the constancy of change, they too often place all the weight of generating visionary possibilities and creativity on only their own shoulders. Or they may include a core group of executives, seeing their broader employee base as peripheral to such creativity and vision.

First, in open and relational theology, life is not static but ever growing and ever perishing, always on the move. And since individual beings have agency and creativity of their own to express, we must always be ready to perceive—and *adapt to*—the sometimes-conflicting forces at work all around us.

Every leader today knows intimately the pace of change in our world. Whether it's the action of a local competitor or seismic shifts on the global stage, we must respond to changing conditions as they occur. Rather than relying on only one or a few leaders to read and understand the environment, what if that role could be democratically distributed to organized groups throughout an organization?

Second, open and relational theology describes a God that seeks for us to enjoy zest and to create value—things that *matter*—in the world. Less complex entities, like rocks and amoebas, may not have much creative license. They may only be able to repeat their immediate pasts. But God graces humans with a much greater capacity for creativity. God lures us to novel futures that are greater than what is currently being lived. We may not always perceive God's guidance—or we may choose to ignore it—but God always provides creative possibilities for zestier futures!

As leaders, we must know our people and know our environments. We must be able to get a sense of when things are shifting, where new opportunities lie, and in what direction we must go. If we make the mistake of only attuning to what is in our current world, we might risk merely repeating the dry and brittle past. That is why as leaders we must also attune to the voice of the future, the Wisdom of God.

What if leaders could embrace the idea that novel possibilities are not just forged within their own brains but are available from divine Wisdom in the flow of life? What if groups could form for tuning into that Wisdom, communicated through dreams and synchronicities?

Third, we exist in relationship. As individual persons, we are formed by, and live within, larger groups and ecosystems upon which we depend. We are not isolated individuals creating our lives out of whole cloth. We are inextricably bound to each other as members of a greater web of life. What we do, how we live, affects everyone in that web.

The isolated leader might create compelling strategic plans that can be imposed on the organization, but as Peter Drucker famously said, "Culture eats strategy for breakfast." In other words, a strategic plan will be dead-on-arrival if the group's spoken or unspoken values, beliefs, and practices do not support the vision that plan describes. Adapting to change requires shared vision, vulnerability, and willingness to fail—qualities that can only be nurtured in communities that trust each other. What if organizations could build true teams that have fostered the qualities required for creative response to changing conditions?

Through my questions above, I have asked us to imagine how groups that work together to read current conditions and generate insight into possibilities for creative response while fostering trust, intimacy, and camaraderie could be invaluable to organizations of all types. Dream groups are such groups. People meeting regularly over time to share dreams and their meanings develop greater intimacy and trust and become more attuned to each other and to what is happening in each other's lives. They seek each other's wellbeing. They are willing to be more vulnerable and generally more open to possibilities.

I dream of a time when organizations might hire Directors of Dreamwork or create Offices of Soul Development. Of course, such ventures carry the same potentials for abuse that abound in human endeavors. Confidentiality must be protected. Personal boundaries must be respected. Within a group framework, applying techniques like projective dream work can help ensure everyone's safety.

It may require a leap of faith, but the treasures of creativity, community, and transformation—and the leadership that arises from them—are there for us when we're ready to dive down deep.

Sheri D. Kling, PhD, is Associate Dean and Executive Director of the Beecken Center of the School of Theology at the University of the South. She is also a public theologian who interweaves spirituality, psychology, and theology for transformation and common flourishing, as well as a singer, songwriter, guitarist, and essayist.

47

The Living Earth as Teacher

JAY MCDANIEL

Listening to leadership from the more than human world helps us to find our place in a way that is more open, more relational, and more than we can ever imagine.

s a young boy, I had many mentors: loving parents, good friends, wise teachers. All taught me something about the open and relational way of living in the world.

But my teachers also included many mentors from the more than human world: hills and rivers, trees and stars. They didn't force me to appreciate or respect them, but they taught me things I couldn't really learn from people or from books. It seems wrong to think that leadership comes from people alone or even from God alone. We forget the other ninety-nine percent of creation. They, too, are our elders who can help lead us.

Lessons from a River

One of the most important of my early teachers was the Guadalupe River in the hill country of Texas. She is 87 miles long, flowing smoothly most of the time from Kerrville, Texas, through the Hill Country, into the Gulf of Mexico. My parents would take me to the Guadalupe River when I was a child, and I was mentored by her color, her smell, and by the way she could hold you if you swam in her. You could never clutch her in your hands, because she was made of liquid. But, like God, you could float in her and be supported.

Often, I would swim underneath her surface and look up at the world above, where my parents were having a picnic. Intuitively I realized that that the world beneath the surface is as real in its way as the world above. It is a world of beauty, of silence, of darkness, and dreams. It is different from the surface world, but complementary to it. Often when I look into the eyes of people and animals, I see this river. All people have rivers inside of them. All people have depth dimensions, even if they do not know it. Our hearts always contain more than our minds can ever understand.

I speak of the Guadalupe River as "she" rather than "it" because, after all, she is named after our Lady of Guadalupe, the mother of Jesus; and also because the word "it" can too easily suggest something lifeless and inert: a mere object for the mental imagination. When I am in the presence of the Guadalupe River, I'm not in the presence of something lifeless. I'm in the presence of something very much alive, but in a way different from animals and other human beings.

The Living Earth

Wherever there is vital energy of some sort, with a power of its own, there is something like life, as I understand life. Of course, the same situation applies to trees, soil, rocks, and maybe even the earth as a whole. James Lovelock puts it this way:

Earth may be alive: not as the ancients saw her—a sentient Goddess with a purpose and foresight—but alive like a tree. A tree that quietly persists, never moving except to sway in the wind, yet endlessly conversing with the sunlight and the soil. Using sunlight and water and nutrient minerals to grow and change. But all done so imperceptibly.

So, here's the point. Maybe the earth is alive in the earth's way, as are all the creatures who inhabit the earth in their ways. The whole idea that there are two kinds of material reality—living things and dead matter—is wrongheaded. It's all alive in some way.

Whitehead and Indigenous Traditions

In saying that nature is alive, I am aligning with indigenous traditions the world over: native American, native African, native Asian, native Australian. None of them drew a sharp line between human life and non-human life, as if only human beings were alive. We have so much to learn from them. I am also indebted to the organic philosophy of the late philosopher Alfred North Whitehead, who also proposed that nature is alive. Whitehead was influenced by contemporary physics and its idea that all things are energy and that energy carries within it a kind of spontaneity or creativity that is vibrant and enduring. Indeed, he believed that what we call feeling is a form of energy and that energy is a form of feeling, such that there is something like life or sentience all the way down into the depths of matter and all the way out into starry heavens above.

A God for All of Life

Whitehead also believed in God. He thought that God is alive, too, albeit in a way that is still different from animals and trees and rivers and the earth and the stars. For Whitehead, God is the very Mind of the universe, and the universe is the body of this Mind. We are small but included in a Life that is much larger than us and yet intimately present to each of us in a loving way. God is, in Whitehead's words, a "fellow sufferer who understands." God's deep nature, thinks Whitehead, is Love.

If there is wisdom in this idea, the question emerges: How can we—you and I—take our place in the larger community of life and how might we be faithful to this Love? What is our vocation, our calling?

The Calling

The very idea that we are "called" by this Love says something about divine leadership. Divine leadership is not a leadership of control, of domination, of brute force. Instead, it is a leadership of invitation, of beckoning, or allurement. It is loving leadership. This means, of course, that we humans need to "lead" as God leads as best we can. And it means that our leading must begin with a deep listening, as it does with God.

The questions suggest something about the content of God's calling. The calling of God to us, and in us, is not to live solely for ourselves, as if our happiness is all that really matters. And it is not to live solely for the sake of the happiness of other human beings, as if the other creatures and the earth itself are mere backdrop for a divine-human drama. The calling of God is that we recognize that we are part of a larger family of life and part of a larger adventure. We are part of a living universe, and our vocation, each in our way, is to play our role in its larger unfolding.

Ecological Civilization

For people like me, and the process tradition in which I stand, response to this calling takes the form of trying to help build and sustain communities of life on our small planet: communities that are good for people, for animals, and for the earth. The building blocks of these civilizations are local communities that are creative, compassionate, participatory, culturally and religiously diverse, humane to animals, good for the earth, and spiritually satisfying—with no one left behind.

This building needs to begin for us as it begins with God: that is, with Love. And we need to remember that Love is not simply about doing things for other people, animals, and the Earth; it is also about listening to their many voices, each of which have something to teach us: about silence, creativity, adventure, play, endurance, hope, vitality, imagination, intelligence, wisdom, beauty, diversity, ecstasy, struggle, cooperation and family. I stress family because, after all, we do belong to a larger family of life, and it is a tremendous mistake to say that we don't. It is time for us to place ourselves humbly in the presence of the larger family of life. Surely it is with this respect and care for the larger community of life that God is leading us, if only we will respond. If we can lead one another into this respect, if we can listen to leadership from the more than human world, I cannot help but think that, in our small way, we are finding our place in a way that is more open, and more relational, than we can ever quite imagine. Almost river-like.

Jay B. McDaniel, Ph.D., is a philosopher and theologian who specializes in Buddhism, Whiteheadian process philosophy and process theology, constructive theology, ecotheology, interfaith dialogue, and spirituality in an age of consumerism. His blog (www.openhorizons.org) aims "to offer ideas that might help people create multi-cultural, interfaith communities that are creative, compassionate, participatory, ecologically wise, and spiritually enjoyable." Jay serves as a consultant for the China Project of the Center for Process Studies in Claremont, California, and is a member of the advisory board of the Institute for Postmodern Development of China.

48

Leading by Listening

L MICHAELS

Leading out of respect for others is better than desire for power over them.

*L*eadership is not what I thought it was. Realistically, I should not be surprised. Few things ever turn out how we originally envision them.
Leadership is a bit tricky, though, especially in a cultural context where the loudest voices tend to be the ones with all the power. If I'm honest, I thought that was what leadership was about—power. It's not.

In what now feels like a former life, I was a business management major. I remember being enthralled with the idea that there are different kinds of power, and the kind that comes with a title is generally referred to as "legitimate" power. I can remember thinking to myself that *this* was the kind of power I needed, because as an Enneagram 1, INFJ, melancholy, choleric, empath, my voice is never going to be the loudest. I will not compete against anyone else for a platform. I really like to win, but I recognize that if the rules of the game require me to be someone I'm not, I can't. With this in mind, I had to find another way. I thought, perhaps, the way was one of captive audiences. There was something appealing to the idea that given legitimate power, others would *have to* listen. They would *have to* follow. However, there are major problems with this theory.

First, possessing a title is not synonymous with having the skills and experience to lead. I'd like to believe that people are chosen, hired, elected, etc. because of their abilities, but this simply is not always (or maybe even often) the case. I'd like to believe that when we step into adulthood we leave behind the injustices of middle school student council nomination popularity contest caliber, but I have seen enough real life examples of the old "it's not what you know, it's who you know" adage to admit this is not true. It's a doubled-edged sword of sorts, because not only does this kind of ascent to leadership put unqualified (often immoral, unjust, or even apathetic—see: did your sixth grade student council representative actually do anything, or did he or she just want to get out of class from time to time) people in positions of power, but it also silences the voices of those who would do a better job.

I used to think the worst part of this was the former. Ascribing leadership to those who are inept or corrupt carries dangerous connotations, to be sure. But in more recent days, I have decided the far more tragic side of this equation is the latter, because silencing robs not only individuals but whole communities (and even wider reaching, all of humanity) of important insight and the kind of compassionate leadership that can only come through the empathy fostered by life lived on the margins rather than in the center of privilege that offers unchecked power based on surface qualifications such as a charismatic personality or an attractive smile.

Second is the realization that leadership is relational, so there are few, if any, good reasons to follow someone simply because a title suggests one should. This can be difficult to unpack, especially for those who have grown up in environments that encourage respect for hierarchal authority and high-ranking offices. The question too often becomes: it is right to respect those who are not respectable because of the positions they hold? I struggle to understand why the answer given to this question is quite frequently a resounding yes, but even more than that, I think it's the wrong question. It puts the burden on those who are treated unfairly. How might things change if, instead, we asked; if leadership is relational, then shouldn't respect be reciprocal?

I am not certain it is possible to lead without caring for the people who are following. In fact, I'm pretty sure it is not. Indisputably, one with legitimate power can make decisions and enforce them, but that can hardly be called leadership, even if people have to acquiesce. Real leadership requires followers who use their own agency to choose to follow. And so, as is so often the case for those who hope to make good decisions that lead to a better world, I began to ask what I might do to be a loved leader, as opposed to a legitimate one. What might I do to inspire others to follow as opposed to further stripping them of that choice in a mad dash to the top of some invisible ladder on which we are expected to step on fingers and kick people in the face instead of turning around to offer them a hand up?

The answer was hard to stomach, again, for myriad reasons. I have come to the realization that the most subversive way a person can lead is to listen to the narratives of those who do *not* possess "legitimate" power. This used to be a frustrating proposal to me, because I have often felt that *merely* listening is not enough. I still contend that this can be a problem, but my experience with listening to others has led me to believe that this is, exactly, what people ask for when presented with the opportunity to ask for what they want or need.

I thought leadership would look more practical. I've never been a fan of pragmatism, but, to be honest, I thought leadership would be more pragmatic. I have looked into the faces of people who are hungry, struggling, addicted, and marginalized because of their very identity, and I have wished that they would ask me to do something that has its roots in temporality or to give them something attached to a price tag, but these are rarely ever the requests of those who are looking for a leader. Instead, they want my time. They want to know that someone believes their stories and actually thinks their experiences matter. Genuine leaders can only lead by first being present to the realities that may or may not be their own.

Only after listening intently for the sake of understanding does it become appropriate for leaders to revisit the narratives for the sake of response, and the right response will never be one that further elevates the leader. There is a humility in leadership that requires those who lead to do so precisely for the sake of others. This is not about being the greatest advocate or the most admired. In fact, those who lead from such a position are often quite superficial when their work is examined. There is a certain degree of irony to this, and it can be exceptionally painful as those who lead poorly draw all of the attention to their enigmatic selves. I have no doubt that personalities such as these can secure a blind following, and history has proven this repeatedly, but the results are usually catastrophic. At its best, this kind of glory hoarding leadership diminishes the people and narratives that deserve a place at the problem solving tables. At its worst, these leaders take whole cultures and societies down roads that lead to assimilation, loss of identity, or even wide scale genocide. It may sound like a stretch until we consider the many times this has actually happened.

And so I think real leadership that respects the humanity of others and makes a positive difference in the world is, perhaps, a bit less sexy than people often hope. It is not denoted by popularity or paparazzi or polls. It might not even be identifiable by large scale movements or a call for change. Instead, it is sitting in the margins with one person, listening to their story, and then finding a way forward, together. It is doing this over and over again, even when no one else notices. It is cheering for everyone instead of competing for the spotlight. We lead by listening, and this makes an impact more like ripples in the water than like waves. It's not flashy, but it endures.

L Michaels is a follower of Jesus, Ph.D. student and teaching fellow at Boston University, author, blogger, editor, and mom to five incredible human beings. She has a B.S.M. from Indiana Wesleyan University and an M.A. and M.Div. (both in theology/spiritual formation) from Northwest Nazarene University. L writes about theology, the sacraments, and ministry to the least of these at Flip Flops, Glitter, and Theology (.com). In her spare time, L likes to binge watch Netflix and Hulu and drink voluminous amounts of Peppermint Bark Mocha (preferably at local coffee shops or by the ocean).

49

Open and Relational Leadership Is Like Coaching a Football Team

JAMES BRADLEY MILLER

Effective leadership conforms to an open, relational, and evolving creation aimed toward love.

*I*t is a part of modern physics lore that Einstein declared, "God does not play dice!" to which Bohr is said to have retorted, "Albert, don't tell God what to do." Of course, neither man was a theologian nor was their debate a theological one. They were arguing about the indeterminacy that seemed integral to quantum theory. As it turned out, Bohr was apparently on the correct side of the argument. Due to the probabilistic character of quantum theory, the cosmos appears to be stochastic, meaning the present is underdetermined by the past.

This does not mean that the universe is chaotic in the common sense of that term. It does not mean that there are not fixed elements in the universe. The simplest example of this is the true die. The true die has six sides labeled with six different numbers. On any throw of the die, one of those numbers will be revealed. All of that is fixed. But, with a true die, one cannot declare with certainty beforehand what number will come up. In principle, there is a one-sixth chance that a particular number will be revealed on each throw.

This probabilistic understanding of the universe suggests an existentialist rather than an essentialist understanding of the cosmos. The universe does not become what it is, it is what it becomes. In addition, it suggests that the universe is not something that has a history, it is its history. The universe is constituted of its relationships rather than an essential thing that has relationships. And those relationships are dynamic. In more Aristotelian terms, the universe's essence is its accidents. So, theologically, the creation is ontologically open and relational.

As the title of this article proposes, coaching football is both an example of and a metaphor for leadership that is fit for an open and relational creation. A football game includes both fixed and probabilistic elements. The size of the field, the formal rules of the game including the number of players on the field at a time, and the plays designed by the coaching staff and practiced repeatedly by the players are fixed elements. But the probabilistic elements are even more numerous.

First, the weather. It can vary in terms of temperature and precipitation and can vary in real time during game play. Then, the defense or offense may not line up exactly as anticipated in the play design, requiring reciprocal adjustments. There are also fumbles and interceptions and broken plays, not all of which cannot be known ahead of time. The rules of the game may be fixed but their application by the officials on the field are not deterministic but often require judgments, which are probabilistic. The odds makers in Las Vegas may have sufficient probabilistic insight such that they can set odds so that they are able to make money from the gambling public. But even they cannot fully protect themselves from outlier outcomes.

If the creation itself is open and relational, what are the fitting elements of leadership? First, it is foundational to understand that the leader plus those being led form a team—an organic or coherent union—not simply an aggregation of otherwise isolated embodied skills. However, such relational, coherent order is not the opposite of indeterminacy. Rather it is the condition of order by virtue of which any outcome affects all. For example, the performance of team members on the field affects not only each individual player's status and that of the team as a whole but also the status of the coach on the sidelines.

Second, it is important to understand that goals in such a probabilistic cosmos are primarily qualitative and not specifically formal. A qualitative goal may be singular but it can be achieved through a variety of forms. This means at least that goals exist as an array of possible outcomes. These outcomes themselves are a part of a more comprehensive array of possible events, some of which will be antithetical to the desired goal. As arrays, the outcomes rarely have equal probabilities, unlike the throw of a true die. The qualitative outcome of a football game is to score more points than the opponent. But that outcome can be large, small, or even nonexistent in the case of a tie. The particular point spread in any case is highly probabilistic.

In preparation for a team effort, the coach needs to assess as best as possible the probabilities of potential outcomes. The strategy of the game plan will depend on that assessment. Ironically, in a particular set of game circumstances, the actions required to achieve the desired goal may not have the highest probability. In addition—even given an initial game plan—moment by moment assessment of probabilities, play to play or for the on-field team members even during a play, are required.

Third, as a consequence of the inherent uncertainty of each play—as well as the game as a whole—a relatively conservative retention of as many options as possible is prudent. A coach who sticks assiduously to a pre-established game plan is virtually certain to lead to a loss. Likewise, a coach that limits his offense only to running or passing plays is also likely to lead to a loss. Burning bridges reduces opportunity. Conservative retention of options provides the best insurance for the ability to respond effectively to changing circumstances.

Fourth, trust is an essential element of open and relational leadership. Trust in a game of football or most human social endeavors has many dimensions. For the game of football there is trust between the coach and the on- field team as a group, between the coach and on-field team leaders (offensive and defensive), between the on-field team leaders and other on-field team members, and amongst the whole panoply of on- and off-field team members.

The on-field team trusts that the coach has developed a potentially winning game plan and the coach trusts that the rest of the team are committed to the game plan. In real time, the on-field leaders trust that the coach, who has an overview of the game, can provide options that are not obvious at field level and the coach trusts that the on-field leaders will act on the options identified. The on-field leaders trust that the other on-field team members will act on their offensive or defensive calls and the various on-field team members trust that their leaders are conveying reliable options from "on high." On every play, each team member trusts that his fellow members will fulfill their assignments.

Lastly, a coach must be open to surprise. Not all surprises are good. In football, an on-field injury is a surprise that can have a negative effect for not only the particular player or game but also possibly for a whole season. A football coach or any other leader has to consider such negative surprises. However, the vast majority of surprises are the inevitable consequence of living in a probabilistic cosmos about which we have limited understanding. Not only that, it is a universe that is still being created. Giving voice to God's creative declaration Isaiah wrote, "Do not remember the former things, or consider the things of old. I am about to do a new thing; now it springs forth, do you not perceive it?" (Isaiah 43:18-19).

In an open, relational, and only partially understood universe being created, openness to surprise is an essential leadership quality. Surprise is the mother of improvisation, whether for a coach calling plays in real time or an on-field player reacting to emergent circumstances.

All analogies have their limitations. A football game is not a scientific investigation, a technological project or a legislative effort. Yet all these human endeavors involve teamwork, a qualitative outcome, conservation of options, trust among participants, as well as innovation. Effective leadership requires conforming to an open and relational, evolving creation.

Theologically, the qualitative goal of the creation is the incarnation of the power of love through the calling Word of God, who is love. And what is the character of that power? The Apostle Paul described it in these words, "Love is patient; love is kind; love is not envious or boastful or arrogant or rude. It does not insist on its own way; it is not irritable or resentful; it does not rejoice in wrongdoing, but rejoices in the truth. It bears all things, believes all things, hopes all things, endures all things. Love never ends." (I Corinthians 13:4-8a)

In a 1936 the Jesuit paleoanthropologist, Pierre Teilhard de Chardin, captured the goal of empowering love when he wrote, "Someday, after mastering the winds, the waves, the tides and gravity, we shall harness for God the energies of love, and then, for a second time in the history of the world, man will have discovered fire" (*Toward the Future*).

I agree!

James Bradley Miller is a retired teaching elder of the Presbyterian Church (USA). He is a co-founder of the Presbyterian Association on Science, Technology and the Christian Faith. Currently, he serves as co-chair of the Broader Social Impacts Committee of the Human Origins Program of the Smithsonian Institution's National Museum of Natural History. He is the author of Where Did I Come From? A Guide for Parents in Science, Evolution, Human Origins and the Christian Faith (2018).

Grace-fully Engaging Young Adults

ANITA MONRO

A college seeks to nurture young adults in values-based, community-focussed, strengths-based, boundary-setting, permission-giving and capacity-building education.

Young adults (16-25 years) are in transition. They're on the move—from high school to college or university, study to work, adolescence to adulthood. Some of them take gap years to travel. Many of them move away from home and family as they go. These moves, though often physical ones from place to place and institution to institution, are also deeply personal. Young adults are becoming their adult selves. It's a time of flux!

Risk-taking is a key element of this transition. Taking opportunities, rising to challenges and discovering limits are all part of this period of incredible growth and development. Uncertainty, possibility and potential open young adults up to vulnerability. It's a hazardous time—physically, mentally, emotionally and socially.

Young adults are the core client group for student accommodation providers. Grace College is such a provider. Our site is on the St. Lucia Campus of The University of Queensland (UQ) in Brisbane, Australia. Our main purpose is "to provide proper accommodation…for women students of the University" (Constitution Para. 3). We are a not-for-profit, for-purpose organization.

We are also a church-related agency. Two churches (The Uniting Church in Australia—Queensland Synod and The Presbyterian Church in Queensland) appoint members of the College Council; two of our objects guide us to "the presentation of…the Christian faith" and encouraging "students to relate their academic disciplines to Christianity and grow in the Christian faith" (Constitution Para. 3).

Australia is a secular, multi-cultural democracy. Our public universities, such as UQ, are secular institutions. They also welcome students from all over the world. The client group of Grace College is multi-cultural, multi-faith, multi-ethnic, and immersed in a secular education context. Our residential community is a microcosm of our context (with the exception that we accept women only).

How can and do we fulfil our objects for this diverse community of young adults in transition? The framework for our operations is a nuanced exercise in public theology. The Christian faith is the foundational narrative for a College story shared by people of many faiths and none, many cultures and backgrounds, and now several generations of alumni.

Our Story

Our College story arises from our motto: "My grace is sufficient" (2 Cor. 12:9). We tell the story of an early Christian worker with an unidentified vulnerability who found comfort in the awareness of the support of a gracious God. We talk about understanding that we are all part of "something bigger" than ourselves, and the strength such awareness can give. We do not expect that that "something bigger" will be God, or at least the Christian God, for every member of our community. For most in the community, we hope that that "something bigger" will at least be the community that they find at Grace College. We work hard to foster such an experience of community.

Our Values

Our College story informs our values. We hold three core values—*community, collegiality* and *care*. Seven characteristics describe how our behaviours embody our living out of those values. These behaviours will make our values *graphic*. We are and will be:

    Generous to others;
    Reconciling in our relationships;
    Aware of what is happening around us;
    Protective of what is important;
    Healthy in our behaviours;
    Inclusive in our community; and
    Committed to living out our values.

OPEN AND RELATIONAL LEADERSHIP

Our Approach

Our story and our values inform our overall approach to that work of personal and community development. Six strategic emphases underpin our approach. Our policies and procedures are:

    values-based;
    community-focussed;
    strengths-based;
    boundary-setting;
    permission-giving; and
    capacity-building.

Our Community

The community of Grace College is firstly the community of young adults that find themselves living with us at any one point in time. That's not where our community ends, however.

This community is part of bigger communities. Our second core value, *collegiality*, points to this broader context. In our immediate context, we share UQ's St Lucia Campus with nine other college communities. The ten colleges together share a whole social, cultural, sporting and community service life.

The College would, of course, not exist without the university and all its infrastructure, including its academic, professional and service communities. The residential community exists in this larger community.

With our student leaders, we also emphasize the corporate community context—the role of College staff, the College Council and a myriad of other support organizations that surround the young adult residential community. Government and regulators even get a mention as we ask our leaders to envisage the interdependent nature of what we are doing.

Many members of the residential community make friends within the community who will travel with them on other significant parts of their life journeys. It might just be the transition to a share-house or a significant career recommendation as the next step on the adult road; or perhaps it will be a lifetime journey through relationships, family, and career with all their ups and downs.

Our alumni testify to the importance of being caught up in that "something bigger" community that supports you through the vulnerable times. If you find one Grace College alumni, you generally find a group of eight or ten friends. Those alumni are part of our broader community too.

Our Strengths

This focus on a "something bigger" community is also a focus on strengths—the abilities that support you through those vulnerable times. We don't forget the unspoken end to our motto quote: "My grace is sufficient [for power is made perfect in weakness]" (2 Cor. 12:9). We celebrate the things that sustain us even in the difficult times; and we recognise that some of those difficult times will be when we let each other down. The bigger picture that sustains us calls us beyond our weaknesses and failures; and offers us the ability to pick ourselves up, start again and keep going. That's one of the reasons why the "reconciling" behavioral characteristic is there: the "something bigger" that sustains us has to be able to help us through our vulnerabilities; and, of course, the story of reconciliation is at the heart of the Christian gospel as the sustaining power for the people of God.

Our Boundaries & Permissions for Building Capacity

Values and strengths that sustain us through vulnerabilities set up limits. Whether it's how we need to risk-manage events to ensure that everyone is safe as well as having a good time, or being mindful of community rules that help to provide a comfortable environment for everyone, the value of boundaries is found in the values of the community and particularly of our "care" for ourselves, one another and the environment. Our boundaries are set from our core—our values.

Boundaries are also permission-giving. They scope out the playing field and prescribe the means for addressing transgressions in a way that brings people back into the game rather than excluding them from it.

Permissions within clearly defined boundaries help to build ability for negotiating fluctuating terrain. This capacity-building is at the heart of the vocation of the College. Grace College is "a safe, inclusive, nurturing home, built on Christian foundations, supporting holistic growth and empowerment for female tertiary students, enriching their paths to academic success and their lives as contributors to the global community" (Vocation Statement). This "safe, inclusive nurturing home" is not "built on Christian foundations" for its own sake, but for the sake of the young adults it serves and the world to which they contribute.

The Christian Formation of Grace College

What we do is a kind of Christian formation although, for many Christians, it would appear to be quite humanist. It is an approach to open and relational leadership that is willing to empty itself of much of the tradition to share the effects of that tradition with people who might otherwise reject its potential.

In this creative theological endeavour for a group of people in transition, we walk a fine-line between scaffolding young people as many of them have been scaffolded in their childhoods and offering the boundarilessness that some of them imagine is the independence of adulthood. Our work is about their formation for the interdependent reality of responsible adulthood. The Christian tradition underpins that work.

Do we always get it right? Not a chance! But do we have a story that will help us to get up, start again and keep going? Absolutely! And that story is the story of a gracious God who sustains us through all our vulnerabilities whether we mention God's name or not.

Anita Monro is Principal of Grace College, a student residence for women at The University of Queensland in Brisbane, Australia. She is an ordained minister of The Uniting Church in Australia. Her doctoral thesis, published as Resurrecting Erotic Transgression (Equinox 2006) proposes a feminist theological methodology that encompasses multiplicity, diversity and ambiguity in hermeneutics, theology and community development. For more information on the Grace College approach, please visit www.grace.uq.edu.au

51

The Uncontrolling Track Coach

CRAIG MORTON

What does it mean to coach athletes from a loving and uncontrolling perspective?

Describing my faith, sharing about my beliefs in Jesus, talking openly about God and prayer are not available to me as a coach in the public-school system or as a part of track club. Certain topics are off-limits. There are boundaries that I respect. And these boundaries entice me to demonstrate my faith rather than talk about it. Issues of liberating love, refraining from control, and trust in the process are pillars in coaching that are supported by faith.

When it comes to athletic performance, there's a certain lack of freedom in basic tasks. There are only so many ways to breathe. Only so many ways to control the movement of the shoulder, of a footstep. Gravity has a knack for being regular which compounds to make routine movements not only predictable, but also limited.

As a track coach, I work with sprinters and hurdlers. There is a fine line between telling an athlete what to do, and helping an athlete discover what it is that they are doing, and having the potential to do. Perhaps it is the sport of track and field. There are no plays drawn up in track and field: no wing formations, cover-two defense, or triple-option. Our strategy is to run fast, throw far, and jump far and high.

Many years ago, we track nerds watched as Michael Johnson ran the 400-meter sprint. Incorrectly! He also ran the 200-meter sprint incorrectly. His back was too erect, there was too little of a forward lean. His arms pounded downward as if he was beating the air like a drum. And his legs, because of his lack of forward lean, looked like he was marching fast, more than running. Thus, his steps were too short and it took him more steps to cover the same amount of track compared to his competitors. His form was weird. He did it all wrong.

Johnson continued to run incorrectly, weird, and wrong. He ran wrong all the way through world records and multiple Olympic gold medals and world championships.

When we work with athletes—elite as well as beginners—awareness of the athlete is almost more important than the technique I can communicate to the athlete. In a day, I will ask a runner ten to fifteen times, "how'd that feel?" and "what did you learn or notice?" There's very little I can do to control the athlete. Coaching is an exercise in limited influence.

Being aware of your body in motion through space is not so much a technique, as it is a way of being. One doesn't do awareness, as much as one becomes aware. Be aware. That is something that I cannot control.

Some parents of athletes, as well as some coaches, try to live through the successes of their athletes. I'm not referring to the experience of sharing their experiences, both joyful celebrations and grievous defeats. Empathy with and living through our athletes are two vastly different things. Parents and coaches may seek their own satisfaction, and in so doing, exercise control over the athlete to meet their own longings, not the athlete's. This is a spiritual and existential issue. The experience of kenosis, of letting go of control (which is elusive at best) allows freedom to the other. Though as a coach I have authority granted me, I cannot use it to control the athlete to meet my expectations.

Opening Up Possibility to the Athlete

More than once I've had hurdlers come and struggle to find the way to get accurate steps in the rhythm to cross over the hurdle without hurting themselves. Some simply require more work, awareness, and development. But others are not hurdlers. Yet, for some reason they may want to hurdle. But their body isn't responding to the techniques necessary to accomplish the task. Then, we coaches work with those kinds of athletes and move them from one track-and-field event to another until that athlete finds the place where they fit and where it works.

Limitations are discovered. As coaches, we guide in the discovery. Some athletes simply want to have fun or develop some type of mastery; winning and losing are not the point. They want to control their emotions, develop personal goals, experience milestones. But when working with elite athletes who are trying to perfect minute movements for high-level competition, then we provide more prompts, tips, and direct coaching. Our job as coaches is to help an athlete become aware of what it is that their body wants to do regardless of what they think they want to do.

The Uncontrolling Love of Coaching

Speaking about coaching track and field is not just some analogy about prayer or about theology. This is about the struggles we go through to find where we belong. Whether it is on the track as an athlete, or in business, academics, and in relationships. When we come to something that feels like a barrier, something that feels like it's keeping us from doing what we want to do, we may ask God to step in to intervene to do something. And God does not always answer those prayers. The infinite number of things that God would have to control may go far beyond God's self-limiting love.

We may be suffering from an illness, or an infirmity, or something about us that just doesn't work and we can do all the work we think possible to make ourselves better. But if you are 6'4" and weigh 320 pounds, you're not going to be a good 800-meter runner and you can pray as much as you want and it probably still not going to happen. Gravity, the laws of thermodynamics constrain. You might be 5' 2" and an excellent sprinter but you're still not likely to get yourself high enough off the ground to become a championship high jumper. Or, as Thomas Jay Oord states it, "God also necessarily upholds the regularities of the universe because those regularities derive from God's eternal nature of love" (*The Uncontrolling Love of God: An Open and Relational Account of Providence*). Gravity, and its sibling, entropy, are the only real competitors in track and field.

While much of Oord's challenge is to understand genuine evil in light of a loving God, "genuine evil" can also be lowered to things of genuine disappointment, existential challenges, losses and personal experiences that compete with our self-understanding. It is not a "genuine evil" that my athlete cannot accomplish a specific race. Also, I will not ask God to alter the "regularities of the universe" to allow this runner to excel. To teach this to an athlete and to attest to a loving God is hard for many to grasp.

Stoicism, Athletes, and Love

Reading the Stoic philosophers, like Marcus Aurelius, Epictetus, Seneca, and others, gives me a helpful posture in the face of the uncontrolling God. God cannot do some things. As a result, I must adapt. Aurelius (*Meditations*) asserts that certain physics cannot be altered. He attributes this to "providence", or simply as we would say, "it's just the way of things." But what is crucial, and what Aurelius does possess, is the possibility of a virtuous response, as opposed to responding with vice.

There may be so many things that I want God to do or do differently, but the limitations that are part of God's very nature are not going to be overturned simply because I want to go faster or jump higher. My role as a coach is to help athletes choose between "virtue or vice." My job is to help athletes understand and to be aware both of what they can do and of what exists for them as a real opportunity. Having uncontrolling love for an athlete puts me in a position to honor and respect the athlete much more than the event or my expectations for her or him. What is best for my athlete as a person?

Oord writes, "A God of everlasting love is always with us, already loving us. But for love to win—in each moment and in the future—we must collaborate. The God of uncontrolling love needs cooperation for love to flourish (*God Can't: How to Believe in God and Love after Tragedy, Abuse, and Other Evils*)." As a coach, my job is to care for the athletes as human beings. To view them as just tools for scoring points in a meet is not loving. To limit their value to a time on a watch, is not loving. But quietly partnering with God and with the athlete honors the athlete.

Prayer doesn't always happen on the track with a bowed head and closed eyes. But there are mantras. Breath prayers. As a coach, I lead the "prayer." Sometimes it is only gratitude. Often, it is the calm question, "how did that feel?" or, "what did you learn?" And sometimes it is just silent compassion when facing disappointment.

The Uncontrolling God wants me to learn to live with wisdom and the drive of the Holy Spirit in this universe. There are disappointments and limitations. These become hurdles to overcome. Not barriers to be removed or sidestepped. Paraphrasing Oord's quoting of Wolterstorff in *The Uncontrolling Love of God*, God is everlastingly present, in our "time-strand." More powerful than an expectation of God becoming present in a specific longed-for outcome is the assurance that the loving God is present now.

Craig Morton, M.Div, Ed.D, is a multi-vocational pastor in Meridian, Idaho. Craig co-pastors a Mennonite congregation, provides church consulting, is a college professor, blogs on Patheos as "RDC Reverend – Doctor – Coach", and coaches for Meridian High School Track and Field and Team Idaho Track and Field Club. Craig co-pastors with his wife, Karla. Together, they have four adult children, and two grandsons.

52

True Leaders are Replaced

SETH PRICE

Many words leadership discussions fail identify this important truth: true leaders should be replaced.

Our world quite simply is bound in a never-ending swirl of leadership and the implications of it. The dance between leader, regime, servant, peasant, follower, subservient, growth, and loss is all wrapped up in the word "leader". The concepts of faith and humility also intersect the definition—or at least one worth caring about—of the term; but why?

I will not define what a bad leader is and I will not say why I believe many end up failing. Why? *That* is a surprisingly simple answer. We need only turn on the television to realize why. Humanity is inherently bound to the emotional attachments to leaders. I believe we innately understand when we sit under the presence of a leader that is not worthy of that role.

What then is the purpose of leadership? What is a leader worth sitting under, worth supporting, and worth listening to? Let us start with that first point: "sitting under".

When I think of sitting under someone so many emotions and stories come flooding back into my mind's eye; many of them are quite beautiful but many are also tinged with fear. Why fear? The answer to that lies in a bit of my own story of leadership.

I came into my current profession just by a lucky draw, a random chance interaction. I am a banker at a bank you may have heard of and was recruited into banking by simply having a conversation with a person who recognized something in me I did not recognize in myself. I remember asking him, "Why did you choose me? I have no experience and little to offer?" His response, "you believe in yourself and because of that you bring others to an ease and this is needed as people deal with their finances; your confidence is needed here."

This was foreign to me, I'm not certain I was confident, yet something I did seemed to manifest in confidence to him. With fear, I had to ask myself, new job or old job? Go with what I know or move to something new? I chose to push into the fear and begin a new career. However, I floundered at this place at first. I was listless. To compound the situation, my manager at the time seemed unclear why she was there and so as an extension of that, I had no clarity in my role. The confidence I brought with me from the prior interaction quickly evaporated. Eventually, that leader left and a new one was installed.

I can remember distinctly the confidence this new leader instilled in his introduction to the team. Giving clear direction of "here is why I am here," he more importantly tasked each of us with that very valuable question, "why are *you* here?" He waited, as we each took a turn attempting to answer this loaded question; it seemed to take forever as we all languished. But in that moment *we*, all of us, found our purpose for being part of a team, any team, THAT team. And it showed in performance; we quickly rose in our jobs and all of us are to this day still in the field. Many have been promoted beyond that small branch and have gone on to realize further dreams. So why did his leadership make such a difference?

He taught us how to find a voice and once found, he didn't try to change it. More than that, he reminded us of it when we needed it the most. What does this mean? Allow me to be more vulnerable; my development as a leader taught me to focus on my team around me, to hear what they're not saying, to see what they don't want me to see. Pride is a dragon we all need to slay, and that dragon keeps us from asking others for help. Partnered with attention and intention, as a leader, I have helped others identify what brings out the best in them—just as I was shown what the best of me is. Will I lose some of my team? Absolutely. In helping them find their voice and strength, they move on to better opportunities. A good leader must be willing to let go.

Here is the crux of the matter of leadership. A good leader learns to let go of power and it is in so doing they elevate the team, community, workplace, etc., around them. I know this sounds like the exact opposite of what you have been led to believe and the exact opposite of the culture that we all grew up in, or at least I grew up in. What does a leader do then upon letting go of tyrannical power? What does the job become? The answer: service. As a leader, your service, humility, and acceptance will elevate others around you to heights they never knew could be reached. They will then become good leaders who teach those under them and you then witness this beautiful manifestation of legacy.

Just as Jesus modeled for us, true power is gained and true leadership is displayed not through suffering, but through service. This means we get our hands dirty, we do all the jobs—especially the ones we feel are below us—modeling all the while what success looks like. Think of that: wash feet, model prayer, display healthy arguments, but most importantly, cede power to those that you are doing life with. There will come a day that you must step aside; your work has reached its climax and the test of a successful leader is this: how have you served those you lead in a way that allows them to surpass you?

The truth is there will be days when the confidence someone recognized in your own life wanes. You might feel lost. You might even feel like your "true North" in God is lost. You may feel like all that was once familiar is suddenly unrecognizable. When that day comes, remember this: when we run through the forest of faith, past the undergrowth that may or may not have burned long ago, when we meet not two but 802 forks in the road, when we wonder which way leads us back to ourselves, back to God, when we are so tired of running... just choose one.

When we are searching for that sweet spot of identity in God, there is no map; someone may try to convince you otherwise, but it's a half-truth. The map they are referring to was "their map" with a different legend and a different starting point. Toss the map, open your heart and mind and your inner compass will hear the call of the Divine. You are right where you're supposed to be. You are here. This intersection with Spirit is only the beginning of your path to great leadership.

Seth Price is the host of the Can I Say This at Church podcast. He lives with his family in Central Virginia and during the day earns a living by working at a bank. Find Seth and the podcast at canisaythisatchurch.com

Toward Developing and Leading Open and Relational Organizations

JOSHUA D. REICHARD

Open and relational theology can develop open organizational cultures, empower holistic teams, and foster mutually transformative growth.

In this essay, I will share some of my own insights in my journey toward becoming an open and relational leader and developing more open and relational organizations, including some practical tools I've appropriated along the way. In prevailing leadership theories, the leader tends to be subject and the followers tend to be the objects. Open and relational theology can help diffuse the subject-object distinctions to develop open organizational cultures, empower relational teams, and foster mutually transformative organizational and professional growth.

Developing Open Organizational Cultures

Open and relational theology helps to inform open organizational cultures. In open and relational *parlance*, coercion and persuasion are two options for conceptualizing the metaphysical nature of power. If leaders value coercive power, they are more likely to develop organizational structures in terms of coercion; but if leaders value persuasive power in terms of love, they may be more inclined to develop organizations with gentler persuasion in mind.

Our conception of power is reflected in the way we lead and the way our organizations are designed. Coercion involves both the coercer and the coerced: that is, an agent that coerces another agent, and an agent that is coerced by another agent. Coercion diminishes the target agent's freedom and responsibility, a violation that most would argue—at least in practical terms—is a moral violation. Coercion is reflected in many traditional aspects of organizational structure and leadership practice.

Preoccupation with the hierarchical and coercive dimensions of leadership tends to foster a "closed" organizational culture. Organizational charts, tight supervision, productivity measures, and rigid goals prevail. On the other hand, "open" organizational culture will be designed around mutually transformative relationships, persuasive interaction, and human flourishing. Open organizational cultures are less driven by leaders who exercise coercive power and depend more on gentle persuasion between members of a cooperative team.

Open organizational cultures have organizational structures built around strong and weak persuasion. Performance evaluations will be less oppressive and more self-directed. Productivity will be measured in more holistic ways. Reporting structures will be looser and more oriented toward team than hierarchy. Needless to say, open and relational leaders will strive toward such open and relational ideals.

I have had the opportunity to experiment with some of these ideas in practical ways. Engaging in 360-degree leadership evaluations (allowing followers to anonymously evaluate their leaders), providing a range of choices rather than directives, and de-prioritizing territorialism are some of the strategies I have employed in my own quest toward developing and leading open organizational cultures.

Empowering Relational Teams

In some of the most innovative technology companies, organizational structure is comprised of complex but sophisticated teams. Successful companies empower work groups over traditional hierarchical structures. Such teams are relationally rich: built around loose power differentials, open communication, mutuality, and opportunities for self and mutual actualization through cooperation. Such teams are empowered to solve complex problems together, collaborate, and cooperate across formerly siloed industrial structures. Stating goals, evaluating goals, and measuring goals are not enough; open and relational leaders must gentle persuade others toward the best possible outcomes for one another, themselves, the organization, and the world.

I have tried both formal structures, such as committees with careful minutes driven by parliamentary procedure, and more informal team-based conversational problem solving. Although I still believe there is a place for some formal structures, team-orientation allows people opportunities to contribute to problem solving in ways they might otherwise be reluctant to engage. While they might not be willing to make or second a formal motion, they might be willing to brainstorm possible solutions if they feel like they are part of a team. Power is expressed through relationships rather than organizational charts. When teams are empowered and develop creative solutions to problems, leaders engage in a kind of *kenosis*: self-giving, others-empowering love.

Open and relational leaders can nurture teams to develop innovative means by which teams can accomplish goals through adaptation and change. Creativity is prioritized over productivity. Envisioning teams in this way provides unique opportunities for shared power over consolidated power, gentle influence over strict coercion, and cooperation over commandeering. In the relational exchange of teams, the "many become one and are increased by one" and more often than not, creative solutions are more than the sum of their parts.

Practically, I have used tools such as the RAPID decision-making matrix to empower team members to make decisions and respect the decisions of others. RAPID comprises designated Recommenders, Approvers, Performers, Inputters, and Deciders for every major decision which must be made in an organization. I have found people appreciate such a matrix because they can respect the roles of their teammates, engage in mutual decision-making, and assume personal responsibility without becoming siloed or territorial. I have found this to be a useful tool for empowering relational teams.

Mutually Transforming Organizational and Professional Growth

Ultimately, open and relational leaders must foster mutual transformation between leaders and followers. Mutual transformation occurs through relational openness, transparency, trust, and vulnerability. Subject-object distinctions between leaders and followers dissolve and leaders change with followers; followers change leaders, leaders change followers and the organization changes as a result. In my experience, engaging in such mutual transformation is not easy; prevailing assumptions about what constitutes strong versus weak leaders are powerful specters which continue to haunt my own journey. However, the most extraordinary moments in my own leadership experience have occurred when I was the most vulnerable.

Mutual transformation requires vulnerability. To be vulnerable is to willingly embrace the pain of love and in so doing, allow that pain to transform both the lover and the loved. Loving from a position of relationality demands strength, for loving is often painful. Such vulnerability reflects humanity's relationship with God and human beings' relationships with one another. Oord calls this kind of deep empathetic love "mutuality" and Hartshorne called it "life sharing."

Open and relational leaders must be willing to submit to change and be willing to engage in helping to change others. In this form of leadership, there is an openness which not only models personal transformation but lives it; not for the sake of the leader as subject changing the followers as objects, but for the sake of mutual transformation. Such openness creates the environment by which trust, synergy, and empathy can be experienced for all members of teams.

I have tried to do this using a three-column chart called "Plus-Delta-Rx." In team meetings, we reflect and assess together: what went well ("plus"), what needs to change ("delta"), and what is the prescription for changing it ("Rx")? Such open discussion allows each team member, including the leader, to embrace change in a constructive way. Together, mutual transformation occurs personally and organizationally.

Conclusion

Open and relational theology can help develop open organizational cultures, empower relational teams, and foster mutually transformative organizational and professional growth. If those of us who embrace open and relational theology can model new forms of leadership in our organizations (business, churches, community agencies, etc.) we can perhaps help forge a new range of leadership theories. Deeply grounded in authentic relationships, open and relational leadership is the greatest and most potent power of all.

Joshua D. Reichard, Ph.D., Ed.S., is the President of Omega Graduate School, The American Centre for Religion/Society Studies (ACRSS) and Dissertation Core Faculty at the American College of Education. He is a well-published scholar, focusing primarily on the interface between Process-Relational and Pentecostal-Charismatic theologies. He is a state licensed school superintendent and a Certified Clinical Sociologist.

The Leadership of a Nurturant God

JOHN SANDERS

Christian leaders should imitate the leadership style of the God who nurtures.

The pastor plopped his Bible down on the table, pointed to it, and said, "I want to know why you put a question mark where God put a period?"

He was upset about my book that surveyed a range of views that Christians hold on the topic of the destiny of those who never heard of Christ. He believed that biblical teaching on the topic was clear, simple, and singular. He did not like it that I rejected his position and, instead, endorsed a range of different views that in one way or another gave hope for the salvation of those who have never heard of Jesus.

The values underlying the different approaches taken by the pastor and me arise from what social scientists call Nurturant and Authoritative values. Nurturants believe it is best to empower people by affirming and loving them. Nurturants prize values such as listening to others, perspective taking, and humility. Authoritatives believe that followers must first obey the leaders before the leaders show acceptance to them. Authoritative leaders need not listen to others because they are the ones in charge and questioning the leader means challenging their authority. They think that perspective taking and humility are signs of weakness. Leaders should simply say, "Because I said so."

Open theism is a variety of Nurturant morality while much of evangelicalism and conservative Catholicism are versions of Authoritative morality. The Apostle Paul implored Christians to "be imitators of God" (Eph. 5:1). Richard Kearney says, "Tyrannical Gods breed tyrannical humans." We imitate the deity we believe in and there are those who believe in an Authoritative God and those who affirm a Nurturant God. Both Gods seek to create humans in their image. I claim that the overall biblical portrait is that of a nurturing God and that Christian leaders should emulate these characteristics. Some examples will show how this works.

Many biblical texts show that God is both responsive to our input and open to our prayers. For example, when God announced his intended judgment on Sodom, Abraham questioned and negotiated with God (Gen. 18). An Authoritative God would have told Abraham: "I am God so shut your mouth." Instead, God patiently listened and considered Abraham's concerns. In another story God and Jacob have an encounter and God wants to leave but Jacob (whose name means "grabber") grabs onto God and wrestles all night long with God. In response, God blesses Jacob and gives him a new name—Israel, which means, "wrestles with God." God approved of what Jacob did. In Exodus, God asked Moses to return to Egypt and liberate the Jewish people. However, Moses does not do what God says. Instead, he raises five problems with God's plan. An Authoritative God would have said, "Go now, because I said so. Do not question my plan or authority!" But the Nurturant God was open to Moses's questions and to each of them God reiterates that "I will be with you." Even when Moses tells God to go "find somebody else," God adjusted the divine plan by allowing Aaron to do the public speaking. Thus, God was flexible and adaptive in working with people.

The way God relates in these stories fits with Paul's description of love in 1 Corinthians 13. Love is patient, kind, and not arrogant. It does not insist on its own way. Rather, love puts up with us, has faith in us, and places hope in us. God does not say, "It's my way or the highway" nor does God display a "take it or leave it" attitude. Rather, God engages us with a give-and-take in which both parties contribute and God practices innovation and employs flexible plans. God works with us like a jazz band which requires improvisation from all the players. At various times, each player takes the lead and the other players have to respond to what the other is doing. Love, says Paul, is not boastful so God does not say, "My music is the only music that matters." Rather, God delights in sharing the stage and seeing what music others produce. Of course, this involves some risk on God's part because we may do things that harm others. Love trusts others but we can, at times, disappoint the beloved.

The Nurturant God listens to our input and is flexible in adjusting plans. God empowers us to participate in the vocation of redemption and delegates responsibility to us for many things. Sometimes we bring God success but we can also let God down. This is how a strong leader operates. Inflexible people who demand their own way are weak leaders. If God is a nurturing leader, then leaders who imitate God will treat others the way God treats us. They will love others by empowering them. They will put faith in others to accomplish a mission. They will hope for a better future.

Philosophers like to speak about God's "great-making" properties by which they mean power and knowledge. God certainly has these but if Jesus is our best example of what God is like, then God's great-making properties include love, empathy, humility, and perspective taking. As God incarnate, Jesus "walked a mile in our shoes." God experienced what it is like to be human.

Genuine leaders are those who learn what other people in the organization are experiencing. In church and in business, leaders should find ways to understand the perspective of others and practice humility by being willing to learn from others. God does not micromanage the church. Rather, God puts divine trust in us. How is that for confidence? It is what church leaders should do as well. One thing that often prevents leaders from doing this is the fear that lack of control may result in others doing things that bring embarrassment on the congregation or organization. But God takes risks with us and we should do the same.

Another implication of the way God works with us is that churches should reject autocratic rulers. If God listens to us and considers our concerns, then leaders should foster democratic structures in order to hear the voices of others. In much of church history, leaders have been authoritarian, and pastors have been little potentates ruling over their piece of the kingdom. They are in charge and seek to control what others believe and do. Making sure that everyone has a voice and providing for some diversity should be a high priority for Nurturant leaders. In the Bible, the metaphor of God as a king is common. But God is quite an unusual king. A king who values what others have to say, exercises flexible strategies, and comes to us humbly in Jesus. This is true kingship and leadership.

One last area of leadership that I want to mention returns us to the story of the pastor criticizing my work for presenting different Christian views on a topic. If God trusts in us and is open to going in directions we want to pursue (as with Moses), then leaders should expect some diversity of viewpoints and practices. We should make room for a "constrained pluralism" of views and practices. We should be able to agree on some general Christian beliefs and practices. Yet, because we do not know everything and do not possess a foolproof understanding of what God wants, we should have humility in our claims to truth.

Throughout history, many church leaders affirmed the Authoritative God and sought to impose monopoly religion on everyone. They established all the correct beliefs and practices, such as those surrounding the Lord's Supper, and anyone who thought differently was exiled, tortured, or burned at the stake. The Nurturant approach affirms a few general Christian truths and allows for a range of views. This is not an "anything goes" approach. Rather, it acknowledges that Christians, from the first century on, have always had some diversity. One can favor a particular understanding of say, baptism, while recognizing that other Christians think differently. In short, one can affirm a specific doctrine or practice as the best and tolerate other Christian views. A Nurturant approach expects some diversity while Authoritative religion fosters monopolies, uniformity, and punishes those who do not conform.

Christian leaders should imitate the Nurturant God. God is love and love is patient, kind, and does not insist on its own way. God values our input and invites us to join the divine band and create some music. God does not micromanage and control us. Instead, God empowers us and takes the risk that we may mess up along the way. In addition, God allows for a range of beliefs and practices—a constrained pluralism. Leaders should emulate these important values.

John Sanders is Professor of Religious Studies at Hendrix College. He is the co-author of The Openness of God, and author of The God Who Risks and the forthcoming Embracing Prodigals. He enjoys basketball and kayaking.

55

I'm Right, You're Wrong

LEMUEL SANDOVAL

Leadership in theological education requires teachers empowering students through dialogue.

"I'm big and you're small. And I'm right and you're wrong. And there's nothing you can do about it." That's one of the most iconic lines from 1996 film "Matilda." Miss Trunchbull, the school principal, will not stand young Matilda correcting her. "Am I wrong? I'm never wrong," the Trunchbull goes on. "In this classroom, in this school... I AM GOD!" What happens just then is so hilarious. A small lizard jumps to Miss Trunchbull's coat and she starts gasping and spinning, trying to get the animal off. You have to watch the movie!

As funny as that may sound, those two lines are still the undercover motto of so many schools, colleges, and universities. Just look at how traditional education is. The teacher possesses all the knowledge and the student has none of it. So, the teacher's role is to provide the right information for the student to swallow. And, voila! Learning has happened. Students just need to take whatever the teacher says as true and that's pretty much it. Now, I'm not minimizing all the effort that is required to pursue formal education. There's homework, and assignments, and projects, and long sleepless nights. Students develop discipline and organization. They make sacrifices and miss out on many things. I know that and celebrate those students who really care enough about their education.

Traditional education tends to consider the teacher as the ultimate source of true information, "In this classroom, in this school... I am God." This leaves the student as ever lacking at least some of that knowledge, until they become knowledgeable enough to occupy the role of the professor.

This model is repeated in seminaries and theology schools, as well as churches and Sunday School classes. There's a particular interest in these contexts to make sure the "right" knowledge is passed on to the pupils. I think this is partly because they are dealing with the sacred and the divine. There's a lot of mystery surrounding God and none would like to fall into heresy trying to explain the divinity. But, without doubt, there are also commitments made to denominations and confessions to keep the so-called "sound doctrine," whatever it may be. So, teachers and professors are required to have the correct knowledge, the correct information, to impart to their classes and correct whoever walks, knowingly or not, down the path of heresy. New opinions are silenced, alternative interpretations are Bible-slammed, tough questions are left unanswered. Students must repeat the correct formulas, the right arguments, the orthodox creeds to be approved. Even teachers who think differently get pushed aside if not removed from their positions. Theology students, whether seminarians, undergrads, or just your regular Sunday School attendees, are boxed in whatever the doctrine, posture or tradition of the educational institution is.

Granted, a good amount of reverence and humility is due when thinking about God. And it is healthy and wise to follow a specific doctrine or theological position for the sake of consistency. But then again, the point is that the typical model starts with the teacher giving the right information and ends with the students accepting it. The teacher remains all-knowing, unaffected. The student ought to be the receiver only, conform to the status quo or suffer the consequences. Because "I'm big and you're small. And I'm right and you're wrong. And there's nothing you can do about it."

This model should be called into question.

My biggest concern with this kind of theological education is that it fosters a view of God in which God reveals almost exclusively to a certain group of people, in this specific case to educators. They and only they have the right revelation, the right interpretation, and the right answer. However, a God who is open and relational is present and continually revealing God's love and nature to everyone. Teachers are not the only ones who can bring insight or a valuable point of view to the classroom. Students who are sensitive and respond affirmatively to God's prompts may have one or two interesting things to say in a theology class. Apart from that, a God who loves everyone teaches us to consider everyone's experience as equally important, so every question, every life story, every concern brought into the room is sacred.

But most of all, the God who always loves, self-gives, and empowers others is an example for teachers to follow in the classroom. The role of the educator can no longer be the know-it-all, right-information provider. A radical change must happen if one is to follow the path of the God who reaches out and touches humanity and all creation. Teachers must become partners with their students in the discovery of the divine. They must empower the pupils for their personal journey with God. Teachers must be liberators.

So, how exactly does a teacher become a liberator? How should professors, educators, faculty members and even school boards lead in theological education? Brazilian educator Paulo Freire proposes a model called critical pedagogy that fits nicely into an open and relational view of God. While Freire didn't focus on theology as an academic discipline, I believe his ideas are helpful in sorting out leadership in the classroom.

First, the teachers and educators ought to have a loving, humble attitude. They must think of themselves "the way Christ Jesus thought of himself. He had equal status with God but didn't think so much of himself that he had to cling to the advantages of that status no matter what." (Phil. 2:5-6) An open and relational model puts the student at the center. The teacher empowers the student in a humble, serving manner, focusing on the student's needs and not on the academic program. This also means that the educator is humble enough to tolerate a student doubting or even challenging her or his ideas.

Second, the educator's role is to identify the context of the students. Where do they come from? What do they already know? What are their aspirations? Their fears? What problems do they encounter daily? What is their own view of God? How is their faith experience? This goes beyond a mere icebreaking exercise. The objective is to make students aware of their situation and guide them into thinking critically about it. This reflection will actually be the basis, the raw material from which the teacher will work in class. That means the lesson plans will undergo constant change to fit the students bring to the table.

Third, the critical open and relational model should be based on the dialogue. Many teachers, if not all, encourage their students to participate in class. Most of the time, though, the participation will consist of doubts or questions, which implies more correction and information giving. The critical dialogue, on the other hand, aims at students questioning themselves and ultimately the typical doctrinal, "orthodox" answers. When the whole group, with the teachers as partners, engages in critical dialogue, they can propose a theology that moves into action, solving the problems they found in their communities and making their efforts relevant to today's world. The teacher leads in this exercise, but in a non-coercive manner: the critical dialogue. Everything counts when it comes to constructing solutions from the exchange of experiences, quotes from books, wild ideas, and previous knowledge. There are many methods to foster dialogue, but the important thing is to recognize that an essential part of the answer to the question is already in the students' hearts and minds. A relational teacher allows herself or himself to be affected by the dialogue, and responds to influence, but not coerce, students to analyze their personal situations, communities, beliefs.

Following this simple and basic clue, teachers and educators can lead their students from every level —college, seminary, Sunday School— towards a well thought, relevant, meaningful, encouraging, and loving theology. Whether it comes to speculating about the Divinity, facing the ethical issues of today's world, analyzing a particular system of beliefs, interpreting the sacred books, or any other theological task, the open and relational model makes space for creativity, respect, hope, unity, and love.

It may be scary at first for teachers and educators not to control what happens in the classroom. Instead of control, classes will be full of self-realization, constant learning, mutual trust, collaboration, happiness, and liberty. Even Miss Trunchbull would attend class.

Lemuel Sandoval is a pastor in Mexico City. His degrees are in Theology and in Music Composition and Arrangement. One of his biggest interests is theological education and promoting critical thinking among the youth. Lemuel loves spending the afternoons out with his wife and daughter, and just discovered a passion for baking sourdough bread.

Seven Tips for Becoming a Better Leader

WM. ANDREW SCHWARTZ

Open-relational leadership means leading by example, empowering others, being adaptable, humble, and showing compassion.

Perhaps you've heard it said, "People quit bosses, not jobs." A bad boss can make an employment situation unbearable. If you don't know what I'm talking about, consider yourself lucky and stay self-employed. For everyone else, I'm sure you can imagine countless scenarios that demonstrate poor leadership. Sometimes it's as innocent as incompetence, other times it's as vicious as abuse. Ever work for a micromanager? You know, the one breathing down the back of your neck and dictating every move as if they don't trust you to handle simple tasks. Or how about the "exceptional" boss, who believes the rules apply to everyone but them? Every day with this person is a lesson in "do as I say, not as I do" hypocrisy. Or how about the employer who needs an EpiPen anytime something "new" is suggested? This is a leader who's stuck in the past and allergic to change. From movies like *Horrible Bosses*, shows like *The Office*, and a variety of viral memes, examples of bad leadership are everywhere.

Often, bad leadership is the result of bad worldviews (including bad theology). What we think about power, perfection, relationality, freedom, and other "big" philosophical and theological principles shape our notions of leadership and the way we structure our organizations. So here are seven insights from open-relational theology that can help you become a better leader.

OPEN AND RELATIONAL LEADERSHIP

1) Leaders are Examples not Exceptions

In open-relational theology, God is not an exception to the nature of reality but an exemplification of it. If the world is interconnected then God is the most connected. If the world is deeply relational then God is the most relational. While some theologies place God outside of the world as we know it, open-relational theology says that God is intertwined with the world—an exemplification of, not an exception to, the ways of reality. Likewise, an open-relational leader is not an exception to the ways of the workplace. One who leads by example is a leader people want to follow. While a "boss" might tell people the way, a true leader "shows" the way. Open-relational leadership invites imitation.

2) Leading for Change Means Changing to Lead

A fundamental insight of open-relational theology is that "all things flow." Life is like a river, and you can't step in the same river twice. To be a leader in a world of change requires being adaptable, flexible, and well…changing. Unlike the mountain, which is thought powerful because it is unmovable, open-relational theology sees the river as powerful because it is adaptable. In open-relational theology even God grows, flows, and changes. As new things occur in the world, God adapts accordingly. Leading for change means changing to lead. A leader that resists change remains out of touch and ineffective. Open-relational leaders "go with the flow," embracing change as a welcome feature of reality. Open-relational leadership means being adaptable and allowing oneself (and one's community) to mature.

3) Leading is Learning

In classical theology, God is often described as "all-knowing." This attribute is thought to make God more reliable. Although we might not see the big picture, if God sees all (including the future) then we have reason to trust in God. When it comes to classical models of leadership, uncertainty represents instability, and this undermines confidence in a leader's capacity to "steer the ship." As a result, classical leaders often pretend to have all the answers. Because they know everything, they have nothing to learn. This type of leader quickly becomes arrogant; closed off to the wisdom of others. By contrast, in open-relational theology God knows all that can be known. But since the future is still open (is possible but not actual), not even God knows the future with certainty. This is the "open" part of open-relational theology. When new things happen in the world, the knowledge of God grows. Open-relational leaders embrace the unknown as an opportunity to learn. Admitting you don't know something isn't a sign of failure, but a mark of good leadership. To lead is to learn. The best leaders aren't know-it-alls, they're the ones who prioritize personal development. From new languages, new skills, or new perspectives, learning is the key to leading toward an open future.

4) Strong Leaders are Vulnerable

Perhaps more than any other characteristic, God is classically associated with power. In fact, some argue that to speak of God is to speak of the most powerful entity—a Supreme Being with "all power." Power is often defined as the capacity to influence, control, or transform others in order to advance one's own purposes: to affect others without being affected. In these theologies, God's power is reflected in God's impassibility (God's ability to affect the world without being impacted by the world). Such power is linear and exerted one directionally. Leader and follower, employer and employee, teacher and student, minister and parishioner, these are all relations that imply a particular power dynamic. The first person in each pairing has more power than the other. Leaders who assume a linear model of power become "my way or the highway" authoritarians who perceive vulnerability as weakness (the opposite of strength). They harden themselves against the influences of the world around them. By contrast, open-relational theology describes power relationally. In this relational model, strength is a matter of both giving and receiving; of affecting and being affected. In open-relational theology, God exemplifies this give-and-receive relational power. This is the "relational" part of open-relational theology. The open-relational God is not an unmoved mover, but the most moved mover. Open-relational leadership is marked by mutual influence. To be a strong leader requires vulnerability. Mutual influence is a source of creativity and novelty. Vulnerability is essential for learning and changing, which are fundamental to open-relational leadership.

5) Leadership Happens from Within, Not Above

As described above, the mutual influence model of leadership is rooted in the notion of relational power. While relational power is bi-directional, it is also non-hierarchical. Classical conceptions of God's power depict God (at the top) influencing the world but never being influenced by the world. This linear power flows top-down. Top-down leaders are repressive and hierarchical. They tend to operate unilaterally (even coercively) to "make" things the way they want. By contrast, an open-relational model of leadership is horizontal and egalitarian. Open-relational theology describes God as working persuasively rather than coercively, working cooperatively rather than unilaterally. Open-relational leaders lead from within, not from above. Whereas the classical leader "runs things" as a top-down authority figure, open-relational leaders guide through interdependent cooperation. Teamwork makes the dream work.

6) Business is Always Personal

Open-relational theology sees the world as a community of subjects, not a collection of objects. A world of subjects is a world of experiencing entities. Experiences are felt as values. While objectifying people might make it easier to fire them (like replacing a cog in a broken machine), this mechanical worldview distorts the true nature of reality as experiencing value relations. Leaders who follow the "it's business, not personal" model objectify others; ignoring their experience. Open-relational leadership recognizes that business is always personal because it involves persons. With personhood comes freedom. To be an experiencing subject (a person) is to possess the freedom of self-determination. Because business is always personal, open-relational leaders don't overpower, they empower. Puppeteers overpower, but people aren't puppets. As free creatures that are creatively self-determining, people must be led through empowerment. That means providing the necessary conditions and support for them to succeed as persons, not machines.

7) To Lead is to Love

In open-relational theology, self-giving love is the central characteristic of God. God does not simply choose to act lovingly (as some theologies contend). From an open-relational viewpoint, God always works in love because it is God's nature to do so. The nature of God is the nature of love—the two cannot be separated. Employers who are who rude, selfish, and inconsiderate are some of the worst. No doubt, kindness can go a long way toward good leadership. But open-relational leadership demands more than being nice on the outside—more than fake smiles. To lead is to love. We are all more than our work, so you can't "hate the worker and love the person." There is no separating the two. An open-relational leader truly cares about the lives of her team members—not just their work. Open-relational leadership means promoting the overall well-being of those you lead.

Conclusion

Ideas matter. Theology matters. Bad theology can inform bad practices. This is true in leadership, as well as other areas of life. Theologies of all-powerful, distant, unmoved divinity set the stage for models of leadership that are hierarchical, one-directional, and incapable of leading in this relational world of becoming. An open-relational model of leadership, informed by an open-relational theology, produces leaders who lead by example, empower others, who are adaptable, humble, and compassionate. Open-relational leadership happens from within, not above, in a spirit of love. If leadership is done right, maybe people stop quitting bosses.

Wm. Andrew Schwartz is a scholar, organizer, and social entrepreneur. He is Executive Director of the Center for Process Studies and Assistant Professor of Process & Comparative Theology at Claremont School of Theology. Schwartz is also Co-Founder and Executive Vice President of the Institute for Ecological Civilization (ecociv.org).

We are All Leaders

MICHELE SNYDER

Each of us is a natural-born leader, whether or not we'd like to be.

If you want to know who is leading you, who is responsible for every victory in your life and every failure, go to a mirror and take a good look at yourself. You are your leader. Leadership is an innate quality, so whether we realise it or not, we are all "Natural Born Leaders". There is not a moment that goes by that you are not leading yourself. If you have a family, you are a leader. If you manage employees at your job, you are a leader. You might even be somewhat of a leader online if you post your thoughts for others to see.

To lead yourself and others well, you must know who you are, and that the Divine furiously loves you. Your self-worth can't come from something that you can misplace or be taken away by someone else. Leading requires a sense of self-worth. Give grace to yourself because the best leaders act with compassion and empathy.

Great leaders have confidence and integrity. They know when and how to apologize; they exercise humility. They want to lift people up and not shoot them down. They see the big picture and communicate it to others well and with passion. A good leader has learned to lead themselves well first. They have self-control. They have battled the inner child and "shadow self," and with that, found maturity and balance. There is still always a struggle for that balance, but they will find it in almost all situations. Leadership is not about acquiring a position; it's more about influence. You must lead yourself well, or you'll never lead anyone else anywhere worth going.

OPEN AND RELATIONAL LEADERSHIP

Parental Style Leadership

If we are parents, we usually lead our children as we do ourselves. We may try to teach our children everything that we believe to be right, but they will learn most by our example. They will emulate it for good or bad. It often seems that they pick up on the wrong things more frequently. However, there are times when they rise above what we've shown them. Sometimes, they end up fighting the same battles that we do. They've watched us closely since we are their leaders. We must get to know them and adapt our parenting to their personality and significant needs; not just childish desires, but real human needs according to who they are, as a good leader would do in other areas.

As parents, we typically fall into two categories, passive and authoritarian. Neither way works in the long term since they don't help children make decisions and to live with the consequences of their actions. The authoritarian is usually non-relational and cold, often dictating what the child must precisely do, say, and think. They manage their children by relying on unquestioning obedience. With this non-relational style, the child will often struggle to feel loved since every aspect of their lives is being managed and controlled. A passive parent, on the other hand, will give their children pretty much whatever they want to make them happy. It is the easier road to go at first, but over time creates a monster who will come out whenever they don't get what they want.

Fortunately, there is a third category. A parent who is a good leader of their children will strive to be an authoritative vs. authoritarian or passive parent. The authoritative style of parenting is relational, warm and leads with love. It helps the child learn from their mistakes and doesn't demand obedience out of fear, but instead trains the child by natural consequences while maintaining a calm and gracious attitude. This style is the most difficult to master, but over time will be the most beneficial to both the parent and the child's well-being.

A Mindset of Leading vs. Management

If we are managers at our work, our goal should be to lead and not micromanage. Great leaders transcend management. Managers are often task-oriented and focus on completing short term goals. They are not visionaries. Unhealthy managers will use their position of power to control and achieve short term results. They can be more interested in being right rather than doing what's right. A micromanaging, demanding boss will sometimes stifle and belittle their employees. They want results, and they will do whatever it takes to get them, often in a cut-throat demeaning way. They fail to see others' true worth. They may regard something in their employees as a weakness when it is actually a strength.

I remember a former boss telling me that I was not motivated by money. She was undoubtedly correct. I am motivated by connection and relationships. Therefore, kindness and compassion go a long way with me. However, a nit-picky, non-relational, self-obsessed, self-serving, arrogant boss would only motivate me to do one thing: QUIT! People aren't robots. They are relational, and desire and need more out of life than just money to buy objects. They desire fulfilment, a sense of self-worth and accomplishment, and a leader who can inspire them, motivate them and help them to accomplish these things. These things will result in achieving much greater success in the end.

Unfortunately, bad management doesn't only exist in the workplace. It is very prevalent in the church as well. I can relate to this since I spent many years in churches with a Reformed Calvinistic theology. There were clear standards and not much room at all for questioning. You turned off your brain, zipped up your lips and got with the program if you wanted to survive. There are many instances that I can recall where a leader was brought in for discipline because they discussed a view held by others outside the church. The most unbelievable thing is that they were disciplined for merely talking about the beliefs even if they didn't condone them! I would label this type of leadership as not just unhealthy but also toxic.

In a sovereignty minded church, the rules are apparent. God submits to God's self, Christ to God, men to Christ, women to men and children to parents. One church I was in plainly told the women that they were free to teach the children in the church up until middle school age. At that point they were only to teach the other females. In that church, women were not only subject to their husbands, but also to all men, which included pubescent middle school boys! That didn't sit well with me. Nor did when the pastor at that very same church yelled at the entire congregation. Baptisms were scheduled for later that evening, and he was agitated because not everyone showed up to baptisms. He ridiculed anyone who wasn't coming to witness them because we were a church family and should behave as such. Don't just "look at the pretty leaves on the trees" he screamed! It was the autumn season, a favorite of many, here in the Midwest. In my opinion, he was not just a toxic leader but also a bully.

These leaders feel superior. They dominate and control with guilt trips and manipulation. They fool others and even themselves into thinking that they do it all for God and the betterment of the church. However, it is usually all about them. They are quite insecure individuals whose lives are a facade. These toxic leaders have an inflated sense of superiority that in some cases sadly stems from an unhealthy understanding of God. No healthy individual wants to be controlled or abused. A healthy person wants to be free to be who God made them and use the gifts that God bestowed upon them. The creator wants us in unity, sharing our unique gifts, lifting each other; and not holding each other down in jealousy and strife.

Healthy Leadership

A healthy leader will see the strengths of others' individuality and does not feel threatened by it. They use their influence to motivate further and become inspired themselves. They empty themselves and serve others. They are sometimes even able to pull out inner gifts of people that they never knew existed. They encourage, inspire, are trustworthy and have integrity. A good leader can make you feel alive since you are free to dream and be yourself. Good leaders have a dream, a vision, and they believe in it with great passion. They motivate others to believe in it too. They magnify people's strengths, not just point out their weaknesses. They serve and do not look to be served as if they are above others. They know who they are, so it doesn't intimidate them to get their hands dirty. They wash others' feet when needed as Christ did as described in the Holy Bible. He could influence the seas to cease raging, yet was more than willing to get down in the dirt for others.

Healthy leaders know how and when to apologize. They have integrity and are excellent communicators. There is a confident strength about them. They don't look to others to fulfil a need that's lacking within themselves. They don't use people to climb the ladder, but rather, they inspire others even as they are about to give up and lose all hope.

Trustworthy leaders have a healthy foundation of love that enables them to lead well. If you want to lead, go to the mirror first, know that the Divine furiously loves you. You are equipped with everything you need to be a good leader. Step out of the shadow, be your true self and help others. Be a leader.

Michele Snyder is the host of The Redheaded Ragamuffin Podcast. She lives in Northeast Ohio with her husband and two children. She works from home and has studied theology for over 20 years. You can contact her at theredheadededragamuffin.com. She would love to hear from you.

The God of Love Compels Me

LEANN M. VAN CLEEF-TRIMMER

The God of love compels leaders be an example of love to all, to respect free will, and to maintain opportunity for restoration.

My life as a Salvation Army officer provides almost daily interactions with people from broad spectrums of life. It is not unusual to start a day among leading business people from the community we serve and to go immediately into a room where there is a man just off the streets, "clean" enough to pass a urinalysis to enter our rehab program with the clothes on his back and little else. The disparities can be staggering and yet at the core the differences are more cosmetic than substantive. At the core, whether dressed in freshly pressed Armani or a second-hand pair of jeans that have been worn for days, these men are the same. Take away the props of wealth or poverty, the social acclaim or the disdain, the mass acceptance or rejection, and at the very core is an individual created in the image of God. At the very core is an individual who has every opportunity to be transformed by the love of God and to become the person that God envisioned he could be at conception. The hope of that truth is essential in the work to which God has called me.

In the earliest years of ministry, I made many mistakes, not necessarily in the mechanics of ministry. I was good at satisfying denominational expectations. The mistakes were in my thinking and in my understanding of my role as a pastor and minister of the gospel. In my immaturity, I imagined that it was somehow my job, my responsibility even, to size people up and "fix" the people that had been entrusted to my care. At this point in the journey, I can only laugh at myself, such hubris! And, such an unrealistic view of ministry and what God had really called me to; it was a self-imposed weight impossible to bear.

The journey from that place and time until now is too long a story to tell here. But the fundamental lessons I learned have shaped who I am and how I lead God's people. The lessons can be summed up easily. The first, and most essential: God loves. God's love is not dependent on human action or inaction. The second: I cannot "fix" people. I can love them, speak truth into their lives, and walk beside them, but never "fix" them. The third: God always honors human free will. That is so when we choose to follow God, and it is true when we choose disobedience. Finally, God never gives up and therefore calls me to walk a long road with people who will often disappoint.

When people come to a Salvation Army rehab, they often refer to it as the "last house on the block." They have worn through the tolerance and good will of family and friends. They have lost job after job. They are well acquainted with the criminal justice system. Any shred of human dignity has been completely consumed by whatever addiction has taken hold of their lives. If they've been on the streets for any amount of time, they've become accustomed to being looked through, not hearing their name called, not experiencing human touch or healthy affection. If they've been in prison, they've learned to keep to themselves, protect their turf and not draw attention to themselves. They can run the litany of their own unworthiness more brutally than anyone else ever could. The notion that they are loved by anyone, much less the God of the universe, is completely out of reach. They can believe that God loves other people, even the guy in the bunk next to his. But that God loves him? That God loves her? The truth of God's love has to be communicated through human agents. It is demonstrated first in the small things, by learning a person's name, saying "hello" when walking by, shaking a hand. Simple kindness restores human dignity. The recovery world speaks about "the gift of desperation," that place where people have nothing left so they are finally ready to accept the help of a power greater than themselves.

The challenge of wealth and success is often that wealthy and successful people are not quite so ready to acknowledge their own deficits, or their need for God. I come back to the thought that at the core we are all the same, and we all need the love and grace of God. It is often more difficult to communicate the need for grace to those who seem to have it all and with whom I interact from a place of asking for help. The approach is different, but the need to understand the love of God for them is the same. The need of the rehab client is obvious, the need of the Board Chairman is hidden under the trappings of success. Jesus said, "It is easier for a camel to go through the eye of a needle than for someone who is rich to enter the kingdom of God" (Mark 10:25 NRSV). Christ compels me to share God's love equally, to those who have and those who have not. The temptation is to overlook the less obvious need. God's love for me compels me to share that love with others.

I am mother to three sons. If parenthood has taught me anything it is that I cannot control another human being. I can guide, teach, suggest, and provide structure and discipline. I can even coerce, threaten and punish. However, at the end of the day I cannot make another human being do what he or she choose not to. Free will is a reality of our humanity. The unhindered exercise of free will is a reality of God's love. And this defines the joys and heartaches of leadership.

Christ calls us to minister his love to people who are gifted with free will. When those we serve choose to join their mind with the mind of Christ, pursuing God's will and purpose for their lives, it is the source of great joy. These people are planted deeply in my heart and mind. These are the people God uses to encourage me to continue to serve.

And when they choose a path that is marked by self-destruction? A path marked by pain? What then? The painful truth is that we must leave people to the consequences of their own choices…while continuing to love. In the parable of the Prodigal Son, we see the example: the father gives the younger son his share of the inheritance and lets him go. We don't know for certain, but I can guess that the father knew roughly where his son was located. He didn't rescue him, didn't interfere, and he waited. He left a door open for him to return and when the son made his way home, the father ran to meet him. We cannot choose for people, we cannot make them choose life, we cannot force them to be Christ followers, but we can leave a door open. And when they make their way back, when they turn around and choose life, we can welcome them with open arms and remind them they are loved and that God has a better way.

My husband, Darren, and I are different. We joked that the recessional at our wedding should be the theme from "The Odd Couple". We complement one another in all the right ways, and he is my daily example of extending God's grace to others and walking a long road with people. Darren does not give up on people, he doesn't rescue them, doesn't make excuses for them, but he continues to see the faintest remnant of the image of God in people. As we minister together, when I am ready to write someone off, my husband reminds me that we do not give up, because God does not give up.

I am reminded of Robert. Robert completed a Salvation Army program, came to church and maintained his sobriety for a while. He made some dicey choices; Darren kept speaking truth in love. Robert made more bad choices, leading to relapse. He would show up at the church demanding help. Darren would meet with him, speak truth in love, and not give what Robert demanded. When he got to the end of his run, Robert parked next to the church and passed out. The next morning Darren made sure he got to detox. Robert went back through the rehab program and his life was completely transformed. Love doesn't give up.

I am also reminded of Gerry who served on our community Advisory Board. Gerry came up poor, The Salvation Army had helped his family when he was a kid and he never forgot it. Gerry served on the City Council; he had made good. He died quite unexpectedly. We were never sure where he stood in his relationship with God. It was never a conversation Gerry was interested in having.

Ultimately, my life, my leadership of others must be defined by love. It does not matter; it cannot matter, whether I am relating to a homeless addict or a CEO. The love of God, the God of love compels me.

LeAnn Van Cleef-Trimmer has served as a Salvation Army officer for 29 years, in congregational ministry and leading Adult Rehabilitation Centers with her husband and partner in ministry Darren. She earned her M.Div. from Northwest Nazarene University. The joys of her life are her three sons and one beautiful granddaughter.

59

Organization as Family?

WM. PAUL YOUNG

Belonging to a common family in which we are seen, known, and loved allows us to recraft systems and organizations without expecting lifeless systems to be what they cannot.

*E*very human is wired for relationship and there is no global expression that is more pervasive and relevant than "family". While many of us have not experienced family as we long for, it is for family we still long. A place to be seen, to be known, to belong, to be safe.

Institutional systems of every sort, economic, business, military, political, and religious, for example, all work toward and promote the values of "family," often in overt standards, mission statements and marketing but even more powerfully in the creation of their ethos and internal messaging. The company, nation, team, church, gang, underworld organization, online gaming community, 12-step gathering can become the "brotherhood" or "sisterhood," and as "family" we identify as members of a community which becomes essential to our sense of worth, value, security, and being.

What is a metaphor? It is a word or phrase applied to something, like an action or object, that doesn't correspond or is not literally applicable. A simile uses the single word "like" to make an attribution, for example, "Our company is *like* a family." A metaphor is much more potent. "Our company *IS* a family." A simile lives in the world of behavior, describing the activity or performance by comparison with something else, but a metaphor is about the "nature" of something, that which is true inherently.

I have a number of friends who are in the military, not a few of them in Special Forces. These individuals develop intense bonds through shared trauma and purpose, often the deepest sense of belonging and being seen they have ever experienced. When they refer to each other as a brother (regardless of gender), you know they mean it in the deep places of their souls. They will literally die for each other. Even if those outside the "brotherhood" are expendable, those within it are not. Often when the "band" breaks up, the member experiences profound loss and dis-orientation, un-moored from that which gave them a place to stand, be seen and belong. They thought they were a family and often will hold onto that belonging regardless of any evidence to the contrary.

I would like to propose that our references to "family" are not to a metaphor but to a simile, and that all of these "belongings"—the church, the team, the nation, etc.—are all similes. Each has attributes that make it "like" family in one way or another. May I go so far as to suggest that even the nuclear family, traditionally defined as mother, father, and children, is itself still a whisper that there is something deeper, wider, higher, more honest, authentic and meaningful than anything we experience as a member of any organization or community, a reality to which all such similes refer. Even our immediate family is still *like* a family, this transcendent assumption that there is and should be a place where I am fully embraced, included, known, seen and loved.

What is that? It is the relationship of and within Trinity. Trinity is *the* definition of family, as it is the true meaning of belonging, of creating, of authenticity, light, love and wonder. Three Persons in face-to-face, other-centered, self-giving adoration and enjoyment. All similes are temporary, but the truth and reality behind them is eternal. The "brotherhood" will disband, or will fail you or you it. The religious organization will disappoint. Your "family" of friends will find someone else who fits better. You will find out that what you thought was love turned out to be betrayal. Your company hired someone more skilled than you. Your parents may not have known how to love well, and you were hurt. Those who should have been safest, failed. Those who could have truly known you, didn't. Yet even in the midst of our relational losses, we still yearn and long for, family.

When Paul the Apostle stands up on Mars Hill in Athens, Greece, and announces, "You are each and all children of God," he is reaching past all simile and into the eternal heart of reality, into our origination and inclusion in "family," from which each family on this earth derives its identity. You are a child of God. You already and have always belonged. Trinity is your family of origin, an identity you may deny, but cannot expunge. This is a love that you will never be able to separate yourself from, except in the embrace of delusion and lie.

Why does this matter, especially to organizational and systemic enterprise? Organizations and institutions exist because human beings created them, human beings bringing to bear all of their inherent longings and desires. If they haven't found family, then they will build one. Where do the values of clarity, empathy, authenticity and vulnerability originate? In the deep places of the human soul, in the eternal, crafted in the image and likeness of Trinity. As human consciousness rises, is it any wonder that these relational values are emerging, being embraced and promoted?

Institutional systems have no life inherently. They "exist" only because human beings empower them. It is true that they seem to "take on a life of their own" but again, that is a dependent sense of life, an extension from the human beings who create and sustain them. If you remove human life from within a system or structure, it has no life whatsoever.

Is it wrong to build a sense of family within the systems and organizations of which we are part? Not at all, as long as we understand that the system itself cannot love, and family is built on love; other-centered and self-giving. You may think you love your job, but your job does not love you. People love, institutions cannot. An organization is a thing, nothing alive. It cannot by its own nature give what it does not and cannot have. If we expect a system to act toward us as family truly would, we will live in a constant state of disappointment and frustration.

One simple application of the distinction between true family and a system: a family always moves at the speed of the slowest, while an institution moves at the speed of the vision, or mission, or leadership. In any family that has health, when a child is born or adopted into its embrace who has a disability or an emotional impediment, that family will slow down and adapt to the weakest member. Love responds to loss, surrounding it in order to bring healing and presence. In an organization, the weakest are hidden away, at best, but more often simply discarded. If you are not someone who can serve the mission, you are not valuable. If you are a drain on resources, you will be "let go."

Yes, there are people who don't fit, who truly are a drain on resources and impediments to the mission of the organization, but how do we love the least of these inside our organizations? If our frame of reference and sense of family is much deeper and broader than the limitations and walls of our institution, then we will always respond first with love because we belong to the same family of humanity, each and all children of God. Our response will not be systemic but one that is kind and loving; relational. You may not be a good fit for this organization, so let us explore and find out where functionally you would be a better match. Who are you? What matters to you? Do you need more education? How can we as members of the same family, help bring clarity to your life about direction and purpose? How can we help you?

What if we build our organization and community "like" family because we assume we belong to a common family in which we are already seen, known, and loved? Perhaps we can then re-craft our systems to express better the reality of family, while not placing expectations on lifeless entities to be what they cannot.

Wm. Paul Young, author of The Shack, Cross Roads, Eve, *and* Lies We Believe About God, *was born a Canadian and raised among a stone-age tribe by missionary parents in New Guinea (West Papua). He suffered great loss as a child and young adult, and now enjoys the "wastefulness of grace" with his growing family in the Pacific Northwes*

Notes

Notes